KITCHING · DER HOFMEISTER

DER HOFMEISTER: A CRITICAL ANALYSIS OF BERTOLT BRECHT'S ADAPTATION OF LENZ'S DRAMA

by

LAURENCE PATRICK ANTHONY KITCHING

1976

WILHELM FINK VERLAG MÜNCHEN

Jutale ja meie poegadele

ISBN 3—7705—1185—9
1976 Wilhelm Fink Verlag, München
Gesamtherstellung: Grafoimpex, Zagreb

"Bearbeitungen"

Ich, zum Beispiel, schreibe manchmal
Bearbeitungen. Manche nennen es auch
Nachdichtungen, und das ist so: Ich mache
aus altem Stoff ein neues Stück und
setze unter den Titel
den Namen eines toten Dichters, der sehr
berühmt ist und von Keinem gekannt, und setze vor
den Namen des toten Dichters das Wörtlein: "nach".
Dann schreiben die Einen, ich sei
sehr voll Pietät, die Andern, ich sei ganz ohne, und was
dem toten Dichter mißglückt ist, das schreiben
sie mir zu, und was mir geglückt ist,
dem toten Dichter, der sehr
berühmt ist und von Keinem gekannt,
und von dem
auch Keiner recht weiß, ob er seinesteils
der Dichter war oder vielleicht der
Bearbeiter.
                          Lion Feuchtwanger

LIST OF ABBREVIATIONS

BBA	Bertolt Brecht-Archiv
BE	Berliner Ensemble
BEA	Berliner Ensemble Archiv
Blei	*Jakob Michael Reinhold Lenz, Gesammelte Schriften,* ed. Franz Blei. 5 vols. München: Müller, 1909.
Briefe	*Briefe, von und an J. M. R. Lenz,* eds. Karl Freye und Wolfgang Stammler. 2 vols. Leipzig: Wolff, 1918.
D	Jacob M. R. Lenz, *Gesammelte Werke in vier Bänden,* mit Anmerkungen, hrsg. von Richard Daunicht. München: Fink, 1967, Dramen I.
GW	Bertolt Brecht. *Gesammelte Werke.* 20 vols. Frankfurt: Suhrkamp, 1967.

ACKNOWLEDGEMENT

A grant from Indiana University and support from The Canada Council are gratefully acknowledged here. My sincere thanks are also due both to the Bertolt Brecht-Archiv and the Berliner Ensemble Archiv for permission to examine and quote from unpublished materials pertaining to *"Der Hofmeister" in der Bearbeitung des Berliner Ensembles.* The friendly cooperation of the staff of each institution was of great benefit. In addition, Mr. Egon Monk kindly gave permission to quote from his unpublished *Notate* located in the Bertolt Brecht-Archiv.

PREFACE

Jakob Michael Reinhold Lenz's tragicomedy, *Der Hofmeister oder Vortheile der Privaterziehung*, was adapted by Bertolt Brecht in 1949/1950 for the Berliner Ensemble. No detailed comparison of the adaptation with its model has been published to date.[1] The purpose of this study is to fill this notable gap in Brecht scholarship with the help of unpublished materials from the writer's *Nachlaß*. These papers, available only in the East Berlin Bertolt Brecht-Archiv,[2] and supplemented by related documents in the Berliner Ensemble Archiv,[3] provide the basis for tracing the genesis of the *Hofmeister* adaptation. The collection of *Hofmeister* papers of the BBA and the BEA is classified and evaluated here for the first time.

Brecht's posthumous papers are also of signal importance in my assessment of the relationship which the *Bearbeitung* bears to Lenz's drama. The documents in both archives prove particularly valuable in the attempt to establish the interpretation of character, situation and didactic intent, as conceived by Brecht and his troupe.

The gradual development of various polemic thrusts in the adaptation can be observed accurately from one level[4] of the manuscripts to the next. This affords the literary historian a unique insight into the creative process in which director, actors and spectators shared during rehearsals in the Berliner Ensemble.

---

1 This work represents a revised version of my doctoral dissertation bearing the same title and written for Indiana University in 1973. A few short studies on the relationship of Brecht's adaptation to its model have been published in several books and learned journals. The two dramas have also been the subject of various East German *Staatsexamensarbeiten* unavailable outside of the German Democratic Republic. See the "SOURCES CONSULTED" under the heading "Works about Brecht and Lenz."

The text of Lenz's *Hofmeister* used in my comparison is that of Richard Daunicht's *J. M. R. Lenz — Gesammelte Werke* (München: Fink, 1967), vol. I, pp. 39—121. Daunicht's is the most reliable edition and faithfully reproduces the first printing of Lenz's *Hofmeister* as published in 1774 by Weygand in Leipzig. Cf. Daunicht, pp. 389—391 for the history of the text. Reinhold Grimm reviews Daunicht's edition in *Monatshefte*, LXI (1969), 181.

2 The Bertolt Brecht-Archiv will subsequently be referred to as BBA. This abbreviation also precedes all file numbers of the catalogued materials in the archive; following the file or *Mappe* number is a slash, after which are given the page numbers, as for example: BBA 1561/1-103. Where I refer to the text of a complete file, only its number is given.

The Houghton Library at Harvard University, Cambridge, Massachusetts possesses a fairly complete microfilm collection of Brecht's *Nachlaß*. Loaned to this library by their owner, Stefan Brecht, the films my be read only with his permission.

3 Subsequently, the Berliner Ensemble Archiv will be abbreviated as BEA.

4 The term "level" is used consistently throughout the investigation to denote any of the five versions or strata of the adaptation, i.e., Level A, Level B, and so

An examination of Lenz's theory of the drama makes clear that the external structure of *Der Hofmeister* — long decried as faulty by the critics — was carefully planned. The juxtaposition of scenes effectively aids in portraying character, illustrating the play's moral lessons, and creating the tragicomic by a technique which resembles counterpoint.

I argue that both Lenz and Brecht conceive of *Der Hofmeister* as a tragicomedy. It is shown, however, that recent critics do not agree whether Lenz's drama may be called a tragicomedy. Their differences stem from their definitions and their points of view. In both Lenz's play and Brecht's adaptation, the comic is the predominant mood. The tragic exists in both plays less in the destinies of the protagonists than — on a symbolic plane — in the fate of the middle class. The techniques which Brecht uses to intensify the tragicomic and its constituent moods are also analyzed.

Brecht adapted Lenz's *Hofmeister* because of the opportunities it offered for trenchant criticism of class society, war, intellectuals and educators. It is primarily from this point of view that the comparison of the two works is undertaken. I identify the changes in the characters and Brecht's reasons behind those changes.

---

on. The terms "copy" and "script" are used only to refer to individual manuscripts which belong to a particular level. As can be seen on page 13, there may exist as many as seven (originally identical, mimeographed) copies of one version, as in Level D.

CHAPTER I

MANUSCRIPTS AND GENESIS OF BRECHT'S
HOFMEISTER-ADAPTATION

Wenn wir an die Aufführung eines klassischen Werks herangehen, müssen wir ...
das Werk neu sehen, wir dürfen uns nicht an die verkomme, gewohnheitsdik-
tierte Art halten, in der wir es auf dem Theater einer verkommenden Bourgeoisie
gesehen haben. Und wir dürfen nicht rein formale, äußerliche, dem Werk fremde
"Neuerungen" anstreben. Wir müssen den ursprünglichen Ideengehalt des Werks
herausbringen und seine nationale und damit seine internationale Bedeutung fas-
sen und zu diesem Zweck die geschichtliche Situation zur Entstehungszeit des
Werks sowie die Stellungnahme und besondere Eigenart des klassischen Autors
studieren. — Bertolt Brecht, "Einschüchterung durch die Klassizität" GW XVII,
1276

Materials in the Bertolt Brecht-Archiv

In a short article "Über das Bertolt Brecht-Archiv,"[1] Hans Joachim Bunge
describes the complex nature of Brecht's *Nachlaß*, and the method used in
cataloguing it. His information is updated and extended concerning Brecht's
plays, in volume I of *Bertolt Brecht-Archiv Bestandsverzeichnis des literarischen Nachlasses.*[2] In her introduction to this catalogue, the editor, Herta
Ramthun, writes:

Der Nachlaß wies keine systematische Ordnung auf. Eine Umordnung wurde dennoch nicht vorgenommen. Er wurde in der vorgefundenen Zusammenstellung ar-
chiviert, um mögliche nicht sofort erkennbare Zusammenhänge nicht zu zerstören.[3]

The *Bestandsverzeichnis* does not attempt a chronology of the BBA materials
for any of the plays:

Die Abfolge der zu einem Werktitel gehörigen Materialien ist nicht als zeitlich
geordnet anzusehen. Es wurden keine Ermittlungen über das Verhältnis verschie-
dener Fassungen zueinander sowie ihre Abhängigkeit von Quellen und anderen
Vorlagen angestellt.[4]

---

[1] *Sinn und Form,* XI (1959), 140—145.
[2] *Band I, Stücke,* Herausgegeben von der Deutschen Akademie der Künste zu
Berlin, bearbeitet von Herta Ramthun (Berlin: Aufbau Verlag, 1969), relevant
to *Der Hofmeister,* pp. 224—232.
[3] Ibid., p. vii.
[4] Ibid.

My first task in documenting the genesis of the *Hofmeister* adaptation was to classify three kinds of archive materials: the BBA files containing copies or fragments of the play and listed in the *Bestandsverzeichnis*, additional BBA files containing various writings about the play, and the less extensive *Hofmeister* materials possessed by the BEA. For the most part, these papers are composed of typescripts and mimeographed copies of the play, in addition to several printed texts; the few handwritten materials consist of brief notes and memos written by Brecht and his collaborator, Ruth Berlau.

The *Hofmeister* materials in the BBA may be divided into two main categories: (A) those listed in the *Bestandsverzeichnis*, and (B) those not listed in it. Each category may be subdivided into two groups.

A. Materials indexed in the "Bestandsverzeichnis"

1. The first and most important group consists of fourteen[5] more or less complete copies of five levels of the adaptation. Four[6] copies are typed, and ten mimeographed. A copy of the *Andruck*[7] — proofs made for the first printing[8] of the *Hofmeister* — may be considered part of this group.

2. The second group of documents is made up of one complete folder[9] and single as well as related pages[10] of corrections, scene fragments, the texts of the four songs of the Majorin in Scene 11, sketches of episodes or scenes, and memos.

B. Materials not indexed in the "Bestandsverzeichnis"

1. This group includes materials tangential to the adaptation: schedules of rehearsals[11] with the time, date, characters, and scene designated; *Notate*,[12]

---

[5] These are BBA files 1561; 541; 546; 495; 542; 540; 545; 544; 539; 1562; 1900; 1563; 2087; 1167. Only photocopies of the BBA original typed, mimeographed, printed, and handwritten materials are normally available for scholarly use in the archive.

[6] The typed copies are BBA 1561; 541; 542; and 540; these are also the earliest versions of the adaptation. The later mimeographed copies indicate the versions used during rehearsals.

[7] BBA 1901.

[8] In Brecht, *Versuche*, Heft 11 (Berlin: Suhrkamp, 1951), pp. 3-78. Subsequent references to this edition will be given as *Versuche*, Heft 11.

[9] BBA 543.

[10] The file and page numbers are: BBA 426/80; 546/100-145; 547/93-97 & 105-106; 1562/102-114; 782/38; 1560/23-32; 1334/55; 1825/30-43; 1528/2; 610/37; 913/76; 1500/1.

[11] BBA 1565.

[12] For examples of the *Notate* of the Berliner Ensemble, see *Theaterarbeit—Sechs Aufführungen des Berliner Ensembles,* edited by Ruth Berlau and others (Berlin:

or brief analyses[13] concerning the stage play and its production, compilations[14] of historical data about social, economic, and political conditions during the reign of Frederick II of Prussia; Brecht's own exegeses[15] of the play; eight typed pages reproducing portions of scenes from Lenz's drama *Die Soldaten;*[16] a photocopy of the table of contents pages of Friedrich Gottlob Klopstock's *Oden,*[17] no longer showing Brecht's [?] underlinings of titles; and a photocopy of *Versuche,* Heft 11, in the first East German edition (Berlin: Aufbau, 1952) in which the underlined portions of the *Hofmeister* text indicate Brecht's literal, thematic, and intellectual borrowings from Lenz's drama.[18]

2. The second group of nonindexed materials consists of two large uncatalogued folders called *"Hofmeister — Rezensionen."* These contain two kinds of documents: firstly, a fairly up-to-date but incomplete collection of over one hundred and seventy newspaper reviews concerning *Hofmeister* productions throughout the world, and, secondly, some carbon copies of typed reviews, poems by Lenz, and factual information about the late eighteenth century.

In addition to the above categories of materials, the scholar may read, with permission, three[19] of Brecht's diary entries and two[20] of his several letters referring specifically to the adaptation.

Suhrkamp, 1961), 2nd revised and enlarged edition, pp. 90-92. Also, see Manfred Wekwerth, *Notate—Über die Arbeit des Berliner Ensembles 1956 bis 1966* (Frankfurt, Suhrkamp, 1967), p. 7f.

[13] BBA 2062/1-40 & /79-93; 1566; 1567.

[14] BBA 1564.

[15] BBA 547/1-92 & /98-104; 548; 1560/9-32; 516/26; these files contain — with one exception — the penultimate and final versions of all the notes appended to the *Hofmeister* in *Versuche,* Heft 11, pp. 56-78, and in Bertolt Brecht, *Gesammelte Werke,* werkausgabe edition suhrkamp (Frankfurt: Suhrkamp, 1967), XVII, 1221-1251. Whereas BBA 1560/9-32 contains *Episierungen* of Scenes 3, 11, 12, and 16, *Versuche,* Heft 11 prints *Episierungen* of Scenes 3, 11, 14a, and of the final episode of Scene 17, but omits such "epic renderings" of Scenes 12 and 16. *Gesammelte Werke,* XVII, fails to include the *Episierungen* of *Versuche,* Heft 11, pp. 67-72. Subsequently, *Gesammelte Werke* will be abbreviated as GW with the appropriate volume number given in Roman numerals, followed by page numbers in Arabic numerals.

[16] BBA 1560/1-8, *Die Soldaten* IV, 6, 7; V, 2, 3, 5.

[17] BBA 2047/1-4: *Klopstocks Oden* (Leipzig: Göschen, 1798), two volumes in one.

[18] BBA 1810/1-82.

[19] BBA 2072/12-13. Permisson to quote the original German of the diaries and letters was withheld pending their publication. Hans Mayer and Ilja Fradkin both quote portions of an important letter of Brecht's of March 25, 1950. The letter is of interest concerning Brecht's reconception of Lenz's tragicomedy as a comedy. Also, the adaptor comments at length on Läuffer as a representative of the *Misere* of the German system of education. See: Mayer, *Bertolt Brecht und die Tradition* (Pfullingen: Neske, 1961), p. 56, and Fradkin: "Die 'Bearbeitungen' von Bertolt Brecht" in *Kunst und Literatur-Sowjetwissenschaft* XVI (1968), p. 167. See the epigraph, Chap. IV, p. 117.

[20] BBA 1280/3; 977/90.

Concerning the genesis of the *Hofmeister* adaptation, only those files listed in category A,1 above need to be discussed in detail. The materials classified in A,2 and B,1 are drawn upon only when they contain relevant dates, facts, or textual information. An examination of the reception of the adaptation, primarily in the German-speaking countries of Europe, and in Denmark and England, lies beyond the scope of the present study. The appendix of this work does, however, include a source list of the newspaper reviews mentioned in B,2.

In order to determine the chronological sequence of the various copies of the *Bearbeitung,* it was necessary, firstly, to ascertain how many distinct master texts or levels of the adaptation existed, and, secondly, to establish which copies belonged to each specific level.

My method of classifying the scripts was to compare all fourteen copies of the adaptation with each other and against the latest edition of the published drama.[21] The scripts were distinguished from one another according to their particular typographical and contextual characteristics. The typographical features of each script examined were as follows: (1) the relative position of initial words in each line of text on the page; (2) the design of the type lettering; (3) the spelling and typing errors; (4) the syllabification of words at line ends; (5) the amount of text on each page. Contextual alterations, such as omissions, additions, and revisions in each script, were investigated as follows: (1) how the act and scene numbers and titles differed; (2) whether scenes or passages from Lenz which do not exist in the published play were still present; (3) whether the handwritten revisions found in one or more copies were incorporated into the typed or mimeographed body of another script or other scripts; (4) to what extent the innumerable textual innovations of the published drama were contained in each of the levels.

The four BEA copies of the adaptation were compared in a similar manner.[22]

This comprehensive method not only determined the particular characteristics of each script, it also clearly established the existence of five levels in the genesis of the play. My classification of the scripts is reproduced graphically in the sequence chart on page 13. Each level of the adaptation is represented by a letter. The progression from one level to another is shown by the respective file numbers on the main arrow. Definitive influence of the text of a specific copy on other copies of the same level or on copies of more than one level is marked by a broken arrow. In the case of BBA 544 and BBA 539 the double-headed broken arrow signifies that each copy

---

[21] GW VI, 2331-2394. This version was also compared to all earlier printings of the *Hofmeister* in *Versuche,* Heft 11 and in Bertolt Brecht, *Stücke* (Frankfurt: Suhrkamp, 1959), XI. The first proofs of the *Hofmeister,* BBA 1901, were made in 1950 by Suhrkamp in Berlin.

[22] A discussion of the BEA materials follows on pp. 14–15.

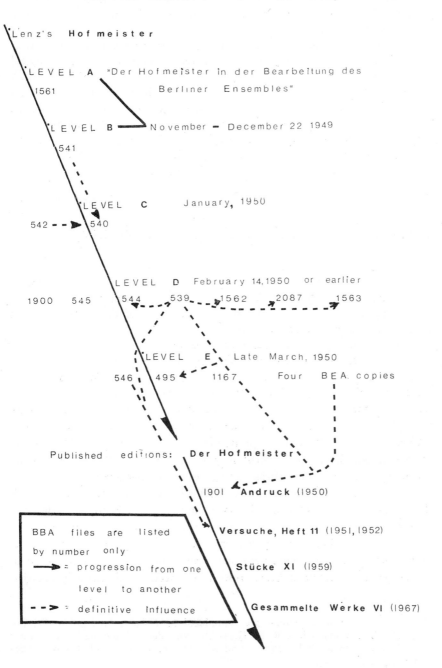

Sequence Chart

The Five Levels of the Stage Play

Lenz's **Hofmeister**

LEVEL A »Der Hofmeister in der Bearbeitung des
Berliner Ensembles«

1561

LEVEL B November – December 22 1949

541

LEVEL C January, 1950

542 ▸ 540

LEVEL D February 14, 1950 or earlier

1900   545   544   539   1562   2087   1563

LEVEL E Late March, 1950

546   495   1167   Four B.E.A. copies

Published editions: **Der Hofmeister**

1901 **Andruck** (1950)

BBA files are listed
by number only
➔ = progression from one
level to another
- -▸ = definitive influence

Versuche, Heft 11 (1951, 1952)

Stücke XI (1959)

Gesammelte Werke VI (1967)

alternately contained innovations which were transferred from the one script to the other. The main arrow stops before reaching the published editions of the *Hofmeister*. Unfortunately, the materials used to print BBA 1901 — the proofs, as well as the particular text used as a basis to revise them — could not be located by the late editor, Elisabeth Hauptmann, at the time of my investigations.

It should be remembered that what appears to be the logical numerical order of the BBA file numbers bears no relationship to the chronological sequence of the text levels in the genesis of the adaptation. As the BBA numbers given to the scripts represent the order in which Brecht's papers were found, it can be seen that the numerical sequence BBA 539 through BBA 548 has only limited significance chronologically: BBA 539, BBA 540, and BBA 541 represent levels D, C, and B, each file being the most definitive on each level. If this order is not fortuitous, it supports the findings of my investigations; if it is, it does not contradict them.

Materials in the Berliner Ensemble Archiv

The BEA collects various kinds of typed, printed, and photographic materials dealing with the production and performance of each drama put on by the Ensemble. The BBA does not possess photocopies of the more important items among the BEA *Hofmeister* collection.

A detailed description of this collection is provided here, because its contents are not recorded in any published index. The most valuable of these documents are the four copies of the level E text, one of which is designated "Eingestrichenes Exemplar," and the other three, numbered 1, 2, and 3, marked "Inspizierbuch." All four copies contain revisions and have the same handwritten corrections. The three scripts of the stage manager offer useful information about all kinds of production details of the play. Because the "Eingestrichenes Exemplar" is kept in a steel safe in the Berliner Ensemble, it is likely considered the official acting version of the adaptation.

There are two BEA copies of the excellent *Hofmeister Modellbuch*, each of which is in two volumes. The two large photo albums of each copy contain altogether some four hundred and fifty photographs (with captions); the pictures were taken during performances.[23] Many aspects of the adaptation take on more profound significance when the *Modellbuch* is consulted, for the published drama indicates few stage directions, theatrical properties,

---

[23] Nearly sixty of these pictures are reproduced in *Theaterarbeit*, pp. 68-79; pp. 97-114. Brecht writes in GW XVII, 1222: "Von der Aufführung wurden unter der Leitung von R. Berlau Photos und Beschreibungen für ein Modellbuch angefertigt ...".

actors' facial expressions, and gestures, but the *Modellbuch* does. Indeed, as John Fuegi notes: "For Brecht, man of the theatre, the literary text gave, in his opinion, only the palest shadow of the play as play."[24]

A large, thin folder in BEA contains photostats of eight sheets of music, of which pages 16, 17, and 75 are taken from Christoph Willibald Gluck's opera *Orpheus und Eurydice* in the Peters edition (n.d.); the other five pages, numbers 22, 23, 79, 80, and 81, are from his opera *Alkeste,* also in the Peters edition (n.d.). Some of this music may have served as the accompaniment for one or more of the songs of the Majorin in Scene 11; but no particular pieces are designated as belonging to a certain song.

There is also a large photo album marked *"Hofmeister — Details;"* unfortunately, it now contains but a few pictures showing close-ups of facial expressions, figures, and costumes.

Three original copies of the *Hofmeister-Programmheft* still exist. One represents a first edition, and two other copies are of a revised second edition.[25] A poster advertising the play is filed together with the *Programmheft;* the latter reproduces portions of a sentimental drawing by Chodowiecki, and of socially critical sketches and engravings by Franz von Goez and William Hogarth, who was long one of Brecht's favorite artists. The poster enlarges an engraving of teachers' heads by Hogarth, examples of which are shown on page 118 of *Theaterarbeit*. A single typed sheet of paper in the same folder as the programs and poster gives the performance dates of the *Hofmeister*[26] in the Berliner Ensemble production when the company went on tour.

BEA 1566/1-126, called *"Der Hofmeister — Notate"* (also on file in the BBA), has analyses of the adaptation and notes taken during rehearsals. Dated, the notes suggest how Ensemble members were to improve their acting.

There are, finally, two large brown folders marked *Hofmeister,* one of which contains typed documents about the on-tour performances of the play. The other folder contains various materials: Max Schroeder's essay and typed copies of data collected for the factual information printed in the *Hofmeister* program,[27] a few typed reviews, and many newspaper criticisms of *Hofmeister* performances throughout the world since 1950. Many of the newspaper clippings have been removed from the BEA collection by the *Arbeitsgruppe Historisch-Kritische Ausgabe der Schriften Bertolt Brechts.* These two BEA folders have largely identical counterparts in the BBA.

---

[24] John B. Fuegi, "The Artful Artificer, Bertolt Brecht: A Study of Six *Bearbeitungen,"* Dissertation, University of So. California, 1967, p. 15.

[25] This second edition of the program is reproduced in BBA 546/146-153.

[26] See *Theaterarbeit,* p. 120 and p. 428. Also, BBA 1563/2 has a list „Daten der Vorstellungen" giving slightly varying dates. The Berliner Ensemble gave the *Hofmeister* a total of seventy-two times between April 14, 1950 and April 17, 1951. Fifty-two performances were given in East Berlin, as well as twenty on tour.

[27] Some of these materials are identical to those photocopied in BBA 1564/1-56.

The genesis of Brecht's adaptation of Lenz's *Hofmeister* can be traced chronologically with a fair degree of accuracy. The primary reasons why Brecht reworked this drama proceed from the founding of the Berliner Ensemble in November, 1949, the subsequent necessity of building up a repertory, and the poet's specific desire to rescue for the stage a socially critical, topical, and grossly neglected German classic.

If we are to appreciate the speed with which the *Hofmeister* was adapted and produced, we should review briefly Brecht's activities during the months just before and immediately after the founding of the Berliner Ensemble.

Brecht settled in East Berlin in the fall of 1949. It is probable that long before his departure from Switzerland, he had definite assurances from the East German authorities that he was to receive the means to establish his own theater company. Possibly these assurances had been forthcoming the previous year when he began rehearsals for the Berlin production of *Mutter Courage und ihre Kinder,* the première of which took place in the Deutsches Theater on January 11, 1949.

The first production of the Berliner Ensemble was *Herr Puntila und sein Knecht Matti,* which opened in the Deutsches Theater on November 12, 1949. Rehearsals for *Puntila* probably started as early as mid-September 1949, if Brecht and his old friend and co-director, Erich Engel, were to have sufficient time to supervise the "13 Vorproben, 48 Bühnenproben, zusätzlich Musik-, Schmink- und Kostümproben"[28] before the opening night. By November 12, at any rate, the *decision* to adapt Lenz's play for the Ensemble was already firm in Brecht's mind.[29]

Always busy, Brecht found time to work on the *Hofmeister* only by asking another old friend, the well-known producer, Berthold Viertel, to assist in building up the company's repertory by directing its second production, Maxim Gorki's *Wassa Schelesnowa*. Five months later, on April 15, 1950, the third play in the company's repertory, *Der Hofmeister in der Bearbeitung des Berliner Ensembles,* as the stage version was called, opened in the Deutsches Theater.

It is possible to assign approximate dates to the various levels in the genesis of the adaptation by virtue of the fortuitous presence of a few dates scattered within the BBA materials, and by making close textual comparisons of the different versions.

As early as December 22, 1949, Brecht wrote in his diary that he had "quickly" finished for the Berliner Ensemble an adaptation of Lenz's *Hof-*

---

[28] *Theaterarbeit,* p. 46.
[29] As we shall see later, Brecht had the *idea* of adapting and producing Lenz's *Hofmeister* much earlier.

meister, a project which he ..ad long had on his mind.[30] Because BBA 541/105, level B of the adaptation, bears the same date as the diary entry, "22. 12. 49," it appears very probable that he was referring to this particular typescript. The calendar date and the adverb "quickly" suggest that BBA 1561, level A of the adaptation, must have been completed sometime between November 12 and December 22.

Level C, like the first two levels, has typed rather than mimeographed copies. This fact may be taken to indicate that BBA 542 and BBA 540, the level C texts, enjoyed a relatively small circulation. Brecht probably finished revising them no later than a week or so before February 14, when rehearsals[31] — using the new level D text[32] — commenced.

Because the second sheet of the stage manager's D level text, BBA 2087/2, notes "Probenbeginn am 14. II. 50," I can posit level D as having been mimeographed in late January or early February.[33] Level D was used at the most for five of the eight weeks of rehearsals. At the very least, it was used for three weeks, that is, until early March, as a corresponding detail between a diary entry and a note in the *Regiebuch,* BBA 539, leads me to believe: BBA 539/67 has, in Brecht's hand, a reminder, presumably to himself: "*episieren* 3. Person!" His diary entry of March 8, 1950, indicates that the actors of the *Hofmeister* needed training in the distanced or "epic" manner of speaking their lines. To this end, the entry continues, several scenes were drawn up in narrative form.[34]

Concerning the time when the level E text was mimeographed there are two pieces of conflicting evidence. Firstly, in BBA 1567, entitled "*Der Hofmeister* — Anmerkungen und Analysen," sheet number seventy has the note: "5. Fassung Anfang März." Should I construe this to refer to what I call level E? The twenty pages of discussion in this file — written by Alexander Koval, who analyzes various scenes of the *Hofmeister* — contain incontestable evidence that the level referred to is an early D text, specifically as represented by the state of BBA 544. However, Koval's discussion of Scene 6 fails to mention the very significant substitution of the excerpt from Kant's *Zum ewigen Frieden*[35] for an earlier quotation from the *Kritik der reinen Vernunft.* The present excerpt was added to BBA 544 during the rehearsals, as emendations in the body of the text clearly show. On the other hand, a

---

[30] BBA 2072/12. Compare the diary entry now published in *Bertolt Brecht Arbeitsjournal,* ed. Werner Hecht. (Frankfurt: Suhrkamp, 1973), vol. II, p. 915.

[31] Cf. GW XVII, 1222: "Geprobt wurde neun Wochen, mindestens fünf Stunden täglich."

[32] It was presumably a copy of level D that Brecht sent to his son, Stefan, in the middle of February, as indicated in one of the father's letters from Berlin-Weissensee. Cf. BBA 877/90.

[33] BBA 1565/1-51, called "*Der Hofmeister*—Probenpläne," shows the scenes, episodes, date, time, and place for rehearsals. BBA 1566/1-126, "*Der Hofmeister*—Notate." represents Brecht's comments on the performance of each actor during the period from February 22 to April 14, 1950.

junior assistant director, Egon Monk, writes the following about "Das Kantzitat"[36] of Scene 6 in his notes on the *Hofmeister:* "Das hier verwendete Kantzitat wurde *erst in den letzten drei Probenwochen* gefunden. Zuvor hatte man an einen Abschnitt über das Ding an sich gedacht."

The quotation from *Zum ewigen Frieden* is contained within the body of the mimeographed level E text; it was not added after level E had been distributed. If I choose to lend more credence to Monk, then Koval is probably wrong in referring to the text which he analyzes as the "fifth" level, implying that it already existed at the beginning of March. Rather, it is more probable that level E, the true fifth level, was not prepared until the last week of March. Should Koval be correct, which I doubt, level D would have to be considered the fifth master text, and some earlier version, of which there is absolutely no trace, would have to have preceded either level A or B. As a final point in Monk's favor, had level E existed as early as the beginning of March, it is most unlikely that Brecht would have continued to use his then superseded level D text, BBA 539, as the *Regiebuch* until the end of rehearsals on April 14, five to six weeks later!

While we have seen that the founding of the Berliner Ensemble in 1949 was the outward stimulus for Brecht to adapt the *Hofmeister,* his interest in doing so goes back much farther. On December 22, he noted that he had had such a thought on his mind for a long time. His imprecision forces us to seek more exact evidence from those who knew him, and from indications in his earlier writings.

Elisabeth Hauptmann, Brecht's lifelong friend, collaborator, and the editor of his collected works, recalled[37] that in Berlin, during the late nineteen twenties, Brecht spoke with interest about Lenz's *Hofmeister.* Although she could not recall the exact year of their conversations on this subject, Frau Hauptmann said that Brecht would have liked to have seen the *Hofmeister* staged. She added that, had he produced the play himself, he would undoubtedly have adapted it, for obvious theatrical[38] and ideological reasons.

---

[34] Cf. BBA 2072/13. Compare the published entry in Brecht's *Arbeitsjournal,* vol. II, p. 918.

[35] Cf. GW VI, 2351, lines 4-11.

[36] "Das Kantzitat" is the title of the discussion found in BBA 2062/11; my italics. The reference to Kant's *Ding an sich* pertains to a short parodistic passage written by Brecht and contained only in BBA 539/45.

[37] During an interview with the present author on February 4 and 6, 1970.

[38] To my knowledge, Lenz's *Hofmeister* was adapted for the stage only once before Brecht. Friedrich Ludwig Schröder simplified the work greatly, omitted the subplot with Fritz and Pätus, and had the Major buy a patent of nobility for Läuffer, who married Gustchen at the end of the play! Schröder's version experienced only one performance in Hamburg on April 12, 1778, another in Berlin on November 26, 1778, and eleven performances in Mannheim between 1780 and 1791. Wolfgang Stammler briefly compared this adaptation with Lenz's original in his 1908 Halle dissertation, "*Der Hofmeister* von Jakob Michael Reinhold Lenz;" cf. pp. 57–61; p. 133. Cf. also Richard Daunicht, ed., *Jacob* (sic) *Michael Reinhold Lenz: Gesammelte Werke in vier Bänden* (München: Fink, 1967), I, 391. Cf.

Apparently it was not until the late twenties that Brecht developed a liking for the poet Lenz. In contrast, Hans Otto Münsterer, a fairly close friend of Brecht in Augsburg and Munich, notes that during the time of their association during the period 1917—1922, Brecht showed less interest in Lenz than in other major German writers of the past:

> Unter den deutschen Klassikern hat Brecht nächst Büchner, Grabbe, Kleist und natürlich Goethe [,] vor allem Schiller geschätzt, dagegen konnte ich ihn für den mir besonders nahestehenden Lenz damals noch nicht recht begeistern.[39]

Brecht's sonnets "Über das bürgerliche Trauerspiel 'Der Hofmeister' von Lenz" and "Über Kants Definition der Ehe in der 'Metaphysik der Sitten' " provide the most valuable evidence of when he may have first seriously thought about specific problems raised by the *Hofmeister*. Although written much earlier, the two sonnets were not published until 1951 in *Versuche*, Heft 11, in the collection "Studien,"[40] which, significantly, was placed immediately after the notes appended to the *Hofmeister*. In an introductory paragraph to this collection, Brecht writes with casual irony:

> "Studien," um 1940 geschrieben, gehören wie die "Chinesischen Gedichte" in Heft 10 zum 23. Versuch. Diese sozialkritischen Sonette sollen natürlich den Genuß an den klassischen Werken nicht vereiteln, sondern reiner machen.[41]

In volume 9 of *Gesammelte Werke*,[42] the two sonnets in question are grouped among poems whose date of origin is given as between 1933 and 1938. BBA 426/80, an early sketch of the sestet of the sonnet "Über das bürgerliche Trauerspiel," was found in a file containing ninety-one sheets of *Galilei* fragments, most of which are dated 1938. The fact that the sketch of the sonnet's sestet was located there may suggest that Brecht was thinking about Läuffer's submission to the ruling powers at the same time that he was working on the scientist's capitulation in *Galilei*.

"Über das bürgerliche Trauerspiel" reveals that already a decade earlier, Brecht had considered some of the main problems emphasized in his adaptation of Lenz's play. For example, he anticipates certain thrusts of the *Bearbeitung* by changing, in the sonnet, the motivation for Läuffer's self-emasculation: where Brecht (in both his works) shows that it occurs out of physical and professional considerations, Lenz made psychological and moral reasons the motives for Läuffer's act. In addition to other stylistic and thematic correspondences between the poem and the adaptation, particular

---

Elisabeth Genton, *Jacob Michael Reinhold Lenz et la scène allemande*. (Paris: Didier, 1966), pp. 64—96.

[39] *Bert Brecht—Erinnerungen aus den Jahren 1917—1922* (Zürich: Arche, 1963). p. 57.
[40] *Versuche*, Heft 11, pp. 79—88.
[41] Ibid., p. 80.
[42] GW IX, 609—610.

19

thoughts and phrases in the play's prologue and epilogue are modelled literally on lines in the sonnet.

A passage from Kant's "Das Eherecht"[43] forms the point of departure for Brecht's ironic sonnet "Über Kants Definition der Ehe," where the philosopher's logic is twisted and led *ad absurdum* in the poem's sestet. The same passage appears almost verbatim in Scene 15 of BBA 1561, the earliest level of the *Hofmeister* adaptation. The only point in common between the sonnet and Scene 15 of the *Bearbeitung* is the quotation, which must rather have appealed to Brecht in its exaggerated subordination of the erotic urge to arbitrary laws of reason and society. There are no signs in the poem that Brecht thought of the passage in connection with Pätus in the *Hofmeister*. (Indeed, even in BBA 1561, the excerpt merely precedes the following literal transcription of Lenz's Act V, Scene 6; no attempt is made at a transition.)

The search in other early works of Brecht for particular themes and figures[44] which recur in the *Hofmeister* adaptation gives no clues as to when he may have first thought of reworking Lenz's play. Such comparisons do, however, yield interesting information about the development of some of his favorite ideas, images[45] and linguistic expressions. That several such figures and images recur in the *Hofmeister* merely attests to a certain predilection.

The Collaborators

Who were Brecht's collaborators for the *Hofmeister* adaptation? The printed and handwritten evidence we possess is not consistent with regard to their

----

[43] *Immanuel Kants Sämtliche Werke in Sechs Bänden, Band 5 Moralische Schriften* (Leipzig: Insel, 1922), p. 390. I was permitted to examine this particular volume in Brecht's library in the BBA. The book mark, a yellow cloth ribbon, was between the very pages where "Das Eherecht" occurs in § 24. It would seem that § 25 served as a basis for the Kant sonnet in "Studien." The two paragraph numbers are underlined in pencil.

[44] Compare for example Gustchen's "suicide" in Scene 13 of the *Hofmeister* with the fate of the "fallen girl" Anna in Brecht's parody of the German domestic tragedy in *Trommeln in der Nacht* of 1922. See the article by Guy Stern: "Brechts *Trommeln in der Nacht* als literarische Satire" in *Monatshefte*, LXI (1969), 241—259. Further research would also involve a comparison of the dilemma and ultimate choice made by Brecht's many teacher figures in plays ranging from the *Lehrstücke* to *Leben des Galilei*, and in the prose piece *Flüchtlingsgespräche*, Chap. III. Cf. also stanza 21 of Brecht's poem "Ballade von der Billigung der Welt," written between 1926 and 1933, GW IX, 473.

[45] Compare the changing symbolism of tree pruning in the Keuner story "Form und Stoff," GW XII, 385 and the action of the Geheimrat in the *Hofmeister*, Scene 8, trimming his box-trees. A discussion of these images occurred in a conversation between the present author and Elisabeth Hauptmann about Brecht's abiding interest in questions of education and upbringing.

individual names. In the *Hofmeister* text of GW VI, the reverse of the title page lists the following collaborators: Ruth Berlau, Benno Besson, Caspar Neher, and Egon Monk. The last name was not included in this list in the *Andruck*, but was added for the first printing of the play in *Versuche*, Heft 11, and in all subsequent editions. Neher designed the sets and was also listed as co-director by Brecht in the *Programmheft* and in *Theaterarbeit*.[46] Besson and Monk were among the four assistant directors. The third, Wolfgang Böttcher, is mentioned only in the *Hofmeister* program.[47] He, like the fourth assistant, a certain Kortner, is not acknowledged in any subsequent editions of the published drama. Kortner is noted together with Monk and Böttcher under "Asst. Regie" in BBA 2087/2. Apparently, neither Kortner nor Böttcher assisted Brecht very much during the rehearsals, at least not enough to be included in the adaptor's remarks concerning the production in the notes to the play.[48]

With the exception of Ruth Berlau and the actors whose innovations or "Kisten" are discussed in *Theaterarbeit* and GW XVII,[49] it is impossible to attribute specific innovations in the adaptation to particular individuals among the collaborators and members of the Ensemble. The only preserved criticisms written by collaborators are, as we shall see below, Ruth Berlau's brief but influential memoranda[50] to Brecht.

When and at what levels of the adaptation did Brecht receive assistance from his collaborators? Elisabeth Hauptmann maintains[51] that Besson and Monk "helped" Brecht "von Anfang an" — whenever that was; this tells us nothing about their contributions, since there are no records of conversations[52] Brecht had with his friends and pupils about problems he faced at any level of the adaptation. It was probably in late December, 1949, that Brecht gave Ruth Berlau a copy of the reworked play for criticism. Thanks to her textual references to the adaptation and to suggestions for changes in the plot, the characters, and the dialogue, we know that she examined — with profound insight — level B, as represented by BBA 541. When her remarks are compared to this copy and to BBA 542, level C, it is obvious that Brecht incorporated several of her suggestions into each text.

---

[46] *Theaterarbeit*, pp. 67, 120.

[47] Here one reads: "Beim *Hofmeister* nahmen besonders Benno Besson, Wolfgang Böttcher und Egon Monk tätigen Einfluß auf die Bearbeitung des Originalstücks, auf die szenische Gestaltung, auf die Arrangements. Sie leiteten Proben, bei denen Szenen entworfen oder ausgearbeitet wurden." The *Hofmeister* program, unavailable in the BBA, may be read in the BEA.

[48] GW XVII, 1221—1222.

[49] *Theaterarbeit*, pp. 102—103; GW XVII, 1241—1242.

[50] BBA 543/43-70. Alexander Koval's "Analysen" of BBA 1567/70-91 and Egon Monk's "Notizen über die Aufführungen—Detailbeschreibungen" of BBA 2062/2-40 do not fit this category; their writing is descriptive, not critical.

[51] In interviews with the present author.

[52] In the present author's interview with Ruth Berlau, January 27, 1970, Berlau mentioned that Brecht, Neher, and their friends often intensely discussed problems of the play at her apartment.

In a letter[53] to Berthold Viertel dated January 17, 1950, Brecht wrote that Neher had begun work on the *Hofmeister,* that the adaptation was finished, and that Gaugler had been induced to come from Switzerland to play the part of Läuffer. Since level B was completed on December 22, 1949, it is probable that the finished *Bearbeitung* referred to in this letter was level B. The letter suggests that Neher and Brecht had worked closely and agreed how to stage the play. The fact that one of Neher's preliminary sketches for Scene 12 — reproduced in *Theaterarbeit*[54] — is signed "N 49" supports my belief that he had collaborated closely with Brecht from November onward.

Apart from the influence of Berlau and Neher, we have no evidence concerning specific individuals who assisted Brecht with level C.

Level D was definitely the first version of the adaptation used during rehearsals, and staging the play was the source of countless revisions.[55] From February 14, 1950, Brecht's emendations and the contributions of his collaborators merge with the many anonymous suggestions made by members of the Berliner Ensemble. Appropriately, Paul Rilla writes:

Lange Diskussionen während der Proben, besonders psychologische, haßt Brecht. Während der mehr als zweihundert Probestunden des *Hofmeisters* gab es zusammengerechnet nicht mehr als vielleicht fünfzehn Minuten Diskussion zwischen Zuschauerraum und Bühne. Er probiert sowieso alle Vorschläge aus. "Wozu die Gründe sagen, zeigen Sie den Vorschlag" und "Sprechen Sie nicht darüber, machen Sie es vor", heißt es. Ist ein Vorschlag gut, wird er übernommen. . . .

Brecht spricht immer laut und ruft seine Vorschläge, meist von unten aus dem Zuschauerraum, den Schauspielern zu, damit alle es hören können. Das tut der Unmerklichkeit seines Eingreifens keinen Abbruch. Beim Inszenieren ist er von Schülern umgeben. Glückliche Vorschläge gibt er sofort weiter, immer mit der Nennung des Vorschlagenden: "X sagt, Y meint." Dadurch wird die Arbeit zu einer Arbeit aller.[56]

Given the possible exaggerations of this devoted contemporary testimony, Rilla's statement makes it abundantly clear why it would be impossible to acknowledge the ideas of individuals in such a long and fluid process as Brecht's rehearsals, of which tape recordings were not made until several years later. Thus it is only fair to describe levels D and E as Brecht's version of Lenz's *Hofmeister* "in der Bearbeitung des Berliner Ensembles."

---

[53] BBA 1280/3.

[54] *Theaterarbeit,* p. 115. This sketch is erroneously numbered as Scene 11 and not as Scene 12 in the first (1952), second (1961), and third (1966) editions of *Theaterarbeit.* This may point to Neher's using a very early copy of level A or B in which the scenes had not yet been numbered definitively for that particular level. (In fact, all the scene numbers given for the pictures on pp. 114, 115, and 117 of *Theaterarbeit* are incorrect, except for Scene 1.)

[55] Cf. BBA 2062/79-93: "Textänderungen während der Proben."

[56] Paul Rilla, "Die Regie Bertolt Brechts," 1952, in *Erinnerungen an Brecht* (Leipzig: Reclam, 1966), Hubert Witt, ed., 2nd edition, pp. 170—171.

Although Brecht assumes the authorship of the drama in the printed edition, all title pages of the BBA and BEA copies of the stage play modestly bear only the above rubric, and not his name. We should remember that no matter what alterations other collaborators suggested, the ultimate authorship must be ascribed to Brecht, since it was he who gave all adopted innovations their final form, whether in any specific level of the stage version, or in the almost identical published drama.[57]

The BBA Copies of the Hofmeister

The important textual innovations of each BBA script are discussed in terms of their contribution to the development of the structure, plot, characters, themes, and language as set forth in the stage play and printed text.

Level A

BBA 1561

This file contains the oldest complete[58] typewritten version of the adaptation. Called *"Der Hofmeister — Alte Fassung,"* it copies literally most of Lenz's play. Before revisions, BBA 1561 was a literal copy of the text of Lenz's *Hofmeister* as printed in the edition of Ernst Lewy: *Jacob Mich. Reinhold Lenz Gesammelte Schriften* (in vier Bänden) hrsg. von Ernst Lewy (Berlin: Cassirer, 1909 und 1917), I, 1—88. This was determined conclusively by a detailed comparison of certain features of the BBA 1561 text with all editions of Lenz's *Hofmeister* published since Ludwig Tieck's edition of 1828.[59] Greatly revised in its present form, BBA 1561 in some passages presages the *Hofmeister* as we know it from GW VI. The pagination, sometimes inconsistent and sometimes lacking, indicates that several scenes of Lenz's play were shortened, reworked, or omitted.

---

57 Concerning Brecht's "sovereignty in his collective play-writing" and play directing, John B. Fuegi has particularly apt comments in "The Artful Artificer, Bertolt Brecht: A Study of Six *Bearbeitungen*," Dissertation, University of So. California, 1967, pp. 69—72.

58 The following pages preserve copies of scene fragments of the level A text: BBA 543/2-6, /12-15, /71, /74, /80-81; BBA 547/93.

59 BBA 1561 reproduces a majority of the particular spellings, misspellings, and other errors as found in the 1909 printing of Lewy's edition. Conclusive proof that Lewy's text was used by Brecht rests in the fact that on pages 46 and 75 of the Lewy text, Wenzeslaus uses a Greek expression. The typist who prepared BBA 1561 for Brecht noted down the page numbers where these expressions occurred, instead of copying the Greek.

BBA 1561 has a prologue and twenty scenes, of which two are newly conceived; the entr'acte first occurs in BBA 541, the epilogue in BBA 539.[60] Deleting some scenes and combining others, Brecht reduces the thirty-five scenes of Lenz's play by half; i.e., material from twenty-four scenes is taken over and combined to make eighteen scenes in BBA 1561.[61] There are no act divisions, nor is the sequence of scenes advantageous for the exposition or indicative of parallels in the action, as is the case in each act of level E of the stage play.

What is particularly interesting about Brecht's intentions in level A is the decisive emphasis he gave to the main plot; in part this was achieved indirectly by omitting those strands of Lenz's main plot and subplot which dealt with Pätus's courtship of Old Rehaar's daughter, Seiffenblase's treachery, Gustchen's childbirth, the discovery of old Marthe, and the reconciliation of harsh fathers and "prodigal" sons.[62] The main plot, which treats Läuffer's hiring and abuse, temptation and fall, castration, capitulation and marriage — while based on Lenz's drama — has already been reconceived and executed in BBA 1561, much as in the printed text, especially in Scenes 7, 12, 14a, b, c, and 17. The parallel subplot of Pätus's intellectual emasculation is only hinted at in BBA 1561, because the episodes which show his idealistic espousal of Kant, his abjuration, and self-subjugation have not yet been added. The similarity between the Platonic union of Pätus and Jungfer Rehhaar and that of Fritz and Gustchen, although suggested by the common motif of "im Geiste zusammenbleiben" is not spelled out, (BBA 543/71), as it is later on.

Similarly, Wenzeslaus's role as a pedagogical model for Läuffer has not yet been elaborated. Bollwerk, who appears only in the sixth and ninth scenes of BBA 1561, is already shown as the crass opportunist. Brecht has not only given many of Pätus's speeches to Bollwerk, he has also changed and exchanged certain aspects of their nature as it was portrayed by Lenz. Now Bollwerk is the blustery, active *Kerl,* while Pätus appears quiet and

---

[60] Because the corresponding scenes have different numbers in the earlier versions of the play, I have, for the sake of clarity, always used the equivalent scene number of the *Hofmeister* text as printed in GW VI. The "Scene Sequence Table," which shows corresponding scenes in the GW VI text and all BBA and BEA scripts, is found in the appendix. It should be consulted during my discussion of the various texts of the adaptation.

[61] See the appendix for the schematic diagram: "Brecht's Condensation of Lenz's Drama." In BBA 1561, as in the printed version, Scenes 1, 2, 12, 13, and 17 all combine two or more scenes or episodes from Lenz. Only Lenz's II, 6 and III, 1 are not yet merged in BBA 1561; this happens only in Scene 11 of BBA 541. One scene of BBA 1561 — the one originally numbered "9" in this typescript — depicts a Halle street with Bollwerk mocking Pätus in front of the latter's girl friends and Fritz. Short, irrelevant to the subplot, and poor comedy, this new scene was dropped from BBA 541.

[62] See the important interpretation of Lenz's *Hofmeister* as a drama of prodigal sons in Albrecht Schöne, "Wiederholung der exemplarischen Begebenheit — Jakob Michael Reinhold Lenz," in *Säkularisation als sprachbildende Kraft* (Göttingen: Vandenhoeck und Ruprecht, 1958), Palaestra, vol. 226, 76—115.

far more gentle than Lenz's Bollwerk. The other characters differ from the original only in some scenes, but not in others. In the first part of Scene 11,[63] the Majorin is depicted as coquettishly singing to Graf Wermuth. However, neither her characterization, nor that of Gustchen, the Major, or the Geheimrat, is consistent from beginning to end of BBA 1561. Thus the sadistic streak of the Berg brothers, which is brought out in the new episode inserted into Scene 16, comes as a surprise. In all, a total of nine new episodes, introducing, for the first time, such themes as war, flirtation, and Kantian idealism, are added in Scenes 5, 6, 7, 11, 14a, b, c, 15, and 16. In most cases, transitions from the inserted passages to the following Lenz passages remain abrupt, whether it is a question of plot, theme or linguistic style. Generally, BBA 1561 is a rather mutilated torso of Lenz's work, mended clumsily here and there with patches of Brecht.

Level B

BBA 541

The texts of levels A and B were initially identical; both BBA 1561 and BBA 541 are typed, rather than mimeographed, texts. At least one of them was a carbon copy, several of which we know once existed.[64] Also, between thirty and eighty percent of the material *before revisions* in Scenes 3, 5, 6, 9, 12, 13, 14a, b, c, 16, and 17 of BBA 541 occurs on pages identical in every typographic respect to similar pages of BBA 1561. While some sections of BBA 541 are quite similar to selections from Lenz and to the new episodes in BBA 1561, others are entirely different. Also, much material taken over from BBA 1561 was extensively revised in BBA 541, and more of the often verbose Lenz text was deleted. The many innovations in structure, plot, character, theme, and language which occur in BBA 541 bring it much closer to the *Hofmeister* text as contained in GW VI.

BBA 541 has a prologue and nineteen scenes, with an entr'acte added after Scene 13, i.e., at the end of the third act. BBA 1561 Scene 9, in which Brecht follows Lenz closely, is much revised.[65] Two other scenes are combined to make up Scene 11. The act division is new and resembles that in the published drama, with the exception of Act II, which includes the new Scene 4, Läuffer's skating episode. A logical but not definitive order for the sequence of scenes is now established; and Brecht comments at length within the BBA 541 text[66] on the most effective position, dramaturgically, of Scene 2.

---

[63] Cf. notes 60 and 61.
[64] Cf. note 58.
[65] The circumstances surrounding the revision of this important scene are discussed in note 68.
[66] Cf. BBA 541/13.

In the already executed main plot, various innovations are made which serve to accent the sexual isolation and willing servitude of Läuffer. More important in this second level of the adaptation is the attention which Brecht gives to establishing a parallelism between the main plot and the two subplots. Thus the three Halle scenes are revised to develop the situations which reveal the disparity between Pätus's philosophical idealism and his unheroic behavior. The reshaping of Fritz's relationship with Pätus in the Halle scenes and to Gustchen in the two Insterburg scenes is only partially successful, since Brecht has not yet hit upon the formula of making Fritz a spiritual disciple of Pätus-Kant and thereby partly motivating his absence from Gustchen. Only later, in BBA 544 of level D, do we learn of Fritz's real reason for not rejoining Gustchen during the holidays: He is afraid of a sexual encounter, and of having to marry her.

In Scenes 12, 14a and 14c of BBA 541, the character and pedagogy of Wenzeslaus are further delineated. They are shown in grotesque caricature when Brecht supplies the pedantic schoolmaster with additional speeches which stress his ready joy in serving the ruling powers. These — in the persons of the Majorin, the Major and the Geheimrat, now more consistently portrayed throughout — are cast further in the Brechtian mould of heartless, class-conscious exploiters of the petty bourgeois. Bollwerk's role as the anti-intellectual, the rapacious bully, and the sexual braggart receives a little more emphasis. Gustchen awakens via Klopstock's odes to her latent sexuality and flirts dangerously with Fritz and Läuffer. And the minor figures of Rehhaar and Karoline,[67] as well as the willing but inhibited middle-class girls at the skating rink, are newly introduced. Most significant among the thematic innovations are the introduction of the emotionally charged Klopstock odes, and the inclusion of additional references to idealistic writings of Kant. Now that the secondary tensions and polemic thrusts have been more clearly established, the adaptation is well on its way to becoming a typically Brechtian *pièce à thèse*.

Level C

Level C is represented by two originally identical typewritten texts: BBA 542 and BBA 540. Most scenes of BBA 542 were revised before those of BBA 540. The changes were then transferred to BBA 540, and the text was further revised. It became Brecht's main working copy and contains considerably more corrections than BBA 542.

---

[67] Whereas Lenz spelled "Rehaar" with one "h", Brecht spells the name "Rehhaar." It is not clear whether the adaptor does so with ironic intent or merely out of carelessness. "Karoline" was a popular name for women during the last quarter of the 18th century. Brecht does not seem to have any ironic intentions in his use of this name.

In BBA 542, the presence of an extra scene, "Halle im Gefängnis," following Scene 9, permits me to date this portion of the adaptation as contemporary with the same section in BBA 541 when it served as the model for the level C text. After level C was typewritten, Brecht must have realized, rather late, that to keep the prison scene was to create unnecessary difficulties in recasting the important Pätus subplot. To motivate credibly Fritz's incarceration in Scene 9, and then to portray it, Brecht found, added nothing to his already radically different characterization of Pätus and Bollwerk. In addition, to follow Lenz's text slavishly here proved too long a digression from the main plot. The problem was solved by omitting the prison scene and its motivation. Surprisingly, Brecht struck them in BBA 541, even though the texts of level C already existed. Likely, they were simply not at hand.[68] Having deleted the troublesome sections from BBA 541, Brecht revised what was left of Scene 9 and made the same alterations in BBA 540. He continued to add new material to this now very different development of the subplot. The scenes in question were, however, left untouched in BBA 542 by these extensive revisions. Hence the extra scene in this text.

With the exception of the above, BBA 542 is only slightly changed in comparison with BBA 541, the parent level. The only significant innovations in BBA 542 are in the character of Wenzeslaus, in so far as short new stage directions serve to accentuate the comic effect of his behavior toward the Berg brothers in Scene 12. New speeches in Scene 14c bring out the irony resulting from the contradiction between the barbarity of his methods and the sublimity of his pedagogical goals.

BBA 540

In all but a few scenes, BBA 540, like BBA 542, resembles BBA 541. In BBA 540, the ninth scene, greatly revised, portrays a Fritz now akin to Pätus in his spiritual nobility; the two unite in seeking comfort in philosophy.

The additions in Scene 12, however, are striking: several new speeches in the form of sudden authoritative commands from Wenzeslaus to Läuffer further reveal the character of each man, as well as adding a touch of ridic-

---

[68] Confusion might result for the researcher, if, in tracing the genesis of the adaptation according to a strictly chronological sequence of levels, he did not take into account the fact that Brecht frequently used whatever level of the adaptation was available at the time new solutions occurred to him. The indexer of Brecht's *Nachlaß*, Frau Ramthun, advised me that such a method is characteristic of many of his works. This not unusual *Salto mortale* of the influence of one level on another is indicated by the broken arrows in several places in the "Sequence Chart" on page 13.

ulousness to the already amusing and tragicomic situation. Here, too, the thematic merging of the three Lenz scenes and of Brecht's additions into a homogenous whole is brought about. The substitutions which Brecht makes for the deleted portions of Lenz's text stress the inhuman aspect both of the schoolmaster's character and of his appraisal of sensuality.

In Scene 8, the addition of Läuffer's final desperate plea, while amusing, indicates that the tensions of the plot have reached their breaking point: the bed scene with Gustchen follows immediately in level C.

A feature of the various copies of this level, and particularly of the later level D, is the meticulous care taken to polish the language by the omission, simplification, and addition of expressions. Also, the spelling and word order were revised with the intention of creating a smooth transition and giving an occasional archaic flavor to new textual insertions.

BBA 542 and BBA 540 are the last versions of the adaptation to be worked on primarily by Brecht himself. BBA 540 was the model for the first acting version of the play, as represented by the texts of level D.

Level D

This level is preserved in seven, originally identical, copies: BBA 1900; 545; 544; 539; 1562; 2087; and 1563. The fact that D is represented by so many mimeographed specimens suggests that it was the first text to be widely distributed for rehearsals. The first four copies of level D were Brecht's own; the fifth belonged to an assistant responsible for accurately noting the revisions worked out and incorporated into Brecht's copies during rehearsals, and the last two scripts were those of the stage manager and the prompter. My sequence of the file numbers indicates the chronological order in which each was revised.

BBA 1900 and BBA 545

These duplicates, sharing half a dozen minor revisions in Brecht's hand, are, in fact, uncorrected or extra copies. The body of their text and the sequence of their scene order are those of BBA 540, level C. As neither BBA 1900 nor BBA 545 records the progress of the adaptation, each is useful only in so far as it preserves the original text of level D. BBA 1900 is complete, whereas in BBA 545, Scene 1 is a fragment, and Scenes 18 and 19 are missing.

BBA 544

BBA 544 and BBA 539 are the two most authoritative copies of the D text because they were Brecht's *Regiebücher*. They contain his extensive hand-written and typed revisions. The corrections of BBA 544 were generally transferred to BBA 539, which through further revision, was to become the one text most comparable to the stage play and the published drama.

BBA 544 alters the position of the beginning of Act II and of Scenes 4, 6, and 9 to resemble the scene sequence as it occurs in the published play.[69] Brecht's reasons for moving up Scene 4 are significant for the exposition of Läuffer's basic situation.[70] Rearranging Scenes 6 and 9, to come at the beginning of Acts II and III, respectively, not only increases the dramatic tension as each scene unfolds, but also establishes in the structure of the work that parallelism which is represented by the dialectical juxtaposition of plot and subplot: Each scene set in Halle is followed by one set in Insterburg.

The rehearsals contributed greatly to the revisions made in BBA 544, Brecht's first *Regiebuch*. The lessons learned during rehearsals made it clear that the three Halle scenes (6, 9, 15) required extensive changes in the character and speeches of Pätus, Bollwerk, Fritz, and Jungfer Rehhaar if Pätus's fall from the moral heights of Kantian idealism to the banal superficiality of a petty bourgeois husband was to be motivated convincingly. Whereas Bollwerk (in Scenes 6 and 9) and Rehhaar (in Scene 9) had to represent the more vital aspects of real life, Pätus and his admiring pupil Fritz had to be shown (in Scenes 6 and 9) as withdrawing from this kind of reality. Consequently, in Scene 6, Bollwerk's several new speeches portray him as thinking about life mainly in sexual terms and scorning the revolutionary ideas of Kant, whom he fails to understand. Pätus takes on the stature of a moral hero in his defiantly enthusiastic defense of that philosopher's writings on freedom and his *Zum ewigen Frieden*, which are referred to in BBA 544 for the first time.[71] Pätus's espousal of this latter work is paralleled by the addition of Frau Blitzer's sympathy for deceased soldiers' families who receive reduced pensions "wegen dem [sic] siegreichen Krieg." (BBA 544/35) As a contrast to Bollwerk's appetite for physical love rather than intellectual disputes, Fritz confesses the increasing attraction which philosophy holds for him.

In conjunction with Scene 7, in which minor revisions now cause Gustchen to appreciate the beauties of nature unfolding in springtime, rather telling passages from Klopstock's odes are added in BBA 544 at the beginning of Scene 9. Here, these poetic selections and another equally telling passage from Gustchen's letter prompt Fritz to give his travel money to Pätus, so that he may pay for Jungfer Rehhaar's abortion. Happy to escape the certain temptation that awaits him in Gustchen's arms, Fritz decides instead to embrace Pätus's "aufwieglerischen Immanuel Kant" (GW VI, 2360), for contemplation incurs less discomfort than amorous involvement. To stress this point, BBA 544 expands the subsequent episode, which contains the reference to the abortionist's fee, and recasts the revered Jungfer Rehhaar as a shameless slut.

---

[69] Cf. the "Scene Sequence Table" in the appendix.
[70] Cf. *Versuche*, Heft 11, p. 58, pp. 74–75.
[71] Cf. Egon Monk's *Notate*, BBA 2062/11.

In the final Halle scene, the inclusion of Pätus's remarks about his examination topic allows Fritz to ascertain the extent of his old friend's intellectual collapse. This particular passage further unites the three Halle scenes by its subtle mention of their three main subjects: Philosophy, war, and fatherhood.

The desperate sexual and professional straits of Läuffer in the main plot are the subject of additional but minor revisions in Scenes 3, 4, 5, 12 and 14c. Among the more important are the individualization of the appreciative but hesitant girls in Scene 4, Läuffer's plea in Scene 5 for a horse, and Wenceslaus's intimation in Scene 12 that the unfortunate tutor can find employment only with him. The addition in 14c of Wenzeslaus's exclamation concerning a "Türkenschlacht" (GW VI, 2381) suggests that it was not until rehearsals had progressed that the latter part of Mozart's Rondo "alla turca" of his *Piano Sonata in A* (K. 331), written in 1778, was chosen as a hilarious musical alienation effect to surround[72] the three short scenes of Act IV.

From many aspects, then, the revisions of BBA 544 reveal that a collective authorship of Brecht and the Berliner Ensemble must be held responsible for the innovations in this adaptation. This is even more true in the case of BBA 539, Brecht's second and more important copy of the *Regiebuch*.

BBA 539

An epilogue is present for the first time in BBA 539. The scene sequence here is the same as that in BBA 544. There are no changes in the main plot, nor in the Pätus and Fritz subplots. Almost every scene in BBA 539 has been very carefully revised, with the result that the depiction of each figure is balanced, vivid, and most eloquent.

Stage directions, for example, are added profusely in Scenes 1, 2, 3, and 12. They contribute enormously to the exposition or clear understanding of the action. In Scene I, the addition of the phrase "Er wird nicht zurückgegrüßt" (BBA 539/4) tells us as much about the Berg brother's estimation of Läuffer as the extensive revisions in their speeches reveal about their class prejudices and the Geheimrat's snobbery. Most of the stage directions inserted into the text of BBA 539 were the fruit of rehearsals. Scene 2, for instance, contains many stage directions unfortunately not included in the published drama. The on-stage positions and the embraces of the lovers in this scene were carefully worked out for the play's performance; these indications, together with the *Modellbuch*[73] photographs, it should be noted, give a much truer interpretation of their situation than can be gained without the knowledge of stage directions. Fritz and Gustchen are shown but a step away from consummating their love. This is hardly conveyed in the printed text.

---

[72] Cf. *Versuche*, Heft 11, p. 64.
[73] Cf. Chapter I, p. 14 of this study for a description of the *Hofmeister Modellbuch*.

As in Scene 2, so also in Scene 3 the movements of Läuffer both in his dance and toward the Majorin are clearly shown in a number of stage directions, some of which are quite lengthy.[74] The intensely sensual proclivities of these four characters are thereby brought out. Similarly, the authoritarian streak in Wenzeslaus receives greater emphasis in Scene 12, both by the insertion of new stage directions and by the inclusion of additional commands putting Läuffer to work. Such interpolations increase, of course, the irony of the situation, while at the same time poviding comic relief. Small extra speeches are recorded throughout BBA 539. Their purpose is sometimes to stress or develop a particular theme or aspect of character, and at other times to parody a certain episode either by adding melodrama, by exaggerating the issue out of all proportion, or by providing a dialectic contrast to something just said or done.

Whereas the previous textual levels gradually shaped the raw material of the adaptation, BBA 539 adds many subtleties to the work. The rehearsals contributed much to the finesse of BBA 539: The most apt expression was found, consistency in character portrayal was achieved, and even more kinds of humor in the action were offered. If a historical-critical edition of the adaptation is ever published, its editors would need to examine BBA 539 closely.

BBA 1562

BBA 1562, called *"Der Hofmeister* mit Korrekturen,"* is a companion text to BBA 544 and BBA 539. The revisions of now the one specimen, now the other, are copied in BBA 1562 either by hand in very neat printing or in retyped pages. The only disconcerting point about this copy of level D is that, contrary to expectation, it fails to note all revisions exactly as they occur in either BBA 544 or BBA 539; rather, it records variants. Possibly, the revisions were only *heard* during rehearsals, and not checked visually against Brecht's written notations.

Among those few additional speeches found only in BBA 1562 and the published *Hofmeister* text, several emphasize the class deference of Wenzeslaus and Läuffer, as well as the effect of the Seven Years' War on the latter's prospects for employment.

BBA 1562 contains a great many stage directions not found elsewhere. Entrances, movements, and exits are carefully recorded for each scene throughout. Also noted carefully are the seasons and the titles summarizing the content or thrust of each scene, such as "Zehnte Szene — Es kam wie es kommen mußte. Insterburg. Gustchens Zimmer. Im Mai." (BBA 1562/46)

---

[74] As for example: "Das Examen ist bestanden. Läuffer ist schweißgebadet, er hat mit äußerster Anspannung den tödlichen Existenzkampf gekämpft. Nun ein großer (langer) Gang auf die Majorin zu, als auf die *Frau* ⟨sic⟩." BBA 539/18.

Such inclusive titles may have served as guides for the *Projektionen,* of which there is no record in either the BBA or the BEA.[75] The most important feature of the stage directions and additional speeches of BBA 1562 is that they shed more light on the character of certain personages. Lise, for example, is shown in Scene 17 to be most curious about Wenzeslaus's interrogation of Läuffer. As the schoolmaster berates the refugee tutor for staring hungrily at her in church, she is eavesdropping at the door. While all maids may share this fault, it reveals Lise's intense interest in Läuffer and her hopes for marriage.

The first reference to Händel's *Largo* occurs in Scene 11 of BBA 1562. It could well be that the idea to have the Majorin play this piece occurred during rehearsals.

Of possible significance in considering the genesis of the epilogue may be the fact that whereas BBA 1562/102 reproduces the *Epilog* of *Der gute Mensch von Sezuan,* the following page, BBA 1562/103, has the *Hofmeister* epilogue as first contained in BBA 539/144. This fact of their juxtaposition, and the similar vocabulary of each, could attest to the difficulty Brecht had initially in finding an appropriate conclusion for the adaptation.[76]

BBA 2087

Other, less important copies of the D level text are BBA 2087 and BBA 1563. The former, called *"Der Hofmeister — Bühnenfassung,"* is actually only the first copy of the stage manager's script, not the final version of the stage play, which is represented by three copies of the level E text, each marked "Inspizierbuch" and kept exclusively in the BEA. Many of the revisions of BBA 544, BBA 539, and BBA 1562 are recorded in BBA 2087, but in variant form. Several minor additions and alterations of words are, surprisingly, unique to BBA 2087 and the published drama. The four songs sung by the Majorin in Scene 11 are added in writing in BBA 2087. This marks their first occurrence.

BBA 1563

BBA 1563 was likely a second copy of the level D "Inspizierbuch." The BBA calls it *"Der Hofmeister — Soufflierbuch."* It may have been used as such *after* the stage manager, R. Thümmel, had received copies of the new level E text. However, the fact that it contains not only the one hundred pages of the play's spoken text, but interperses an additional eighty pages containing the stage manager's production notes, indicates that it was or-

---

[75] The *Projektionen* are mentioned only in passing in *Versuche,* Heft 11, p. 64; the slide for Scene 12 of the *Hofmeister* is reproduced in *Theaterarbeit,* p. 115.

[76] Variants of an early version of the *Hofmeister* epilogue occur in BBA 543/30.

iginally his copy. Also, BBA 2087/2, the page showing the cast, has "Diene-mann" as the prompter; there is a similar notation in BBA 1563/3. It is prob-able that BBA 1563 was only the first copy of the prompter's book. Likely, the "Eingestrichenes Exemplar," an E level text, present only in the BEA, was the prompter's final copy. This is a reasonable suggestion since in it all but the spoken and sung texts have been deleted. The revisions in BBA 1563 were not kept as up-to-date as those in BBA 2087. Certainly, neither copy can be considered as authoritative as BBA 539.

Level E

The text of this level is represented by seven, originally identical, mimeo-graphed copies: BBA 546, BBA 495, BBA 1167, and four scripts in the BEA, of which one is called "Eingestrichenes Exemplar," and the other three, numbered 1, 2, and 3, are marked "Inspizierbuch."

BBA 546

BBA 546 is perhaps the most important of all level E texts. A comparison of the revisions incorporated into the typewritten text of level E in BBA 546 with the handwritten revisions of BBA 544 offers convincing evidence that BBA 544 has fewer revisions than BBA 539: BBA 544, for stenographic reasons, had to be out of circulation for some time while the level E text was being typed and mimeographed. Once it was completed, BBA 544 was returned to Brecht. In the meantime, BBA 539 had served as his *Regiebuch*. Sub-sequent to the preparation of the E level texts, Brecht continued to use BBA 544 *as well as* BBA 539 for noting changes in the play. This reconstruction of the circumstances surrounding the level E text also explains why hand-written revisions were transferred from BBA 544 and BBA 539 into the level E texts even after the text of level E had been mimeographed.

A most interesting discovery was that the file BBA 546 contains a total of one hundred and fifty-three pages. Not all of these represent the original mimeographed state of level E; only pages one to ninety-nine do. The epi-logue, which would have followed page ninety-nine, is missing in BBA 546. Pages one hundred to one hundred and fifty-three were simply placed under-neath page ninety-nine, although that was not their intended order. In BBA 495 and BBA 1167, copies of these pages were inserted in the proper place, and thus superseded the original, now revised pages. Pages one hundred to one hundred and thirty-eight are unique to the three level E texts in the

---

77 Compare the "Scene Sequence Table" of Scenes 16 and 17 in BBA 546, 495, and
1167 in the appendix.

BBA; they do not exist in the copies of the E level text in the BEA. However, their mimeographed revisions are identical with the handwritten emendations contained in the BEA level E texts. What is particularly striking about these mimeographed pages is the fact that they also bear the corrected scene numbers which now correspond to those of the printed drama. Specifically, the revised Scene 17 in the level E text (the *last* scene of the printed text) was originally Scene 16 in the stage play.[77] It was decided only after the last main rehearsal that the scene with Fritz's reunion (Scene 17) should precede Scene 16, and that Läuffer's "happy end" should conclude the play: "Erst nach der Hauptprobe entschieden wir uns, das Stück mit Läuffer abzuschliessen." (BBA 2062/93) Clearly, then, pages one hundred to one hundred and thirty-eight were retyped and mimeographed only *after* this decision. It is remarkable that none of the E level copies in the BEA contains any of the thirty-nine definitive pages. Although these pages were not inserted in their correct order within the BBA 546 text, they were in BBA 495 and BBA 1167. Also, the fact that they were *mimeographed* indicates there were a large number of copies of the E text which were to have had these pages inserted into them.

But what of pages one hundred and thirty-nine to one hundred and fifty-three? These can be divided into two groups. The latter group is textually less interesting, consisting, as it does, of eight photocopies of the second edition of the *Hofmeister* program. Of greater significance is the first group. Its pages, one hundred and thirty-nine to one hundred and forty-five, are additional revised sheets (even correcting some belonging to the group composed of pages one hundred to one hundred and thirty-eight) which were to replace the superseded pages of BBA 546. They contain some of the last revisions of the text of the *Andruck* and are found in the first published text of the play. Thus these pages are more definitive, in the sense of a critical edition, than the *Andruck* itself. In other words, they have speeches and stage directions which appear to have been added to the text of the adaptation only after the printing of the *Andruck*. This raises several questions which can perhaps be answered only when more materials, now in private hands, become available: (1) Which level (and which copy) served as the model for the *Andruck*? (2) Which text served as the definitive version for correcting the *Andruck*? (3) In whose possession are these slightly divergent texts?[78]

----

[78] It is my belief that an E level text into which the revisions of pages one hundred to one hundred and thirty-nine had been inserted was used as the model for the *Andruck*. It is likely that the papers of Elisabeth Hauptmann, the late editor of the *Hofmeister*, may contain the texts editorially important for the published play. In February, 1970, they could not be located for examination, although Frau Hauptmann was sure that they still existed.

The level E texts BBA 546 and BBA 495 were Brecht's own copies. BBA 495 contains many minor handwritten corrections. However, it is not as complete as BBA 1167, called *"Der Hofmeister — Text für Modellbuch — Mappe Berlau."* This copy has corrections in Berlau's hand, and, given the unordered state of the pages in BBA 546, it is the most reliable of the three BBA level E copies. BBA 1167 is more interesting from a photographic than from a textual point of view, for cross marks were placed at those points of the action where photographs were taken for the *Hofmeister Modellbuch*. A comparison of the photographs in the *Modellbuch* of the BEA against these crosses confirms this fact. The speeches next to the crossmarks provided the basis for the one-line caption found under most pictures in the *Modellbuch*.

The BEA Copies of "Der Hofmeister"

Level E

All four BEA level E copies must be considered the most definitive versions of the stage play. They contain a majority of the revisions of BBA 539 which are written in by hand. In addition to BBA 2087, each of these four copies contains the four songs of the Majorin. As noted earlier, the three copies of the stage manager's script contain much information about the different properties and tasks involved in the actual production of the play. Otherwise, these copies have no textual additions not already discovered in BBA 1167, BBA 539, or the first copy of the stage manager's script, BBA 2087.

The Proofs: BBA 1901

BBA 1901, called *"Der Hofmeister — Suhrkamp 1950 — Berlin — Andruck Mappe Berlau,"* has twenty-eight pages. It is the proof copy for the first publication of the *Hofmeister* in *Versuche*, Heft 11; only the text of the play is represented by these twenty-eight pages, and not the "Anmerkungen," "Episierungen," or the essay "Über das Poetische und Artistische." BBA 1901 contains no corrections. When comparing it to all printings of the *Hofmeister* text in *Versuche*, Heft 11, in *Stücke* XI, and in GW VI, we see that only minor portions of speeches, printing errors, and punctuation must have been revised in some other copy of the proofs which is now no longer available. The printing errors were not completely banished until GW VI.

The differences between the text of the stage play and the text of the published drama are few in number. Whereas the acting version reproduces the four songs of Scene 11 and has more stage directions, the published work has neither these songs nor as many stage directions.[79] It does have some speeches which are slightly lengthened or altered. The acting version deletes the Majorin's song at the end of Scene 16, but the printed piece retains it.

As this cursory description of the various levels of the adaptation has shown, tracing the genesis of the work was a complicated matter. Although the facts we possess tell a great deal about the adaptation, we shall probably never definitely know who was responsible for particular innovations, nor how and when certain of them came into being.

If a *Materialienband* — such as already exist for most of Brecht's major plays — is eventually made for the *Hofmeister,* the BEA level E texts and the original materials of the photocopies contained in the BBA will have to be consulted. The present BBA photocopies are not always completely legible; and neither the first few lines nor the last few lines of the original pages are always reproduced in the photocopies. If a critical edition listing all the variants is ever undertaken, the presently unavailable, and possibly important, unpublished *Hofmeister* scripts still very likely owned by Benno Besson, Ruth Berlau, Egon Monk, Caspar Neher, Elisabeth Hauptmann or their respective heirs, should be examined.

---

[79] For example, the stage direction: "Er wird nicht zurückgegrüßt" exists only in BBA 539/4 and the published drama (GW VI, 2335).

CHAPTER II

GENRE, EXTERNAL STRUCTURE AND PLOT
OF LENZ'S DRAMA AND THE ADAPTATION

Die shakespearisierende Szenentechnik der Sturm-und-Drang-Dramatik opponierte gegen die in gesellschaftliche Regeln eingezwängte ständische Enge, indem sie gegen allen dramaturgischen Regelzwang opponierte. Aber Lenz opponiert auch gegen eine stoffliche Verflüchtigung, wie sie ihm die Zeitmode auferlegt. Mit einer dichten und deftigen Milieu-Aufnahme holt er die weitesten szenischen Sprünge ein. Was sein realistischer Griff zusammenrückt, rückt die Bearbeitung zurecht; sie führt thematisch durch, was Lenz dem Stoff anheimstellt. — Paul Rilla, "Analyse der Bearbeitung," *Theaterarbeit*, ed. Ruth Berlau et al. (Dresden: VVV Dresdner Verlag, 1952), pp. 81—82

Lenz's Theory of Tragicomedy

J. M. R. Lenz never formulated a coherent theory of tragicomedy as such. Certain remarks which he made about the tragic and comic genres and their characteristics suggest that he was trying to describe the nature of a drama whose comic and tragic scenes, significantly juxtaposed, delineate the structure of an intermediate genre, tragicomedy. And when his remarks on theory are interpreted in light of his dramatic production, it appears that he understood by the term *Komödie* what some critics call tragicomedy.[1]

In letters written in June and October, 1772 to Salzmann, Lenz consistently designates (what critics take to be) his *Hofmeister* as a "Trauerspiel."[2] The term does not convey the true generic nature of the play, however, for Lenz excuses himself, qualifying his use of "Trauerspiel" with the parenthetical statement: "(ich muß den gebräuchlichen Namen nennen)." (*Briefe*, I, 25) The Berlin manuscript of 1772 shows a change, possibly a progression, in Lenz's thought. Here he specifies the genre of the play as a "Lust- und Trauerspiel." This subtitle is crossed out, however, and replaced by "Ein

---

[1] René Girard suggests that Lenz's theory of tragicomedy must be deduced from the dramatic works themselves: "Aussi importantes qu'aient pu être, à maints égards, les tentatives de Lenz pour élaborer un certain nombre de définitions, il n'a jamais été en possession d'une dramaturgie dont son théâtre serait le reflet. Contrairement à ce qui se produit dans l'oeuvre de Lessing, la démarche du créateur a, chez Lenz, une primauté absolue sur la réflexion théorique ... Ce n'est qu'en analysant les oeuvres dans lesquelles, des comédies adaptées de Plaute aux *Soldats*, s'élabore progressivement la tragi-comédie, que l'on peut en saisir véritablement la structure et la portée." Cf *Genèse d'une Dramaturgie du Tragicomique* (Paris: Klincksieck, 1968), p. 188.

[2] Cf. *Briefe von und an J. M. R. Lenz*, eds. Karl Freye und Wolfgang Stammler (Leipzig: Wolff, 1918), I, 25, 58—59, 62. Subsequent references to Lenz's letters are given in the text, showing volume number and page.

Lustspiel." And finally, the edition of 1774, published by Weygand, shows the subtitle "Eine Komödie."[3]

Apparently, Lenz does not intend the same generic meaning with the terms *Lustspiel* and *Komödie*. Rather, he understands by *Komödie* a kind of play tending toward tragicomedy. He not only differentiates between *Lustspiel* and *Komödie* but, more importantly, advances a new concept with the term *Komödie*, by which he understands plays that emphasize now the comic and now the tragic mood.[4] Girard interprets Lenz's attempts to define the genre of *Der Hofmeister* as follows: "Cette oscillation dans la désignation du genre de l'oeuvre correspond à l'élaboration d'une technique dramatique particulière qui lie, de façon spécifique, des modes d'expression réputés contradictoires, voire incompatibles."[5]

Lenz's views on tragedy and comedy, as expressed in *Anmerkungen übers Theater* and "Rezension des *Neuen Menoza*," aid somewhat in trying to establish what he understands by *Komödie*. The *Anmerkungen*, to be sure, deal primarily with tragedy; nevertheless, Lenz states that comedy should concentrate on situation and event rather than character: "Die Hauptempfindung in der Komödie ist immer die Begebenheit,..."[6] On several occasions, he repeats that *character* is the substance of tragedy, *action* the fabric of comedy. Lenz considers that characters serve the development of the action in comedy:

> Die Personen sind für die Handlungen da — für die artigen Erfolge, Wirkungen, Gegenwirkungen, ein Kreis herumgezogen, der sich um eine Hauptidee dreht — und es ist eine Komödie. Ja wahrlich, denn was soll sonst Komödie in der Welt sein? Fragen Sie sich und andere! — Blei, I, 254.

----

[3] Lenz also changed his mind as to the generic label of *Die Soldaten*, published as "Eine Komödie" in 1776. He originally intended to use "Eine Komödie," as evidenced by a letter of September, 1775 to Herder: "In guter Prosa: 'Die Soldaten', eine Komödie, habe ich Dir über Darmstadt zugeschickt..." (*Briefe*, I, 131) Later, fearing social embarrassment for himself and others, he requested Zimmermann in a letter of March, 1776: "...den barokken Titel Komödie... vor den Soldaten wegstreichen zu lassen und statt dessen darauf zu setzen: Ein Schauspiel von Steenkerk aus Amsterdam." (*Briefe*, I, 191)

[4] A similar view is expressed by Girard: "Le terme de 'Komödie' habituellement utilisé pour désigner les comédies de Shakespeare, est suffisamment vague, dans sa consonance étrangère, pour recouvrir une réalité plus complexe que la désignation habituelle de 'Lustspiel'. Il permet, en outre, de marquer la différence avec la comédie traditionelle ('Lustspiele nach dem Plautus') tout en orientant la pièce de façon plus précise que ne le fait le terme de 'Schauspiel', généralement employé à l'époque." Cf. *Genèse*, p. 227, note 11.

[5] Ibid., p. 227.

[6] Cf. *J. M. R. Lenz — Gesammelte Schriften* hrsg. von Franz Blei (München und Leipzig: G. Müller, 1910) in 5 vols., I, 252. Subsequent quotations from Lenz's theoretical writings all refer to Blei's edition and will show the editor's name, volume and page number after the quotation.

Here, *Komödie* seems to be synonymous with *Lustspiel*. In Lenz's dramatic practice, however, events generally serve to illuminate character, the main focus of Lenz's tragicomedy. Guthke, too, sees Lenz's emphasis on the action in comedy as predisposing this genre to the tragicomic:

> Für unseren Gesichtspunkt ist hier deutlich, daß, wenn Lenz das Strukturgesetz der Komödie als "Handlung" bestimmt, damit dem Eingang von Tragischem in die Komödie Tür und Tor geöffnet ist, da "Begebenheiten" fast unumgänglich solche vielfältige Schattierung annehmen.[7]

It seems that Lenz soon tires of theorizing about what he does not yet see clearly himself; he eventually begs the question: "... es ist so eine verdrießliche Sache, von Dingen zu schwatzen, die sich nur sehen und fühlen lassen, über die nichts gesagt werden will —." (Blei, I, 255)[8]

Lenz's views on comedy, as expressed in the important and more helpful "Rezension des *Neuen Menoza* von dem Verfasser selbst aufgesetzt," come close to defining *Komödie* as a genre which should tend toward tragicomedy. Lenz proposes here, that because society in his era exhibits barbaric as well as refined tendencies, it is content neither with mere comedy nor with pure tragedy.[9] For Lenz, pure tragedy in conceivable only in times when the most refined civilization is a general condition of mankind. The more primitive man's culture, the closer his comedies are to the purely low comic. Guthke notes that in contrast to the comedy of antiquity, Lenz sees the comedy of his own era as "... hervorgegangen aus und bestimmt von einem bereits sittlich gebildeteren und feinsinnigeren Publikum, [sie] hat ernste Bestandteile in sich aufgenommen."[10] *Komödie*, as Lenz understands the term, appeals, or should appeal, to those who wish to be entertained as well as to those who seek edification in the theater. The mixture of the tragic and the comic should be conducive to all the spectators: "Ich nenne durchaus Komödie nicht eine Vorstellung, die bloß Lachen erregt, sondern eine Vorstellung, die für jedermann ist. Tragödie ist nur für den ernsthafteren Teil des Publi-

---

[7] Karl S. Guthke, *Geschichte und Poetik der deutschen Tragikomödie* (Göttingen: Vandenhoeck und Ruprecht, 1961), p. 52.

[8] Theodor Friedrich, an expert on Lenz's dramatic theory, warns: "Indessen — wir dürfen der Theorie ⟨Lenzens⟩ von der Komödie nicht prinzipielle Bedeutung geben. Sie dient nur als Staffage für die Theorie von der Tragödie, und kommt so wenig aus der Tiefe, daß sie Lenz nicht einmal zur Überleitung zu Shakespeares Lustspiel benutzt." Cf. *Die "Anmerkungen übers Theater"* des Dichters Jacob Michael Reinhold Lenz — Nebst einem Anhang: Neudruck der "Anmerkungen übers Theater" in verschiedenen Typen zur Veranschaulichung ihrer Entstehung — (Leipzig: Voigtländer, 1908), p. 87.

[9] In this regard, Walter Hinck comments: "Nur im Rahmen der tragisch-komischen Mischform erscheint ihm ⟨Lenz⟩ wesenstreue Spiegelung der ungestaltet-uneinheitlichen deutschen Gesellschaft möglich. Der gesellschaftlichen Heterogeneität entspricht im ästhetisch-dramaturgischen Bereich die gattungsgesetzliche Heterogeneität." Cf. *Der neue Menoza* (Berlin: de Gruyter, 1965), p. 82.

[10] Op. cit., p. 53.

kums, ..." (Blei, II, 333) If the tragedy tends to idealize its subject, the *Komödie* seeks to reproduce it realistically and in a socially critical manner:

Komödie ist Gemälde der menschlichen Gesellschaft, und wenn die ernsthaft wird, kann das Gemälde nicht lachend werden. Daher schrieb Plautus komischer als Terenz und Molière komischer als Destouches und Beaumarchais. Daher müssen unsere deutschen Komödienschreiber *komisch und tragisch zugleich schreiben*, weil das Volk, für das sie schreiben, oder doch wenigstens schreiben sollten, ein solcher Mischmasch von Kultur und Rohigkeit, Sittigkeit und Wildheit ist. So erschafft der komische Dichter dem Tragischen sein Publikum. — Blei, II, 334 Italics mine.

Taking stock of the progression in Lenz's theory, one might say that his *Hofmeister,* initially called a "Trauerspiel" for want of a more accurate term, possibly contained too great a mixture of the comic and the tragic to be considered a tragedy in the sense entertained by Lenz later on in the "Rezension." In contrast, the term "Lust- und Trauerspiel" of the intact Berlin manuscript of 1772 may be approximate to what Lenz really means here by *Komödie.* In the light of these statements, Lenz's choice of "Eine Komödie" as the generic label for *Die Soldaten* also seems to have been carefully considered, particularly if he understands by *Komödie* a socially critical, tragicomic play. Such does, indeed, appear to be his understanding of the term as revealed in his letters. In July and August, 1775, he writes that he wishes to portray society as realistically and critically as possible, and to show social classes "wie sie sind;" he is writing for "das ganze Volck," and hopes to combat the "Verderbniß der Sitten" that is so widespread. (*Briefe,* I, 115—116) To Herder he writes of *Die Soldaten:* "Es ist wahr und wird bleiben ..." (*Briefe,* I, 119) and "Das ist nach dem strengsten Verstand wahre Geschichte ..." (*Briefe* I, 124)

The characters in *Die Soldaten* are far less caricatured than the figures in *Der Hofmeister.* The former play has a tragic outcome, whereas in the latter, such an outcome is averted. Nevertheless, Lenz calls both plays "Eine Komödie." As he uses this term, it can apply to plays with differing admixtures of the comic and the tragic mood, for *Der Hofmeister* — as will be shown — must be read as a primarily comic play with tragic overtones, as a tragicomedy in which the comic is the dominant mode. Conversely, *Die Soldaten* tends toward being a tragic play with comic overtones; it is a tragicomedy in which the tragic prevails over the comic.

The Tragic, the Comic and the Tragicomic
in Lenz's "Hofmeister"

As the above examination of Lenz's theory has suggested, his use of the term *Komödie* may well be tantamount to what some critics call tragicomedy. In the following considerations of the tragic, the comic and the

40

serious, together with a review of critical opinion, I shall try to show that for Lenz *Komödie* is indeed synonymous with tragicomedy.

Lenz's *Hofmeister*, although tending toward the tragic mode, stops short of tragedy and is, instead, distinguished more by the use of the comic, the ridiculous, the farcical, the burlesque and the absurd modes. The tragic element is not realized in the destinies of individual characters but manifests itself only as the "nearly tragic" in various situations experienced by Gustchen and Läuffer, and in the intended suicide of the unwed mother The truly tragic manifests itself indirectly in the behavior of Pastor Läuffer and his son (II, 1) *in their function as representatives* of the intellectual and of the servile middle class.

If the tragic results from the failure of the protagonist — struggling nobly — to preserve his dignity and his ideals in the face of adversity or against insuperable odds, then his fate may be considered tragic. The protagonist Läuffer is no tragic figure because he has such a weak character. The noble struggle to preserve ideals is absent from his actions. His is little more than a banal, half-hearted protestation that he deserves a minimum of financial reward and the opportunity to seek sexual gratification. The fact that he readily allows himself to be used and abused by the Major's family and Wenzeslaus is hardly tragic. The spectator cannot admire Läuffer for cowering and crawling instead of resisting. His servile behavior and, particularly, his self-emasculation render it difficult for the spectator to identify with his sufferings. Lenz fully intends that we should be repulsed by the tutor while, at the same time, being horrified at the abuse and exploitation that such a middle-class intellectual must endure if he is unwilling or unable to find different employment. It seems clear that Lenz is documenting here the "tragedy" of the German middle class. For all his anguish, Läuffer remains an essentially comic figure. The fact that he also symbolizes the "tragedy" of the middle class, makes him, by implication, a tragicomic figure. (Such a conception of Läuffer as a symbol also reflects, of course, Lenz's didactic intentions.)

As I attempt to show below, Guthke tries, often unconvincingly, to see the misfortunes of Läuffer as tragic. Lenz may wish the spectator to feel a certain pity for the protagonist's misfortunes and frustrations but the primary effect Lenz seems to intend is the comic. Lenz's irony frequently prevents the spectator from dwelling for long on the tragic implications of Läuffer's fate. The best example of this fusion of the comic and the tragic effects may be V, 3 where the spectator is horrified by the tutor's castration but forced to laugh because of the unexpected, preposterous reaction on the part of Wenzeslaus. (Ironically, the schoolmaster congratulates Läuffer, mistaking the tutor's motive in castrating himself.)

If the comic is the product of an unexpected kind of behavior which contrasts sharply with what the spectator normally could and should expect in a given situation, then much of what Läuffer, the Major, Gustchen,

Wenzeslaus and Pätus do and say is indeed comic. But the extent to which the spectator or the critic experiences the comic as ambivalent will naturally depend on his concept of what is tragic and what is comic.

The Critics and the Generic Question

Ever since the publication of Lenz's *Hofmeister* in 1774, critics have been unable to agree about a generic classification for the play.[11] Sometimes the impression given is that they are as embarrassed for a simple answer as was Faust when asked by Margarete: "Glaubst du an Gott?" (line 3426)

What accounts for this hesitancy in giving a satisfactory answer? *Der Hofmeister* is a complex generic phenomenon in its protean juxtaposition of varying shades of the comic and the tragic, the serious,[12] the grotesque and the absurd. The comic and the tragic are often ambivalent and sometimes fuse to produce the grotesque and the absurd. There is, perhaps, no simple, constantly, even universally, accepted generic description which would do justice to the sum total of the ambivalent situations and events in the thirty-five scenes of Lenz's play! To a certain degree, Girard and Guthke, the most important recent critics of the tragicomic in Lenz's drama, fail to agree on what constitutes the tragic mood. Whereas Guthke stresses the tragic effect — as he claims Lenz and other Storm and Stress writers understood it — and maintains that Lenz undeniably succeeds in *Der Hofmeister* in writing "komisch und tragisch zugleich," Girard tends to follow the definition of the tragic which I have given above but never once designates the play as a tragicomedy. (Girard, too, requires that the protagonist struggle nobly to preserve an ideal and the dignity of man.) Furthermore, Girard is primarily interested in the comic aspects of the characters and their behavior, and takes care to point out the indebtedness of Lenz's dramatic techniques to the comic tradition in literature.

---

[11] Girard discusses various critics, cf. *Genèse*, p. 283, pp. 288—291; Guthke does so also, cf. *Gesch. d. dt. Tragikomödie*, pp. 55—65; also Rosanow, *J. M. R. Lenz, der Dichter der Sturm- und Drangperiode* (Leipzig: Schulze, 1909), pp. 194—195; Rosanow also prints excerpts from the contemporary reception of *Der Hofmeister* on pp. 206—211; cf. Korff, *Geist der Goethezeit* (Leipzig: Koehler und Amelang, 1966), 8. unveränderte Auflage, vol. I, pp. 246—247.

[12] The serious, as revealed in various situations experienced by Läuffer in Lenz's drama, may be defined as that which causes grave concern in the protagonist without, however, eliciting in the spectator that horror, empathy or intense anxiety which the tragic mode may inspire. Lenz's I, 4, for example, illustrates what I consider the serious, the unfortunate, the regrettable. The Major ruthlessly takes advantage of Läuffer's material dependence on him by requiring the tutor to perform more duties while, at the same time, reducing his salary. Such exploitation is regrettable but hardly tragic, for it lacks not only those spiritual effects described above, but also that quality of finality, of what can never again be made what it once was.

This fundamental difference between the French and German critic brings to mind a line from Brecht's ironic sonnet "Über das bürgerliche Trauerspiel 'Der Hofmeister' von Lenz: "So wirds ein Lustspiel drüben und hier keins." (GW IX, 610) Here, the disparity between the French and the German view of social freedom, the destiny of the middle-class individual, and the degree of social emancipation already achieved accounts for the choice of genre in the dramatization of the theme. The grounds for disagreement between Girard and Guthke are, however, aesthetic, rather than sociological. Girard — as we shall see — suggests that "...le raisonnement de K. S. Guthke nous semble cependant pécher par un abus de terme."[13]

A prescriptive poetics satisfies few modern critics, and Guthke is certainly one of them in resisting normative definitions: "Was tragisch und was komisch ist, entpuppt sich plötzlich als bedingt durch den historischen, bildungsmäßigen, weltanschaulichen Standpunkt des Betrachters, und eine grenzenlose Relativität der Begriffe tut sich auf."[14] He notes "...daß sich die berufensten Kritiker bis heute nicht einigen können, ob bestimmte dichterische Gestalten tragisch sind oder komisch, etwa Shylock, Don Quixote..."[15] and, one might add, Läuffer.

Guthke calls the *Hofmeister* a tragicomedy, suggests that there is no absolutely normative vantage point from which to designate a play as tragicomic, and advises against too strict a definition of this generic type.[16] He rejects the notion that the alternation of comic and tragic scenes is characteristic of the genre and bars the dramatist from using the technique known as comic relief in order:

> ...to decrease the tension of our tragic involvement by temporarily diverting our attention to something entirely different. There is no chance with this kind of succession of the tragic and the comic for the synthetic view, for the very principle of the psychology of comic relief is that the comic scenes are experienced alternately with the tragic ones.[17]

To Guthke's way of thinking, the synthesis of the tragic and the comic is the distinguishing characteristic of true tragicomedy:

> Only when both directions in the heightening of effect are integrated can we speak of the complex and yet simple phenomenon of the tragicomic. In it the comic and the tragic are identical and mutual conditions of each other ... it may well be that the tragic is more tragic and the comic is more comic in the tragicomic fusion.[18]

---

[13] *Genèse*, p. 288.
[14] *Gesch. d. dt. Tragikomödie*, p. 16.
[15] Ibid., p. 17.
[16] Ibid., pp. 16—17.
[17] *Modern Tragicomedy — An Investigation into the Nature of the Genre* (N. Y.: Random House, 1966), p. 58.
[18] Ibid., p. 59.

Although the tragicomic may be only episodic, it can set the prevailing mood and determine the dominant interpretation of the action:

> Denn wenn auch nicht jeder Moment des handlungsmäßigen Ablaufs als tragikomisch gestaltet werden kann, so doch die tonangebenden Stellen, und wie auch in der Tragödie nicht jeder einzelne Augenblick von sich aus tragisch ist, sondern viele Momente nur zur Hinleitung auf das Tragische dienen, so wirken die tragikomischen Höhepunkte in der Tragikomödie ebenfalls wie Lichtquellen, von denen aus das Tragikomische auf das Gesamt (sic) ausstrahlt, das Vorangehende ins rechte Licht setzend und die Auffassung des Kommenden prädisponierend.[19]

Guthke describes Lenz's tragicomedy as follows, intimating that what may seem to be a crude juxtaposition of the tragic and the comic is actually a synthetic positioning of the two:

> Denn in ihm [dem integrierten Tragikomödietypus Lenzens] sind die entgegengesetzten Elemente noch klarer und scheidbarer als in anderen Bauformen des gleichen Genres, aber nichtsdestoweniger sind sie zur Objektivierung des Phänomens des Tragikomischen integrativ bezogen, nur eben in gewaltsamer, klaffender Weise, wie es der Dramatik eines Lenz überhaupt entspricht....[20]

When calling Läuffer and his situation "tragic," Guthke tends to qualify his use of the term, arguing that although modern critics may not call the tutor's lot tragic, Lenz most certainly did:

> Und sprach Lenz von Tragödie, so kann er schlechterdings nichts im Sinne gehabt haben als die dargestellte *Gesamtsituation,* die sich "tragisch" auf den Hofmeister Läuffer auswirkt, der in ihr gefangen ist: rettungslos ist dieser junge Mann den demütigenden Unannehmlichkeiten seines Standes ausgesetzt, Unfreiheit, Zwang, ist sein unabdingbares Los, und gleichgültig, ob wir heute dies als tragisch oder nur traurig empfinden: Lenz hat stark herausgearbeitet, daß dies im Sinne der Genie-Geistigkeit Tragische den Hofmeister mit voller Gewalt trifft.[21]

Guthke is more convincing, however, when he labels as tragic Läuffer's abdication of his human dignity and of his rights to personal and intellectual freedom (as described by the Geheimrat in II, 1): "Für die Mentalität der Stürmer und Dränger ist einem Menschen in solcher Situation sein wesentlichstes Sein tragisch verneint."[22] Guthke is of the opinion that Lenz turns what is basically an almost naturalistic tragedy into a comic tragedy in two ways. Firstly, Lenz places his comic type-characters in "tragic" situations:

> Einmal: die Figuren, die diese für den Hofmeister im Sinne des Sturm und Drang tragische Lage konstituieren, sind die komischen Typen aus der sächsischen Verlachkomödie ... Durch diese komischen Typen ... erscheint also Läuffer in aller "Tragik" bereits wieder im Zwielicht ...[23]

---

[19] Guthke, *Gesch. d. dt. Tragikomödie,* p. 15.
[20] Ibid., p. 58.
[21] Ibid., p. 59, italics mine.
[22] Ibid., p. 60.
[23] Ibid., pp. 60—61.

Secondly, Lenz makes these comic characters the "tragic" victims of the action:

> Die führende Strukturschicht dieses tragikomischen Dramas besteht vielmehr darin, daß die tragischen *Opfer* dieser Situation selbst komische Figuren sind, ja Karikaturen.... Dieses Gestaltungsprinzip ist auch auf die Opfer: auf Läuffer, das verführte Gustchen und ihren erschütterten Vater angewandt.[24]

Girard, on the other hand, does not describe any of Läuffer's situations before the castration as tragic, as for example when he says: "La situation [de Läuffer en I, 4] n'est pas tragique, mais infernale et dérisoire; elle correspond parfaitement à la description qu'en donne le conseiller dans la scène 1 de l'acte II,..."[25] The French critic notes that Lenz "...fait du séducteur la principale victime d'une comédie sentimentale."[26] Girard does imply that he considers the castration tragic, but he emphasizes the comical and farcical elements of the situation and the dialogue which render the tragic grotesque: "La rhétorique de Wenzeslaus [en V, 3], les images employées, l'accumulation des superlatifs créent une rupture énorme à l'intérieur même du dialogue; un comique aristophanesque sert de contrepoint à la tragédie."[27] Agreed, there is a tragic element in Läuffer's castration, but the tutor cannot, in Girard's opinion, meet a tragic end after this, for "...il est inconcevable que le public s'identifie à la destinée d'un eunuque."[28]

In fact, Girard doubts whether the so-called tragic situations of Läuffer in *Der Hofmeister* can really by classified as tragic when they are perhaps only serious, i.e., regrettably unfortunate and lacking in spiritual depth. Girard's argument is pertinent, for — as Guthke shows[29] — the comic mood tends to predominate with the result that: "...le tragique...se réduit parfois au sérieux et au poids angoissant des situations."[30] Girard maintains that:

> ...contrairement à l'affirmation de K. S. Guthke, l'interaction permanente du comique et du tragique ne renforce pas, dans le cas précis du *Précepteur* [!], la virulence de l'un et l'autre des termes, mais tend au contraire à se dépasser elle-même en une synthèse qui fait avorter la comédie comme la tragédie. L'action du *Précepteur* nous conduit fréquemment au seuil de l'un ou de l'autre de ces genres, elle ne s'enferme jamais totalement dans l'un d'entre eux.[31]

----

[24] Ibid., p. 61.
[25] *Genèse,* p. 238.
[26] Ibid., p. 239.
[27] Ibid., p. 269.
[28] Ibid., p. 279.
[29] *Gesch. d. dt. Tragikomödie*, p. 65: "⟨Es⟩ ist nicht zu verkennen, daß sich im *Hofmeister* das Komische des Schicksals Läuffers etwas stärker geltend macht als das Tragische, das manchmal zum nur Ernsten, Schweren abgeschwächt erscheint. Das absolut gleichgewichtige Sich-Geltendmachen der beiden Elemente des Gleichen ist jedoch ein selten erreichter Bestfall, und die vorhandenen Tragikomödien bewegen sich fast alle in einem Spielraum der fluktuierenden Akzentverteilung. So auch bei Lenz selbst."
[30] Girard, p. 288.
[31] Ibid., p. 288; cf. also p. 421.

While Girard grants the existence of the tragic and the comic as separate modes, his denial that they fuse in the tragicomic clearly reflects his opinion that *Der Hofmeister* is not a tragicomedy. Contrary to Guthke's repeated affirmation, Girard maintains that Lenz does not regard Läuffer's end as tragic, for the Storm and Stress author sees no solution to the tutor's difficulties:

> L'individu médiocre succombe sous les coups d'une société hiérarchisée et stratifiée Toutes les tentatives pour se faire une place dans cet univers ou pour forger une éthique qui permettrait de survivre sont vaines... En refusant toute solution idéale, toute intervention transcendante, d'ordre métaphysique ou moral, Lenz récuse tous les genres dits "bourgeois" que pratique son siècle. Ce qui n'implique pas qu'il rejette, théoriquement, tout recours à la tragédie. Mais vivre tragiquement, est réservé à des natures d'exception capables d'affirmer leur liberté et d'affronter la marche du monde. C'est dire que la tragédie est exclue de l'univers trivial de la vie quotidienne, dans laquelle Lenz fait évoluer ses personnages.[32]

Girard views Läuffer's marriage as farcical to the point of absurdity: "L'ultime initiative du précepteur: réparer la castration par le mariage est une nouvelle illusion qui transforme un comportement condamnable en un comportement absurde."[33] Girard concludes that Lenz describes Läuffer's highly improbable end in a sober, realistic manner, i.e., as opposed to sentimentally glossing over an unfortunate fact of life:

> Toute tentative pour plaquer une issue tragique sur une situation commune est, pour Lenz, un recours arbitraire à un art idéaliste, qui projette sur la réalité des solutions illusoires.
>
> . . . .
>
> Lenz n'a pas décrit — et n'a pas voulu décrire — autre chose qu'un ensemble de contradictions réelles dans le cadre limité de la vie quotidienne.[34]

Girard does, however, admit the momentary existence of the tragic, but only in the sense in which Dürrenmatt describes its possibility in the essay *Theaterprobleme:*

> Doch ist das Tragische immer noch möglich, auch wenn die reine Tragödie nicht mehr möglich ist. Wir können das Tragische aus der Komödie heraus erzielen, hervorbringen als einen schrecklichen Moment, als einen sich öffnenden Abgrund, . . .[35]

In Girard's opinion, *Der Hofmeister* constitutes but one of several stages in the genesis of Lenz's dramaturgy of the tragicomic; the play does not reflect the attainment of this kind of drama. Guthke, on the other hand, insists that the tragic does exist throughout the *Hofmeister,* and that, because

---

[32] Ibid., p. 289.
[33] Ibid., p. 280.
[34] Ibid., p. 289 and p. 291, respectively.
[35] Cf. *Theaterprobleme* (Zürich: Arche, 1955), p. 48.

46

of its repeated juxtaposition with the comic, the structure of the play must be regarded as that of a tragicomedy. As the divergent views of the two critics clearly suggest, whether Lenz's *Hofmeister* may be called a tragicomedy must depend in each case on the arguments of the critic, his degree of subjectivity, and the broadness of his definitions.

Brecht's Views on Generic Aspects of Lenz's "Hofmeister" and the Adaptation

Much of what has been noted earlier about the tragicomic phenomenon *per se* — especially Guthke's remark that the tragicomic influences one's conception of the past action and predisposes one's view of the action to come — also applies to the tragicomic as it occurs in Brecht's adaptation of the *Hofmeister*.

The tragic and comic aspects of the characters and action in a particular scene of the adaptation may become ambivalent or increasingly so as a result of the influence of the preceding or following scene, i.e., the juxtaposition of the scenes contributes significantly to the peculiar generic character of the drama. This occurs, for example, in the configuration ["Liebe in Stellvertretung" (GW XVII, 1245)] of Scenes 9 and 10, or in the configuration of the three "happy ends" of Scenes 15, 16, and 17.

As the sonnet "Über das bürgerliche Trauerspiel 'Der Hofmeister' von Lenz" indicates, Brecht not only conceives of Lenz's drama as a middle-class tragedy but also as a comedy. The last line of the poem's sestet reads: "Des Dichters Stimme bricht, wenn er's [die Geschichte der Selbstentmannung, d.h. der Selbstunterwerfung] erzählt." (GW IX, 610) This verse suggests that Lenz wishes to share his anguish with the spectator when contemplating the tragic situation of Läuffer, and by implication, that of the middle class as a whole. Despite the fact that Brecht emphasizes Lenz's horror and despair in this last line, the tone of the poem is equally comic: pity merges with amusement, mockery, vulgar humor and scorn. The poem thus becomes tragicomic in tone and actually describes the Berliner Ensemble's adaptation of the *Hofmeister* more accurately than Lenz's drama; and the distressed voice of the poet is also that of the social critic Brecht.

In the epilogue, Brecht describes his adaptation as a comedy. The first line of the epilogue reads: "Und das war nun der Komödie Schluß." (GW VI, 2394) The adaptor may be using the term "Komödie" in several ways. Possibly, he uses it loosely to mean play, or perhaps he has in mind Lenz's term for tragicomedy "Komödie," used as the generic label for the original play. Most likely, however, he simply intends it to mean a comedy which, despite its serious, and possibly tragic, moments, remains highly amusing and entertaining.

In the situations of the three unfortunate lovers, Läuffer, Pätus and Fritz, tragic effects consistently blend with comic effects to produce the tragicomic mood. Each character experiences the tragic in the most ridiculous, hilarious situations. In the amusing Scene 10, for example, Läuffer has seduced Gustchen and muses aloud, cynical yet helpless, that his situation, instead of having become easier to bear, now threatens disaster. The tragic aspect in this episode, comments Brecht, "... muß doch bei Läuffer [und nicht bei Gutschen] liegen: Sie darf ihm immerhin die Stellvertreterin der anonymen Natur, er muß ihr Stellvertreter eines ganz bestimmten Mannes, Fritzens, sein." (GW XVII, 1232)

Brecht also states that the adaptation is a tragicomedy when he comments on Läuffer's situation in Scene 3:

> Die Szene erhält ihre Bedeutung durch Gauglers [des Darstellers] Kunst, die aufsässige, brutale Vitalität des niedriggeborenen Läuffers in den Schnürstiefel der feudalen Etikette geschnürt aufzuzeigen. Der Keim der Tragikomödie ist nun angedeutet. — GW XVII, 1250 "Das aufsässige Menuett"

Brecht frequently uses the tragicomic, as in this scene, to illuminate and identify the sociological focus of the play. And in the note entitled "Stückwahl" — which describes Lenz's *Hofmeister*, and by comparison, the adaptation — the adaptor again couples the sociological viewpoint with the tragicomic mood, or as he calls it, the serious and the comic (which he conceives of as ambivalent):

> Noch hat die Idee [das Idealistische, wie in den Werken des reifen Goethes und Schillers] nicht das Stoffliche [das Sozialkritische] vergewaltigt, es entfaltet sich üppig nach allen Seiten, in natürlicher Unordnung. Das Publikum befindet sich noch in der großen Diskussion; der Stückeschreiber gibt und provoziert Ideen, gibt uns nicht das Ganze als Verkörperung von Ideen [die, wie in der *Iphigenie*, zum Beispiel, der sozialen Wirklichkeit fremd sind]. So werden wir gezwungen (oder instand gesetzt), die Vorgänge zwischen seinen Personen zu spielen und die Äußerungen davon abzusetzen — wir brauchen sie nicht zu unseren eigenen zu machen. Auf diese Weise sind die Personen auch nicht entweder ernst oder komisch, sondern bald ernst, bald komisch. — GW XVII, 1221

Here, Brecht considers that the tragicomic has the function — among others — of producing in the spectator an intellectual objectivity which permits him to examine social evils. (To be sure, Brecht also employs the tragicomic effect to inspire empathy in the spectator as well as to alienate him from the action and the protagonists.) The carefully worked-out gestures and movements of the actors, the desperate situations, the confrontations of one class with another — all contrast with the rhetoric, which, as Brecht was fond of saying, had been all too often used to conceal social evils by treating the aesthetic and idealistic.

In the adaptation, Brecht heightens the comic and the tragic while also creating the synthetic phenomenon of the tragicomic more frequently than does Lenz. Brecht adds a number of new comic episodes and situations to the main plot (as in Scenes 4, 5, 7, and 11), to the Fritz subplot (as in Scene 2) and writes an almost completely new Pätus subplot which abounds in the tragic, the comic and their synthesis, the tragicomic mood (Scenes 6, 9, 15). On occasion, the serious and the potentially tragic in Lenz are replaced by the comic in the adaptation, as is the case of the theme of the suicide of the seduced girl.

Secondly, Brecht intensifies the tragic in Lenz's depiction of Läuffer by endowing the episode of the castration with symbolic relevance; the tutor's act is made to symbolize the tragic self-crippling of the German educator throughout modern history. As noted earlier, Dürrenmatt suggests that the modern dramatist can show the tragic only as a fleeting, horrifying moment within the primarily comic. Brecht frequently employs a similar technique, as for example in Scene 14c. Here, as elsewhere, the language may be comic, but the event spoken about, as well as the implications of what is said are tragic. This is illustrated by the rhapsodic reaction of Wenzeslaus to the news of Läuffer's castration: "Kann man weiter gehen? Für Euer persönliches Fortkommen seid unbesorgt. Pflicht getan." (GW VI, 2383) Brecht notes that the rapid transition from the tragic to the surprising remarks of Wenzeslaus is necessary "... für den Fortgang der Komödie, weil nur so das individuelle, medizinische Moment vernichtet werden kann, ..." (GW XVII, 1237)

As indicated, Brecht also renders Läuffer's self emasculation much more ludicrous than Lenz. The adaptor gives preposterously ironic reasons for the castration; further, he makes the contradictions between Wenzeslaus's speech and behavior more obvious to the spectator. Wenzeslaus, too, is given tragic as well as tragicomic significance in the adaptation. His pedagogical mission is, for example, to produce "riesige Untertanen" (GW VI, 2371), a terribly perverted goal which has "tragic" implications for generations of students. Here, the tragic also exists on a grimmer level from which the comic is absent, namely, the abstract level of the tragedy of the middle-class intellectual and German schoolmaster.

Finally, the comic episodes involving Pätus in II, 3 of Lenz's drama are retained in the scene of student life (Scene 9) in the adaptation. The comic aspects of his character and exploitation have become ambivalent in Brecht's play and, consequently, are endowed with tragic depth. In addition, the action of the Pätus subplot parallels some of the action in the main plot and the Fritz subplot. Its comic, tragic and tragicomic moments function as a commentary on these same moods as in the main plot and the Fritz subplot, adding perspective while driving the author's point home.

Like Wenzeslaus and Läuffer, Pätus and his pupil Fritz act in a most comic manner regarding what is really tragic, namely, abandoning their intellectual freedom and, with it, their rights to free speech. Brecht notes the following about portraying the behavior of Fritz and Pätus on stage: "Zu zeigen wäre hier, in einer leichten und komischen Art, die eigentliche Form der Selbstentmannung der deutschen Intellektuellen bürgerlicher Kreise, . . ." (GW XVII, 1230—31) Perhaps what is most tragic, or at least, unfortunate for mankind, is not that Pätus and his kind remain unharmed by their intellectual cowardice but that they remain unaware of the historical consequences of their apolitical idealism and become insensitive to the evil they help to perpetuate. Brecht remarks that Pätus and his type have ". . . persönlich im Tragischen nichts verloren . . ." (GW XVII, 1247)

In summary, the result of surrounding tragic effects so completely as Brecht does in the adaptation with all forms of comic effects is twofold. The spectator becomes intensely aware, via the disparity of modes, of the social evils which the author wishes to castigate. Secondly, the spectator is given the possibility to be amused by seeing his faults portrayed in hilarious caricature. Via the comic, the author "sweetens" the unpleasant-tasting medicine that is self-scrutiny. In this sense, Brecht continues the tragicomic tradition begun by Lenz, and, like his predecessor, employs it in the hope that it will help contribute to social reform.

The External Structure: Lenz's Theory

Counterpoint: One Unity for Three

This analysis of the structure of Lenz's *Hofmeister* builds on the poet's views on the drama, as recorded in his theoretical writings and letters. I note that criticism of the external structure of Lenz's *Hofmeister* must take into account the fact that Lenz develops a new concept of form based essentially on the following considerations. Lenz makes the scene into an autonomous structural unit of the drama. He regularly alternates the setting and the plot strands in order to establish significant patterns in the scene juxtaposition. The counterpointing of situation, event, character, moral lesson and generic mood are functions of this scene juxtaposition, i.e., the structure is carefully designed to add depth to the portrayal of character, to create a complex unity of the action of the various plot strands, and to engender the tragicomic. After examining Lenz's views on the drama, I show that he only partially succeeds in formulating in the abstract what he later develops as definitive structural principles in the dramatic works themselves.

Like Goethe in the essay "Zum Shakespeares Tag" (1771),[36] Lenz, too, rejects the three unities in the tragedies of the French neoclassicists as unnatural and objects to most of Aristotle's strictures concerning tragedy. Responding to the new literary taste of the era, Lenz champions the dramatic structure of Shakespeare's plays as well as his masterly characterization. Lenz's views on these matters are set forth somewhat disjointedly in *Anmerkungen übers Theater*, which, likely begun in 1771, was published, after several revisions, in 1774.[37]

Rejecting the unity of action and particularly the unities of time and place, Lenz substitutes a single all-embracing unity which — not coherently defined in the *Anmerkungen* — permits the dramatist to adopt a ubiquitous view of society:

> Ist es nicht die *eine* [Einheit], die wir bei allen Gegenständen der Erkenntnis suchen, die eine, die uns den Gesichtspunkt gibt, aus dem wir das Ganze umfangen und überschauen können? ... behalten Sie Ihre *Familien*stücke, Miniaturgemälde, und lassen uns unsere Welt .. Welch ein größer und göttlicher Vergnügen, die Bewegung einer Welt, als eines Hauses?
>
> [Blei, I, 237]

The unity which Lenz is trying to describe here is less an objectively identifiable subject or set of rules than an intuitive concept: "Der Dichter und das Publikum müssen die eine Einheit fühlen, aber nicht klassifizieren. Gott ist nur eins in allen seinen Werken, und der Dichter muß es auch sein ..." (Blei, I, 237)

Lenz comes closer to defining what he means by "die eine Einheit" when he discusses the unity of action deemed necessary by Aristotle. Lenz conceives of unity as a series of events which, succeeding each other rapidly, complement each other by comparison and contrast:

> Er [Aristoteles] sondert immer die Handlung von den handelnden Personen ab, die *bongré, malgré* in die gegebene Fabel hineinpassen muß, ... bei den alten Griechen war's die Handlung, die sich das Volk zu sehen versammelte. *Bei uns* [Lenz] *ist's die Reihe von Handlungen, die wie Donnerschläge auf einander folgen, eine die andere stützen und heben, in ein großes Ganze zusammenfließen müssen*, das hernach nichts mehr und nichts minder ausmacht, als die Hauptperson, wie sie in der ganzen Gruppe ihrer Mithändler hervorsticht.
>
> Blei, I, 238 Italics mine

---

36 Goethe writes in "Zum Shakespeares Tag": "Ich zweifelte keinen Augenblick, dem regelmäßigen Theater zu entsagen. Es schien mir die Einheit des Orts so kerkermäßig ängstlich, die Einheiten der Handlung und der Zeit lästige Fesseln unsrer Einbildungskraft. Ich sprang in die freie Luft und fühlte erst, daß ich Hände und Füße hatte." Cf. *Goethes Werke*, ed. Trunz (Hamburg: Wegner, 1960), 4th edn., vol. 12, p. 225.

37 The dates of composition of the various parts of *Anmerkungen übers Theater*, as well as Lenz's indebtedness to Lessing, Mercier, Herder and Goethe, are discussed in: Theodor Friedrich, ed., *Die "Anmerkungen übers Theater;"* Hans Wolffheim, *Die Entdeckung Shakespeares* (Hamburg: Hoffmann und Campe, 1959), pp. 265—268; Girard, *Genèse*, pp. 149—188.

The italicized portion [in German] of the above quotation represents one of the most precise statements that Lenz makes to describe his — as yet not fully developed — dramatic technique. What he outlines here is the technique of counterpoint, whereby events and situations in one strand of the action parallel and complement those in another strand. It is the most important principle on which the external structure, i.e., the juxtaposition and grouping of scenes, and the development of the action in *Der Hofmeister* are based. Lenz sees "ein großes Ganzes," an overall or complex unity of the drama, in this parallelism which enables comparison and contrast of situations, characters, generic moods, and moral lessons.

Lenz is also theorizing here that, despite its diversity, the action is supposed to develop the figure of the (tragic) hero. In *Der Hofmeister*, however, the action portrays a number of significant characters via their relationships to one another, and shows them in as many similar situations as possible.[38]

Autonomy of the Scene

Whether it is a question of the action in *Der Hofmeister, Der neue Menoza* or *Die Soldaten,* the unity of action is broken up by atomizing the main plot and the subplot into several strands which develop in a rush of often significantly juxtaposed scenes of varying length. In Lenz's dramas, the scene itself becomes an independent structural unit — as can also be observed later in the plays of Brecht. For both dramatists the division of the plot into acts seems less important than the particular juxtaposition and alternation of scenes. Girard observes that with the translation of *Love's Labour's Lost* in 1774, Lenz develops a technique:

> ... à laquelle il restera fidèle, qui fait de chaque scène un élément autonome et étroitement circonscrit, relié par un procédé d'amplification ou de contraste à la scène suivante qui, elle aussi, se suffit à elle-même, avant de s'insérer dans l'enchaînement de l'ensemble. Cette technique déplace l'intérêt de l'acte vers la scène, et la comédie se présente désormais comme une succession de séquences limitées, chargées d'une signification propre; l'acte n'est plus que la survivance d'une technique dramatique traditionelle.[39]

For this reason, the act and scene division in Lenz's *Hofmeister* must obviously lack the harmony of proportion and organic neccesity of the French

---

[38] As Girard notes, Lenz's theory does not necessarily correspond to his practice: "Il est remarquable que *la création dramatique* de Lenz ne prend jamais appui, contrairement à sa propre définition du drame moderne, sur l'évolution dynamique et autonome du héros central, mais sur des situations et des relations à partir desquelles les personnages apparaissent dans la complexité de leurs réactions individuelles." *Genèse*, pp. 163—164, Italics mine.

[39] Ibid., p. 192.

tragédie classique. Lenz's adherence to the principles of counterpoint and autonomy of each scene sufficiently explains why he neither develops the action logically nor groups the scenes according to neoclassical aesthetics.

Action in the Service of Character Portrayal

As noted, Lenz's juxtaposition of scenes is anything but haphazard. It is determined by his wish to compare and contrast similar situations (and developments of the themes and moral lessons) in the main plot with their counterparts in the subplot. One function of this counterpointing of events is to add relief to the depiction of character, as Girard points out:

> D'une part, le comportement des personnages n'"illustre" pas l'événement, mais au contraire, l'événement est là pour provoquer les réactions des personnages: c'est ainsi que le motif de la séduction reproduit quatre fois (Läuffer-Gustchen; Pätus-Mlle Rehaar; v. Seiffenblase-Mlle Rehaar; Läuffer-Lise) est à l'origine d'attitudes très différentes chez des personnages tels que Läuffer, Pätus, Fritz et von Seiffenblase: l'événement sert de réactif, mais l'intérêt est fixé sur les réactions des personnages.[40]

Bruno Markwardt considers Lenz's emphasis on character rather than action an important achievement in the history of German poetics:

> Das Folgende ist von Lenz erstmalig in der deutschen Dramaturgie mit voller Klarheit gewonnen und kunsttheoretisch ausführlich vermittelt worden: die Einsicht in die Überlegenheit des Charakters im Verständnis zum Geschehen, zum „Ereignis" und zur „Begebenheiten"-Abfolge.[41]

Lenz himself states quite definitely that to portray the characteristic, or even to caricature, represents the supreme task of the dramatist:

> ... nach meiner Empfindung schätze ich den Charakteristischen, selbst den Karikaturmaler zehnmal höher als den Idealischen, hyperbolisch gesprochen, denn es gehört zehnmal mehr dazu, eine Figur mit eben der Genauigkeit und Wahrheit darzustellen, mit der das Genie sie erkennt, als zehn Jahre an einem Ideal der Schönheit zu zirkeln .. — Blei, I, 235

Certainly, this profession of faith is well reflected in Lenz's sensitive character drawing (the Major, Wenzeslaus) in *Der Hofmeister.*

On the other hand, Roy Pascal seems to ignore or tacitly rejects these relevant statements of Lenz when he writes that the Storm and Stress author's best works *[Der Hofmeister* and *Die Soldaten]* "... are spoilt by inequalities

---

[40] Ibid., p. 252.
[41] *Geschichte der deutschen Poetik, Bd. II, Aufklärung, Rokoko, Sturm und Drang.* Grundriß der germanischen Philologie, ed., H. Paul (Berlin: de Gruyter, 1956), p. 407.

and crudities, by the lack of discipline so characteristic of his whole character. He had a keen sense of comedy, of incongruity, but the characters of his plays often turn into caricatures."[42] The incongruities and the caricatures are, however, just what Lenz goes to such great lengths to portray. In his plays, the incongruities encourage in the spectator an objective criticism of the strengths and weaknesses of the *dramatis personae* and their motives. The caricatures prevent an idealized characterization. Together, they hold up for scrutiny and reform the evils of society as revealed by the protagonist's contradictory traits and vices. In addition, the presentation of incongruity and caricature permits Lenz to view alternately as well as concomitantly the serious and the comic aspects of his protagonists.

In 1775, one year after the publication of his *Anmerkungen,* Lenz reiterates his position concerning the characteristic more clearly and strongly than before. He declares in "Rezension des *Neuen Menoza*":

> Ich habe gegen diesen Menschen [den Prinzen Tandi] gewöhnliche Menschen meines Jahrhunderts abstechen lassen, aber immer mit dem von mir einmal unumstößlich angenommenen Grundsatz für theatralische Darstellung, zu dem Gewöhnlichen, ich möcht' es die treffende Ähnlichkeit heißen, eine Verstärkung, eine Erhöhung hinzuzutun, die uns die Alltagscharaktere im gemeinen Leben auf dem Theater anzüglich, interessant machen kann. – Blei, II, 337

A diversity of characters requires diversity of action, and both, claims Lenz in his *Anmerkungen,* imitate nature: "... die Mannigfaltigkeit der Charaktere und Psychologien ist die Fundgrube der Natur, hier allein schlägt die Wünschelrute des Genies an. Und sie allein bestimmt die unendliche Mannigfaltigkeit der Handlungen und Begebenheiten in der Welt." (Blei, I, 244)

Lenz is not interested in portraying character for its own sake but in making character portrayal serve the moral lessons of the drama. His new concept of form serves no less an ambition than to bring about moral and social reform. He outlines this plan in a letter of July 1775 to Gräfin Sophie von La Roche:

> Sie sollen einmal ein Stück von mir lesen: *die Soldaten.* Überhaupt wird meine Bemühung dahin gehen, die Stände darzustellen, wie sie sind; nicht, wie sie Personen aus einer höheren Sphäre sich vorstellen.. Ich will aber nichts, als dem Verderbniß der Sitten entgegen arbeiten, das von den glänzenden zu den niedrigen Ständen hinab schleicht, und wogegen diese die Hülfsmittel nicht haben können, als jene. – *Briefe,* I, 114—115

Character and Probability

Lenz continues to advocate his ideal of realistic drama in the brief essay "Von Shakespeares 'Hamlet' " of 1776 where he reminds the reader that

---

[42] *The German Sturm und Drang* (Manchester: Manchester Univ. P., 1967), p. 34.

Shakespeare permitted himself — in exceptional cases — to take liberties with the unities of time and place in order to portray character better:

Man bedenkt nicht, daß er [Shakespeare] mitnichten der einzige sei, der das getan, daß schon die Alten und wohl niemand mehr als Aristophanes die Szene verändert.. Man vergißt, daß auch Shakespeare die Veränderung der Szene immer nur als *Ausnahme von der Regel* angebracht, immer nur höheren Vorteilen aufgeopfert und daß, je größer die dadurch erhaltenen Vorteile waren, desto mehr Freiheit man in dem Stück dem Dichter gestatten mußte und zu gestatten gar kein Bedenken trug. — Blei, IV, 217

Lenz justifies the dramatist's right to such artistic freedom and states it programmatically in this brief essay:

Wie gesagt ... das Interesse ist der große Hauptzweck des Dichters, dem alle übrigen untergeordnet sein müssen — fordert *dieses* — fordert die Ausmalung gewisser Charaktere, ohne welche dies Interesse nicht erhalten werden kann — unausbleiblich und unumgänglich Veränderung der Zeit und des Orts — so kann und muß ihm [dem Interesse] Zeit und Ort aufgeopfert werden.. — Blei, IV, 217.

Altering the settings from scene to scene, believes Lenz, is an advantageous means of creating the artistic illusion that we are witnessing reality on the stage. Unity of place, he protests, is artificial, for, in a drama which strictly observes this rule, all the characters are made to appear in the same place on stage one after the other in what for Lenz is a marionette-like manner: "— wo um aller Götter willen bleibt da Wahrscheinlichkeit, die erste, unverletzlichste, heiligste Grundregel aller Poeterei, aller Täuschung und alles Vergnügens [?]" (Blei, IV, 220)

Lenz insists on portraying the events which lead up to a climax in the action; he advocates sacrificing the unities of time and place if portraying such events further increases probability:

Und Wahrscheinlichkeit, kann sie *ohne Darstellung der Ursachen gewisser Folgen* bestehen [?] Wie also wenn um gewisse Handlungen, gewisse Situationen, ich will nicht sagen glaublich — um begreiflich zu machen, gewisse andere Handlungen und *Situationen vorhergeben müßten*.. Wenn diesen Handlungen und Situationen zehnmal lieber Zeit und Ort aufgeopfert, als meine Sinnlichkeit auf Unkosten meines gänzlichen Verstandes belogen würden? — Blei, IV, 220—221

He maintains that it is even easier to imagine change of time and place when new settings are shown on stage: "Soll ich mir dies [die Ursachen der Folgen] itzt *denken* — und warum denken — weil ich mir keine Verwandlung der Szenen denken kann? weil ich mich nicht in Gedanken von einem Ort zum anderen versetzen kann [?]" (Blei, IV, 221)

Act and Scene Division in Lenz's "Hofmeister"

The detailed exposition of Lenz's aesthetic and dramaturgical views has shown that far from being indifferent to form, the Storm and Stress dramatist actually entertains a new concept of form.[43] This new concept is developed clearly in *Der Hofmeister,* as well as in *Der neue Menoza* and *Die Soldaten.* In each of these plays, Lenz intentionally violates the unities of time and place in order to contrast scenes which portray characters in similar situations and show how the behavior of one figure differs from that of another. In the absence of a strict unity of action in each play the strands of action in the main plot and the subplot progress in a largely parallel and sometimes jerky fashion as one setting alternates with another. This jerkiness in the progress of the action in *Der Hofmeister* does not always exist, for some events may be interpreted as occurring simultaneously, as, for example, Läuffer's seduction of Gustchen in II, 5 and the Majorin's attempted seduction of Graf Wermuth in II, 6.

Lenz does not convey the impression that he was interested in the staging of his dramas. Nevertheless, one is tempted to speculate whether he might have insisted on a few of the scenes of *Der Hofmeister* being played concomitantly. In the *Anmerkungen,* Lenz theorizes that a regular and rapid alternation of settings from one scene to the next is normal but less desirable than an all-embracing view afforded by simultaneity of experience. In this impression of simultaneity lies the unity he seeks:

> Unsere Seele ist ein Ding, dessen Wirkungen wie, die des Körpers sukzessiv sind, eine nach der andern . . . . so viel ist gewiß, daß unsere Seele von ganzem Herzen wünscht, weder sukzessiv zu erkennen, noch zu wollen. Wir möchten mit einem Blick durch die innerste Natur aller Wesen dringen, mit einer Empfindung alle Wonne, die in der Natur ist, aufnehmen und mit uns vereinigen. — Blei, I, 228

Lenz's technique of the rapid alternation of setting and plot strand, the technique of counterpoint, must be regarded as his attempt to achieve this ideal of simultaneity. Certainly, flashing from one setting to another — an established technique of the art form of the motion picture — becomes the basic structural characteristic of *Der Hofmeister, Der neue Menoza* and *Die Soldaten.*

Indeed, Lenz's use of the juxtaposition and sequence of scenes to develop several strands of action at once seems strikingly narrative in manner. Girard supports such a view:

> C'est essentiellement la technique épique propre aux romanciers anglais du XVIIIe siècle, et en particulier à Fielding, que Lenz transpose au théâtre . . . [Le sens général de *Tom Jones*] . . . ressort, comme dans *le Précepteur*, de la juxtaposition d'expériences multiples qui s'éclairent réciproquement par le parallélisme et le contraste.[44]

---

[43] For a discussion of the structure of Lenz's *Hofmeister* as "open form" see Volker Klotz, *Geschlossene und offene Form im Drama* (Munich: Hanser, 1960), pp. 150—153.

[44] *Genèse,* p. 253. The recent article by E. P. Harris, "Structural Unity in J. M. R. Lenz's *Der Hofmeister:* A Revaluation" in *Seminar* VIII (1972), 77—87, builds

The juxtaposition of scenes in Lenz's *Hofmeister* reveals a high degree of conscious craftsmanship. The settings for all six scenes of Act I are in the Major's house or in front of it in Insterburg. In Act II, there begins what is to become a carefully designed alternation of scenes throughout the remainder of the drama. The regularity of the change in the settings is not disturbed by the artificial grouping of the scenes into acts. In Act II, Scenes 1 and 2 are set in Heidelbrunn, Scenes 3 and 4 in Halle, Scenes 5 and 6 in Heidelbrunn and Scene 7 in Halle. Act III also exhibits a regular pattern; Scene 1 and 3 are in Heidelbrunn, and Scenes 2 and 4 in Wenzeslaus's village school. A different setting in each scene is presented in Act IV. Here, Scenes 5 and 6 are really one and the same. Act V also exhibits an astonishingly regular alternation. Scenes 1 and 3 are set in Wenzelsaus's school, Scenes 2, 4, 6, and 8 in Leipzig, Scenes 5 and 7 in Königsberg, Scenes 9 and 10 again in the schoolhouse, and Scenes 11 and 12 in Insterburg. (A similar, carefully designed regular alternation of scenes may be observed throughout Lenz's *Der neue Menoza* and *Die Soldaten*.)

Girard has shown that Lenz's technique of counterpointing situations, characters, and events establishes close links between the various strands of the subplot and the two strands of the main plot:

> ... on peut considérer la "comédie des étudiants" comme une action-commentaire s'inscrivant en contrepoint dans le déroulement des deux actions principales; elle éclaire, à partir de points de vue différents, à des niveaux divers, les motifs dramatiques désormais familiers au spectateur et établit, par le jeu des analogies thématiques, une connexion entre des lignes de force qui ont tendance à se disjoindre.[45]

The spectator does not really know specific details about Läuffer's experiences at the university, but the subplot, with its settings and action in the university towns of Halle and Leipzig, provides a fair indication of the economic, social, and moral forces which contributed to making him what he is. Girard notes that Läuffer's past is unfolded before our eyes, following the technique of counterpoint: "À l'origine des péripéties malheureuses de l'existence de Läuffer, se retrouvent les composantes de l'existence de Pätus: la pauvreté, l'isolement dans la société, la quête d'un plaisir inaccessible."[46]

There are other important instances of Lenz's use of counterpoint. One notes, for example, specific thematic reasons for the particular juxtaposition of several scenes. The cowardly musician, Old Rehaar, refuses to duel with Pätus and defend his honor and that of his daughter (V, 2). In the following scene (V, 3), Lenz shows us the emasculated Läuffer — in V, 1, he fainted

---

on Girard's analysis and demonstrates that Lenz's drama exhibits great structural precision. Investigating the play's dramatic situations, Harris affirms that the "system of contrasts and parallels which Lenz provides here is a remarkable structural entity." (p. 83)

[45] *Genèse*, pp. 252–253.
[46] Ibid., p. 255.

when he recognized the child, which Marthe brought him, as his own. Like Old Rehaar, the tutor is incapable of accepting the responsibility of his paternity.[47]

At some point or other in the course of the action, all of the characters are represented in a scene, the situation or theme of which is treated in a comparable or contrastive manner elsewhere. Gustchen, the seduced girl, has just been saved from drowning (IV, 5) when we overhear Fritz criticizing Pätus for trying to seduce Jungfer Rehaar.[48]

A final instance of Lenz's use of counterpoint to achieve a unity of the various plot strands and to contrast characters and moral attitudes may be seen in a juxtaposition of V, 9 against V, 11, and V, 10 against V, 12. Just as Läuffer is cross-examined by a harsh and tyrannical Wenzeslaus as to his intentions concerning Lise in V, 9, so Fritz, too, in V, 11, is cross-examined as to his intentions concerning Gustchen. However, the Geheimrat is a loving and forgiving father who welcomes his prodigal son home and praises his honorable and earnest desire to marry Gustchen. In contrast, Wenzeslaus banishes Läuffer and mocks his desire to marry Lise.

Act and Scene Division in Brecht's Adaptation

Whereas the unconventional external structure of Lenz's *Hofmeister* owes much to the author's iconoclasm as well as to his use of counterpoint for various effects, the structure of Brecht's adaptation was definitively conceived with the exigencies of the stage in mind.[49]

When Brecht and the Berliner Ensemble adapted Lenz's drama, extensive changes were made in the action. These changes were obviously designed to simplify the external structure in Brecht's play. The simplicity of the grouping and sequence of scenes in the adaptation derives from Brecht's concern for the unity of the action within the main plot and within each of the two subplots, the latter created out of Lenz's single, choppy subplot. In the adaptation, Lenz's occasional use of counterpointed themes and events becomes a more consistently applied structural principle. Hence, Brecht also achieves

---

[47] Ibid., pp. 256—257.

[48] Ibid., p. 259.

[49] In his notes to the adaptation and in his diary, Brecht states that he much appreciates Lenz's aesthetic intentions in *Der Hofmeister* and its Shakespearean flavor. Strangely, Brecht recommends that one should read Lenz's play in order to learn how to perform Shakespeare! It would seem more appropriate to read the plays of the Elizabethan playwright himself. Friedrich Gundolf, for example, thinks little of Lenz's understanding of Shakespeare and even less of his success in emulating the Elizabethan. Cf. *Shakespeare und der deutsche Geist* (München: Küpper, 1959), 11. Aufl., pp. 222—225.

a clearer overall unity of action because each development in one plot strand is counterpointed by a similar event in each of the other plot strands. This is particularly the case in Acts II, III, and V of the adaptation where the action and setting alternate regularly from scene to scene, the one scene clearly pointing up the other.[50] Also, far fewer events are portrayed in the adaptation and the length of the scenes is fairly uniform. As a result, the course of the action is much smoother than in Lenz's *Hofmeister*.

The newly achieved balance and proportion in Brecht's plot structure contribute greatly to the presence of a certain elegance and classical simplicity in the act division and scene juxtaposition. In the adaptation, the parallelism, the functional position of the parts of the dramatic action, is made more clear than in Lenz's work.

In Lenz's and Brecht's play, the scene generally is a complete, fully consistent unit of action. Whereas some scenes in Lenz's *Hofmeister* (V, 1 and 8) are fragmented units of action, each scene in the adaptation is complete in itself and has its own exposition, rising action, climax(es) and resolution. The Berliner Ensemble acting scripts and programs actually refer to each scene of a Brecht play as a *Bild*. This is significant because it indicates — as noted earlier — that the primary structural unit is not the act but the scene.

Given the dramatic effectiveness of the interchangeable position of a number of the scenes in Brecht's *Hofmeister*, and granted the fact that his Scenes 3, 4, 8, and 13 could be omitted without weakening the major thrusts of the drama — these considerations indicate that the *course* of the action, the interplay of event and character, and not the ultimate *outcome* of the action, are the determining interests in the adaptation. Such considerations also confirm the importance of the scene as an autonomous structural unit.

Brecht divides the nineteen scenes of the adaptation among its five acts as follows: Act I has five scenes, Act II has three, Act III five, Act IV three, and Act V three. Lenz divides his thirty-five scenes into five acts in this manner: Six in Act I, seven in Act II, four in Act III, six in Act IV, and twelve in Act V.

Broadly speaking, Act I in the adaptation serves as an exposition, Act II shows the rising action, Acts III and IV develop the climaxes and the decisive action in the two strands of the main plot and in the two subplots, and Act V contains the resolution to the action of both subplots and the second strand of the main plot. Strictly speaking, there is no simple unity of action as such within four of the acts because in them the setting, characters, and plot strand always change with each scene; more important, however, is the

---

[50] Throughout this investigation I give the act and scene numbers when referring to Lenz's drama but only the scene numbers when speaking of Brecht's adaptation. It may seem strange but Brecht's Scene 7, for example, is really the second scene in Act II. Although the adaptor made act divisions in the *Hofmeister*, he numbered the scenes of the play consecutively from the beginning to the end. See Appendix B, a schematic diagram entitled "BRECHT'S CONDENSATION OF LENZ'S DRAMA."

counterpoint, the parallelism of like developments in the action of the main plot and each of the subplots. This parallelism is found in Act III, Scenes 9 and 10, and especially in Act V, Scenes 15, 16, and 17. Only Act IV possesses unity of action, for the events in it are restricted to developing and resolving solely the tensions of the latter strand of the main plot, i.e., the portrayal of the intellectual self-emasculatiaon of Wenzeslaus and Läuffer.

A prologue and an epilogue frame the adaptation, distance it from the spectators and serve to remind them with moral urgency of the significance of the drama as a historical document and of its relevance to present-day affairs. The entr'acte between Acts III and IV has a similar distancing effect on the spectators. Its significant function is to divide the play at that point in the action where the major climaxes in each of the subplots and in the first strand of the main plot have been reached. Even more than the slides and signs used to announce new settings and different seasons, the entr'acte interrupts the flow of the action. It does so in order to compress time and summarize the intervening events so that a new development in the major action, Läuffer's experiences in the house of Wenzelsaus (Act IV), and the closing scenes of the subplots and the main plot may be prepared.

Time and Place in the Adaptation

Appropriately, Brecht sets the action of the adaptation in approximately 1774, the same year as the publication of Lenz's *Hofmeister*. The Major comments in Scene 1 of the adaptation: "Potz hundert, die sieben Jahre Krieg sind noch nicht verwunden im Land." (GW, VI, 2335) He is referring to the Seven Years' War (1756—1763), which, judging from his remark, apparently took place several years before the action of Scene 1 commences. Brecht's desire to set the action of the play shortly after this war is evident not only from frequent references in the dialogue to a recent war, but also from several selections in the play from works by Klopstock, Händel, Mozart and Kant. Some of the works excerpted were either already popular or were published within a decade or so of the year in which Lenz's play was printed.[51]

---

[51] The prologue and the epilogue in the adaptation refer the audience to times other than 1774. There seems no apparent reason why, in the prologue, Brecht should write that his play was composed "einhundertfünfzig Jahre zurück" GW VI, 2333) rather than one hundred and eighty, which would be more accurate. The vagueness of the historical reference is intended perhaps to encourage the spectator to think of political events of the late 18th and early 19th centuries and public reaction to them. The spectator compares Läuffer's behavior and its implications for society to the revolutionary spirit shown by the French in 1789 or by German student societies at a later date. Also, the various reactions of the German middle class to the French Revolution and the Reign of Terror as described by Goethe in *Hermann und Dorothea* suggest themselves.

The duration of the action in the *Hofmeister* adaptation is about two and a half years. In the Berliner Ensemble stage version, Brecht was much more careful than in the printed version to indicate by signs and within the dialogue the time and the exact season in each scene. In the printed version, the time is made known either in the scene title (which BBA 1562, called *"Der Hofmeister"* mit Korrekturen," records for most scenes), or in the dialogue.

Whereas it requires careful probing on the part of the reader to determine time and the passage of time accurately in Lenz's *Hofmeister*, Brecht's more specific treatment of time in the adaptation is necessary for staging the play, simplifying the plot strands, and making some of the action of Lenz's drama more plausible. It is, for example, much more credible that Läuffer and Gustchen quickly succumb to the growing power of their sexual appetites — not after two years of temptation as in Lenz's work — but after the short space of the winter months, during which Läuffer has tried and failed to find someone other than Gustchen.

The exigences of stage production also require a certain economy in the number of settings which a play may use effectively before it confuses the audience. Brecht reduces the twenty settings of Lenz's model to nine. In each scene of the adaptation, he specifically designates where the action takes place. Four settings occur three times, two settings are used only twice, and three settings are required only once. Unless an event is unique, such as Gustchen's pretended suicide by drowning, Brecht's repeated use of the same setting adds depth to the action by increasing the appreciation of the spectator for the milieu in which familiar characters recur.

Because Brecht limits the number of settings and uses some of them several times, place becomes an active factor in the characterization of particular individuals. Thus, we can associate the Geheimrat, a thoughtful man of leisure, with his garden and box trees, the Majorin, an exuberant amateur talent seated at her spinet, with the society of the salon, Läuffer, a servile teacher, ruler in hand, with the schoolroom, and Gustchen, an emotionally aroused reader of love poetry, the Bible and romantic tragedy, with her bedroom. Hence, where and with which material objects an individual is repeatedly seen may say a good deal about his character and what is to be expected of him.

––––––––

On the other hand, the reference to time in the epilogue is more exact. With the phrase "Vor hundert Jahr" (GW VI, 2394) Brecht may be alluding to the spread of revolutionary fervor in 1848, the fall of Metternich, or even to the idealism and failure of the Frankfort Assembly of 1848 to draw up a workable plan for national unity and political liberty. Brecht's second reference to time und vor zehn Jahr" (GW VI, 2394) clearly points to the outbreak of World War II and the diminishing opposition of intellectuals against the leaders of the Third Reich. Brecht maintains unambiguously that the problem of the apolitical intellectual who "kowtows" to authority is still with society "vielerorts" (GW VI, 2394), i.e., in West and, presumably, East Germany, too.

Plot Strands

The action in Lenz's *Hofmeister* is divided into a main plot and one largely independent but rather fragmented subplot. The main plot consists of two complementary strands, of which the first centers on the relationship between Läuffer and Gustchen and her family and the second on the relationship between Läuffer, Wenzeslaus and Lise. For the sake of convenience, these two lines of action will be termed Strand A and Strand B, respectively.

In Brecht's adaptation, the greater portion of the action in Lenz's main plot is retained. The main plot may still be divided into two distinct strands; Strand A, as in Lenz, concerns the relationship between Läuffer and Gustchen and her family; Strand B develops the tutor's relationship to Wenzeslaus and Lise. Brecht omits from Strand A the rather static scenes between the Major and the Geheimrat in which they discuss their grief and their misfortunes; he also deletes the scenes with the old and blind Marthe in Strand B. These scenes contain some of the most contrived and fragmented action of Lenz's play. There, Marthe is a key figure in indirectly supplying the impetus for Läuffer to castrate himself. In Brecht's adaptation, there are different reasons for Läuffer's self-emasculation. Also, the tutor neither knows of nor sees Gustchen's baby.

The action of Lenz's subplot centering on Fritz advances in five major stages: (1) Fritz and Gustchen exchange vows of loyalty when parting, (2) Fritz meets Pätus and is later jailed, (3) Fritz forces Pätus to act honorably toward Old Rehaar, (4) the Geheimrat rescues Jungfer Rehaar from Seiffenblase, and (5) Fritz and Pätus return to Insterburg, are reconciled with their fathers and reunited with their sweethearts.

Whereas I posit five stages of development in the action of the complicated subplot in Lenz's play, Brecht's adaptation has two distinct subplots, whose lines of action frequently parallel each other and the action of the main plot. One subplot deals with Fritz's amorous interest in Gustchen, his association with Pätus, and his reunion with Gustchen. Another subplot, thematically more important,[52] and almost an entirely new creation of Brecht, presents a greatly altered Pätus in conflict with the demands of his Kantian idealism and the exigencies of real life. Because Brecht wishes to show Pätus as the counterpart to the spineless private tutor of the main plot, he makes major revisions in Lenz's subplot, omitting all of stages three and four, as well as large portions of stages two and five.

Subsequently, I shall discuss the progression of the action in the two strands of the main plot, the Fritz subplot and the Pätus subplot in the

---

[52] Subsequently, the two subplots in the adaptation will be referred to as the "Fritz subplot" and the "Pätus subplot."

adaptation. The degree of Brecht's indebtedness to Lenz's drama is determined, and his major innovations in the action are pointed out. A fuller treatment of Brecht's often radical changes in the characterization of the various figures is reserved for Chapters III and IV.

The Action in Brecht's Adaptation

The Main Plot — Strand A

The action in Strand A of the main plot in Brecht's adaptation is developed in Scenes 1, 3, 4, and 5; Scenes 7 and 8; Scenes 10, 11, 12, and 13. (Scene 12 also contains the beginning of the action in Strand B of the main plot.)

The first five scenes of the adaptation contain the exposition and initial incidents of Strand A of the main plot. The same is true of Act I of Lenz's *Hofmeister*. In Scene 1 of his adaptation, Brecht combines and greatly alters the first two scenes of the model. Now, Läuffer no longer characterizes himself and the Geheimrat at length in a monologue, as he does in Lenz's play. Rather, the salient information of his monologue is compressed and conveyed in a revised dialogue between the Major and the Geheimrat. Silent, Läuffer remains in the background. While bowing obsequiously when the brothers pass in conversation, he utters a barely audible curse.

Whereas Lenz emphasizes the Geheimrat's progressive attitude toward public education and shows the brothers heatedly arguing about their ideas, Brecht portrays them as conservatives, has them agree on Läuffer's fitness as a tutor for Leopold, and stresses the attitudes and behavior of the two social classes represented. Hence the violence of the quarrel and its excitement, present in Lenz's Scene 2, are absent from the adaptation.

Brecht's Scene 3 — the next scene to carry the exposition of the main plot further — closely resembles I, 3 of Lenz's *Hofmeister* and shows Läuffer's desperate struggle to please the Majorin. The would-be tutor feverishly dances a minuet[53] and a *pas de deux* to the accompaniment of the Majorin at her spinet. Whereas Lenz seems to refer to the dances only in passing, Brecht elaborates and interrupts the action by having Läuffer execute several dances. The adaptor often illustrates in gesture and movement certain events or situations which are suggested only by a few words or casual references in Lenz's play. Thus Brecht makes the action of the plot visualize ideas pertaining to the theme.

---

[53] The best source of factual information concerning the music used in Brecht's adaptation of the *Hofmeister* for the Berliner Ensemble is Fritz Henneberg, *Dessau-Brecht — Musikalische Arbeiten* (Berlin: Henschelverlag, 1963), pp. 460—461.

As in Scene 1 of the adaptation, the action of Scene 3 also stresses the class barrier between Läuffer and the nobility. Hired because he is cheap, he is cruelly made to realize that he cannot expect to be treated better than a servant and has to leave the salon for contradicting an aristocrat, Graf Wermuth. A few minor additions to the dialogue bring out more clearly than in Lenz's Scene 3 the fact that Graf Wermuth visits the Major's home because he is a suitor for Gustchen's hand.

Brecht's Scene 4 contributes further to the exposition.[54] Its action pointedly illustrates Läuffer's sexual isolation in Interburg. While Läuffer demonstrates his skill on the ice, the adolescent girls watching him make it clear that his desperate hunger for female companionship cannot be satisfied among his peers. The scene has a dual function; it is a unit in the exposition and it also provides the spectator with a period of relaxation between the rather tense scenes (3 and 5) in which Läuffer is brutally exploited by the Majorin and the Major, respectively. The skating scene is a presentation of the beauty of stylized motion. According to the photographs of the *Modellbuch* and the oral communication of Frau Ramthun of the BBA, the graceful choreography of Läuffer's simulated skating constituted a high point in the spectator's aesthetic enjoyment while serving as a refined artistic counter-comment on the crass realism of Läuffer's frustration.

The action in Brecht's Scene 5 much resembles that of Lenz's I, 4. It also serves the exposition and establishes the tensions important for the rising action of the main plot, which starts in Scene 7. In both dramas, the Major's efforts to educate his son, Leopold, prove futile and end in brutality. Brecht elaborates the militaristic aspect of the Major's character here in Scene 5 by creating a new episode in which the Major reprimands Läuffer for having failed to stress the glory of battle and the heroism of Frederick II in the Seven Years' War. Läuffer is more interested, however, in escaping from his loneliness in Insterburg and pleads for the use of a horse for a few days once every three months. (The plea, a short new episode added here by Brecht, prepares for the tutor's unsatisfactory encounter with the Geheimrat in Scene 8.) The Major's harshness toward his son contrasts with the gentleness he bears toward his daughter. Solicitous, but uncompromising, he asks Läuffer to teach Gustchen the Catechism, reminding him to treat her gently. Brecht also intends the reminder to be construed as a pun: "Ich sags Ihm, damit Er sie zart anfäßt." [sic] (GW VI, 2347) Lenz's Major threatens violence in plainer words: "... wer meiner Tochter zu nahe kommt oder ihr worinn zu Leid lebt — die erste beste Kugel durch den Kopf. Merk' Er Sich das." (D I, 48)

---

[54] Brecht finds the basic situation of Scene 4 — girls ridiculing a sexually-frustrated man — in Lenz's II, 4. The idea of showing Läuffer skating was probably suggested to the adaptor by Klopstock's ode "Winterfreuden." an excerpt of which formerly introduced the action in Scene 6 in BBA 541/25.

Most of the devices which Brecht used when revising either the plot, scenes, episodes, characters or language of Lenz's play can be discerned in the first five scenes of the adaptation. Their frequent use throughout the drama establishes them as definite principles which underlie all of Brecht's alterations. As noted above for Scene 1, Brecht may omit or combine entire scenes, thereby pruning the dialogue while retaining the action and the ideas of the original in a more compact form. Or, as in Scene 2 — which will be discussed in detail later — he combines two scenes and advances them, i.e., moves them up, in addition to greatly revising their content. With regard to Scene 3, it was observed that the characters of the Majorin and of Läuffer are elaborated, i.e., Brecht develops and translates into action for the stage play their particular talents which Lenz mentions only in passing. Scene 4 exemplifies Brecht's use of the technique of addition. He sometimes adds a whole new scene, the action of which, as here, illustrates a certain situation more intensely. Scene 5 offers examples of Brecht's use of elaboration of the character of the Major. The discussion of the various lines of action in subsequent acts will show additional devices underlying Brecht's alterations, such as postponement, and the division and recombination of episodes or scenes.

The action of Lenz's II, 2 forms the latter portion of Brecht's Scene 7. Here, the rising development in the action in the new first half of the scene shows Läuffer in emotional turmoil. Under the spell of Gustchen's physical attraction, he has become the helpless victim of the teasing of his likewise sexually aroused pupil, who pretends to recite the Catechism in all innocence. Unable to endure her flirtation any longer, and annoyed, too, that she is his superior in rank, the tutor rushes from her room to avoid the torture of her presence.

In Scene 8 of the adaptation, the Geheimrat points out, perhaps correctly, but very unsympathetically, to Pastor Läuffer that all private tutors are the victims of their own lack of ambition. He refuses to influence the Major not to exploit Läuffer shamelessly. In II, 1 of the original, Lenz indicates only by means of a letter from Läuffer to the Geheimrat that the Major denies Läuffer the horse. Brecht makes effective drama with this plea, extending and illustrating the motif of the letter with the person of Läuffer, who is now present in Scene 8. When Läuffer objects that the Major has broken his promise to lend him a horse, the Geheimrat cruelly mocks the tutor and the reason for requesting the animal.

The confrontation with the Geheimrat, while adding to the dramatic appeal of the play, intensifies the anguish which Läuffer suffers from being unable to escape from Insterburg. He fears that he will be unable to resist Gustchen's temptation much longer.

Brecht selects from Lenz's II, 1 only those lines from the Geheimrat's idealistic discourse on the uselessness of private tutors which point up the lack of opportunity available to such persons as Läuffer. Also, he omits the Geheimrat's constructive proposals on how to improve education and abolish the necessity for tutors. The adaptor presents a one-sided view of Lenz's Geheimrat since he wants to show only the *Misere* of the German system of education.

Scene 10 the adaptation brings the first of four climaxes in the development of Strand A of the main plot. There is little action in this scene, as is also the case in the equivalent scene in Lenz's drama (II, 5). Läuffer and Gustchen, their love-making over, lie in bed together, each preoccupied with his own worries. Brecht alters the dialogue in places to indicate more forcefully than Lenz that despite the physical closeness of the lovers, each character remains mentally and spiritually as distant from the other as ever.

Vulgarization of a thought, moral value, or mood is frequently the purpose of Brecht's linguistic changes. One such change is singled out for comment here, because it suggests the course of the later action. In the adaptation, reference is made to Abälard in Rousseau's novel *La Nouvelle Héloïse*. Whereas Lenz discreetly suggests Abälard's fate in a brief remark by Läuffer: "Es könnte mir gehen wie Abälard" (D I, 67), Brecht revises the dialogue so that Gustchen, as though reciting, spells out at length and in elevated language the whole crudity of Abälard's punishment. Such jesting on Brecht's part cannot be called merely foreshadowing Läuffer's self-emasculation. The adaptor does not wish to hint vaguely at what might happen in order to excite the spectator. He aims, rather, to forestall any such emotional tensions by leaving no doubt in the spectator's mind as to what is in store for Läuffer.

The action of Scene 11 in the adaptation develops in three definite stages. In the first, the Majorin is seated at her spinet and sings various songs, some with erotic implications, to Graf Wermuth. This episode has been added by Brecht, partly as an ironic comment on the action of the previous scene, and partly as a musical-literary parody.[55] Graf Wermuth has returned

----

[55] The Majorin plays the spinet and sings in an attempt to seduce the aging aristocrat Graf Wermuth. The Count visits the household in order to court Gustchen, but finds that (as always) he is detained by the Majorin. (We should remember that in Scene 10, Läuffer and Gustchen were shown together in bed.) Wermuth has no choice but to listen and wait in the hope that Gustchen will appear.

The songs of the Majorin are French pastoral love lyrics arranged to selections from Christoph Willibald Gluck's opera *Orpheus und Eurydice*. The phallic imagery of one of the songs seems totally incongruous with the sedate and harmoniously restrained measures from Gluck who celebrates a pure, spiritual love. The Majorin sings, for example:

> Ach, wenn doch mein Schätzchen
> ein Feigenbaum wär!
> .//.Also tät ich drauf steigen
> wenn er noch so hoch wär!.//.   BBA 2087/70

to see Gustchen, but the Majorin, jealous of the attention paid to her daughter, seeks to entertain the aging Count herself and dispel her boredom. Equally bored, Graf Wermuth repeatedly tries to make the absent Gustchen the topic of conversation.

The second stage of the action in Scene 11 is based on revised portions of Lenz's II, 6. Brecht's Majorin, complaining of how her husband neglects her for agricultural interests, is interrupted by his return from the fields. As though signalling his entry, as well as the sad discovery of Gustchen's seduction in the last stage of the action in Scene 11, the Majorin begins to play Händel's *Largo*! Her objections to the Major's neglect awaken his concern, not for her, but for Gustchen and he asks where she is. This is too much for the Majorin; accused rightly by her husband that she cloisters Gustchen, she angrily leaves the drawing room to fetch her.

Pretending to be embarrassed by the family quarrel, Graf Wermuth asks to leave, but the Major requests him to stay. The brief quarrel between husband and wife is but an overture to the scandal shortly to be discovered. The interval between the departure and return of the Majorin is occupied by several lines of dialogue supplied by Brecht. In contrast to the Major's chauvinistic conviction that Prussian interest in French financial backing and Italian ballet only serves Prussia's decline, Graf Wermuth remains optimistic, suggesting that such international relations may improve the country: "Unter uns, Major, ich habe immer gedacht, ein kleiner Abstecher hin und wieder nach Sodom frischt das Blut auf." (GW VI, 2367) His suggestion, couched in a metaphor with implications of an erotic nature, has immediate relevance to Gustchen's situation — but only for the spectator. Her health has improved wonderfully since her intimacies with Läuffer began.

The third stage of the action, in Scene 11, is based on the compressed action of the latter half of Lenz's III, 1, and deals with the Majorin's hysterical account of Gustchen's affair with Läuffer, as well as the Major's reaction to this news. In Lenz's III, 1, the reasonable, sensible Geheimrat

----

The musical humor provided in this scene reaches a peak when the Majorin begins to sing Orpheus's aria: "Ach, ich habe sie verloren," for the spectator knows — but the Majorin and the Count, in particular, do not know — that Gustchen has just been seduced!

One is tempted to ask whether Brecht planned this episode of the scene as a veiled yet hilarious parody of Thomas Mann's ironic story entitled *Tristan*. Mann's Spinell and Frau Klöterjahn seek spiritual union in an unreal world of delicate aestheticism. Wagner's music creates the illusion of an ideal world in which the lovers attain mystic fulfillment. In contrast, in Brecht's drama, Gustchen and Läuffer are already united, but only sexually; Gustchen tried unsuccessfully to elevate the physical experience to an *Erlebnis im Geiste* (cf. GW XVII, 1244) by imagining that Läuffer is Fritz. It is not difficult to envisage Brecht wishing to poke fun at Thomas Mann's already satiric mood painting. It is effective but perhaps too subtle comedy to juxtapose the sublimtiy of Wagner played by the fragile Frau Klöterjahn against the earthy vitality of the Majorin who persists in her attempt to seduce Graf Wermuth at least in song, if not in reality.

was present when the Majorin announced the scandal. Brecht drops this calm and rational figure from the scene and replaces him by the egoistic Graf Wermuth, who becomes an unsympathetic but highly interested witness to the Major's family tragedy.

At this point, the action of part A of the main plot reaches its second climax. Enraged and bent on revenge, the Major becomes physically violent. He shakes his wife, sweeps the music from the spinet with his stick, and, abusing his unconscious spouse verbally, he drags her away, shouting and raging as he smashes open the doors of the salon. Graf Wermuth still remains on stage, struck speechless by the intensity of the moment. He lets fall the rose that he has been holding and sniffing during the entire scene, and, with a mild "Parbleu," steps over it to leave.[56]

There is no fine dividing line in Brecht's adaptation between the end of the action of Strand A in the main plot and the beginning of the action of Strand B. The action of B begins as Scene 12 opens, but one of the two last major developments in the action of A occupies the dominant position in this scene.

The action of Strand A reaches the most important of several climaxes with the shooting of Läuffer in Scene 12. The action of the first third of the scene is taken over by Brecht with only a few omissions from Lenz's II, 2. In the model as well as in the adaptation, Graf Wermuth pursues Läuffer, who has just found refuge from the Major in the school operated by Wenzeslaus. Intent on capturing Läuffer himself, the Count bursts in unannounced. Thwarted in his desire and driven out of the school by Wenzeslaus, Graf Wermuth returns later the same day, bringing the Major and the Geheimrat. (In Lenz's IV, 3, Graf Wermuth does not return until a year later.) Their sudden intrusion in the last third of Scene 12 differs little from the action in Lenz's IV, 3, only the first half of which Brecht retains.

In the adaptation, the Major is unable to control his anger when he perceives Läuffer, and shoots him in the arm. Prevented from firing a second pistol at the tutor, the officer learns, to his surprise and alarm from Lise, the ward of Wenzeslaus, that Gustchen has left a message for him at the nearby inn, indicating that she can be found at the village pond. The Major interprets her message as a sign that she intends to commits suicide. Hoping to rescue her, he storms away, followed by the Geheimrat and Graf Wermuth.

Brecht's Scene 13, like his Scene 1, combines two short adjacent scenes of Lenz, the action of which occurs at the same time in the same place. The action of Strand B of the main plot is neglected in Scene 13, while that of Strand A is concluded. Because Brecht radically changes Gustchen's reasons for being at the pond, her actions are necessarily different, too. Whereas in Lenz's IV, 5, her suicide attempt is the serious act of a desper-

---

[56] See the corresponding photographs of the BEA *Hofmeister-Modellbuch* and the appropriate stage directions in BBA 1562/53.

ate, emotionally and mentally distraught person, in Brecht's Scene 13, her attempt at suicide is only pretended; in addition, it is carefully planned, as is indicated by the message which Lise delivers in Scene 12.

In Lenz's *Hofmeister*, Gustchen threw herself into the pond in expiation of her guilt to appease the angry father she saw in a dream. In the adaptation, she regrets her loneliness, Fritz's absence, her pregnancy and the seemingly interminable wait before her father hears her message and comes after her. Finally, when quite certain that rescue is at hand, she removes her shoes, places them on the ramp, pointing them in the direction she will take, and walks backwards into the pond, keeping a cautious eye out for her father. His excited searching in the water for her is balanced by the calm, emotionless discussion between the Geheimrat and Graf Wermuth, who look on from a dry vantage point on the ramp. Gustchen's ruse succeeds; her father pardons her, and, as in Lenz's play, all ends well. The action in Strand A of the main plot is now over. (The fact that Gustchen is shown sewing infant's clothing in the entr'acte immediately following Scene 13 concerns only the action in the final episode of the Fritz subplot in Scene 16.)

The Main Plot — Strand B

The action in Strand B of the main plot in Brecht's adaptation is developed in Scenes 12, 14a, b, c, and 17.

Brecht's long Scene 12 is a combination of three scenes from Lenz's drama, namely III, 2 and 4, and IV, 3. The adaptor retains most of the action of each of these three scenes, but omits Wenzeslaus's lengthy, moralistic digressions about personal habits and the job of a private tutor. Also, Brecht strikes out the comic episode of Schöpsen, the surgeon-barber of Lenz's IV, 3, who is to cure Läuffer's gunshot wound.

In Lenz's play, the action of III, 2 and III, 4 occurs on the same day, that of IV, 3 a year later. In the adaptation, time in Scene 12 has been greatly compressed and the events occur within a few hours of each other. Brecht's skilful joining and reduction of the three scenes taken from Lenz's play makes for a smooth, swift pace of the action in the adaptation.

In Brecht's play, Läuffer, fleeing from the Major, Graf Wermuth, and the Geheimrat, begs Wenzeslaus for protection. No sooner has the old schoolteacher made him welcome than he suddenly gives orders to the poor tutor, putting him to work and establishing a master/servant relationship. These orders are Brecht's innovations and are interpolated without transitional speeches into the dialogue taken over from Lenz. (The commands in question are discussed in Chapter III.)

As in Lenz's drama, Graf Wermuth intrudes, for he has spotted the fugitive Läuffer inside. Wenzeslaus soon gets rid of the aristocrat, driving him out with a torrent of words and, as photographs in the Berliner Ensemble *Modellbuch* show, brandishing his quill pen in the face of the surprised man. Wenzeslaus enjoys only briefly the illusion that the pen is mightier than the sword, for Wermuth soon returns. Läuffer, given tasks to perform even while eating, is told in all seriousness that work is good for his morals.

The second in a series of surprises in this scene occurs in a short episode added by Brecht. Here, Wenzeslaus suddenly begins to march violently up and down while vociferously instructing Läuffer about the pedagogical goals of the German schoolmaster. The fact that Wenzeslaus's exaggerations apparently contradict his character is intended to disturb the spectator. (This, too, is discussed at length in Chapter III.)

Läuffer has no opportunity to welcome or protest the old man's plans for his future because the Major, accompanied by the Geheimrat and Graf Wermuth, bursts in and shoots at him. Wenzeslaus assumes a tone of righteous indignation and argues with the Geheimrat as they stand facing each other, the fallen Läuffer lying neglected on the floor between them.

Leaving the Major and the Geheimrat to care for the wounded tutor as best they can, Brecht's Wenzeslaus rushes off to sound an alarm: "Ich lauf nicht nach dem Gevatter Schöpsen, ich lauf die Sturmglock läuten!" (GW VI, 2373) (This differs from Lenz's IV, 3 where Wenzeslaus runs to get the surgeon and to bring farmers to help drive out the intruders.)

The Major is just about to shoot Läuffer again, this time for refusing to tell him the whereabouts of Gustchen, when Lise rushes in with the beer which Wenzeslaus had ordered earlier for Läuffer. Lise's appearance in this scene, rather than in Scene 14a, is Brecht's somewhat contrived innovation. Her entry here has a twofold function. She tells the Major the coy story of Gustchen's message,[57] which she overheard in the inn as she was fetching the beer, and thus prepares logically for the action of Scene 13. Secondly, Lise's befriending Läuffer indicates that his trials with the fair sex are not yet over. (In Lenz's drama, she appears only once, in V, 10; this scene is taken over in the adaptation to form the latter half of Brecht's Scene 14a. The fact that we see Läuffer and Lise together before the courtship episode in Scene 14a serves to make their mutual interest in each other in that scene much more probable than is the case in Lenz's drama.) At the close of Brecht's Scene 12, Lise is standing next to the tutor, dressing his wound, when he wonders aloud, disgusted with the callous treatment he has received from the Major: "Wo bleibt meine vita sexualis?" (GW VI, 2374)

In the adaptation, the rising action, climax and falling action of Strand B of the main plot are developed in Scenes 14a, b and c, respectively. Scene 14a resumes the action of Strand B after the intermediate Scene 13, which

---

[57] The report of Gustchen's message to the Major is one of several examples in the adaptation of the narrative or epic style that Brecht taught the budding actors of his newly founded Berliner Ensemble in 1950. See also the maid's report of the reunion of Fritz with Gustchen in Scene 16. See Chapter I, note 15 and note 34.

sees the conclusion of the action of Strand A of the main plot. The entr'acte after Brecht's Scene 13 indicates that Läuffer has spent a year under Wenzeslaus's moralistic tutelage, performing and even relishing the menial tasks assigned to him.

Whereas Lenz devotes little space to depicting the brief love scene between Lise and Läuffer in V, 10, Brecht prepares and illustrates this situation in the action of the first third of Scene 14a by the addition of a new episode. The latter two thirds of his scene represent in concentrated form the action of the first half of Lenz's V, 10.

As Scene 14a in the adaptation begins, it is a cold, stormy night in November. Lise, prompted by her sincere but undefined infatuation for Läuffer, repeatedly visits him, interrupting his work. Apparently unwittingly, she arouses his desire for her. He is only too receptive to the charm of her appearance and naive manner. His desire to possess Lise conflicts with his sense of sexual guilt and his feeling of moral responsibility to fulfill the duties thrust on him by the domineering Wenzeslaus. The course of Läuffer's inner conflict to resist Lise and devote himself to his work is illustrated by his repeated efforts to make her leave.

At this point, the adaptor appends the slightly revised initial half of Lenz's V, 10. In this segment of the action in the adaptation, Läuffer hungrily questions Lise about her previous experience with men and learns to his great delight that she would be happy to marry him. Almost smothering her with unrestrained kisses, he is interrupted by Wenzeslaus, who sees in him only the seducer of innocent girls. The old schoolmaster refuses to accept the tutor's protestations that his intentions are honorable; he also rejects Läuffer's lame excuse that Lise's irresistible charms led him to embrace her so wildly. Brecht concludes this scene by adding a new speech to be spoken by Wenzeslaus. Pointedly, the schoolmaster warns that Läuffer has not only abused his profession, but has also forfeited a certificate of recommendation for the second time and must leave the following morning.

Written especially by Brecht for the adaptation, Scene 14b takes the form of a lyrical monologue in which Läuffer gives voice to the stormy inner conflict between the wish to satisfy (physical) desires and his even stronger and ever-present need for material security. Läuffer reviews his present situation, judging his desires and actions not with the values of the natural man but with the frightfully pernicious sexual and pedagogical values which Wenzeslaus has instilled into him during his past year of slavery. In a great curse, reminiscent of Faust's curse and spiritual despair (*Faust I*, 1583—1606), Läuffer damns his natural urges and condemns all striving to satisfy personal ambition as incompatible with his role as teacher. He accepts with savagery what seems to him the only alternative to being himself and consequently having to languish in abject poverty. He castrates himself.

The action of Scene 14c in the adaptation is similar to that of Lenz's V, 3 but Brecht condenses the dialogue, shortening Lenz's scene by more than half. The wintry storm, which raged outside in Scenes 14a and 14b has subsided, giving way to calm, and covering the landscape with a mantle of pure snow. Brecht's nature imagery here is a symbol of the cooling of the tutor's passions and of the barrenness of his intellect. The violent outburst of Läuffer's feelings subsides as the storm abates; his self-emasculation leaves him forever empty of all emotional and intellectual vigor.

Fearing that he may die, the tutor confesses his deed to Wenzeslaus. Surprised, the schoolmaster no longer rejects him; on the contrary, his former rejection of Läuffer now becomes a sincere, heartfelt approbation, just as in Lenz's drama. The latter half of Scene 14c, an addition of Brecht's, develops the action as follows. Wenzeslaus learns the motives for Läuffer's castration and exclaims that the tutor's decision to emasculate himself has made him unconditionally acceptable to all authorities to whom he might apply for a position. Läuffer as much as admits that this is his opinion too, for he asks Wenzeslaus to read a letter he has written to the Major.

Brecht uses the device of the letter to present in an ironic and exaggerated manner the change in the tutor's thinking. Läuffer assures the Major that under no circumstances will he think independently, and promises full compliance with the officer's wishes. Wenzeslaus's joy at Läuffer's total self-abnegation is matched only by his boundless optimism for the tutor's prospects of employment.

Scene 17, the concluding episode in the action of Strand B of the main plot and the last scene of the adaptation, combines the action of V, 9 and 10 of Lenz's drama. With only minor additions, the first half of Brecht's Scene 17 represents Lenz's V, 9 in condensed form. In the second half of Scene 17, the text of Lenz's V, 10 is considerably reduced; Brecht adds several new short speeches but otherwise the action and the "happy end" of Lenz's play are retained.

The action of Scene 17 is as follows. Several weeks after finding in the castrated Läuffer his intellectual son, Wenzeslaus, disturbed at the tutor's interest in Lise at church that morning, questions him about the sermon. Läuffer pretends to have been pleased by Wenzeslaus's thoughts on the necessity of present suffering for the sake of future bliss. When he refuses to admit that he is still sensually attracted to Lise, Wenzeslaus confronts him with the fact, arguing that she would never be satisfied with a eunuch. To the surprise both of Wenzeslaus and Läuffer, Lise — who eavesdrops, as maids in literature generally do — enters and insists that she would indeed be satisfied with Läuffer, and even more happy if she did not have to feed children in addition to the poultry. Wenzeslaus recognizes with regret that Läuffer is unwilling to become quite the ascetic model teacher that he, Wenzeslaus, would like him to be. His scorn has no meaning for Läuffer, who is confident that as slave, eunuch, and husband he is eminently well qualified for a good position as teacher.

In the adaptation, Brecht divides the extremely involved, single subplot of Lenz's *Hofmeister* into two subplots. Major changes concerning the characters and the deeds of Fritz, Pätus, Bollwerk, Seiffenblase, Jungfer Rehaar and the Geheimrat are necessary in order that two subplots can be established. On the whole, very little of the action of Lenz's subplot is found in the adaptation. The action of Brecht's Fritz subplot borrows much from stage one of Lenz's subplot, a little from stage two, and only a letter episode from stage five, thus omitting stages three and four completely.

In the adaptation, the action in the Fritz subplot develops in Scenes 2, 6, 9, 15, and 16. Its course in Scene 2 of the adaptation is largely the same as in Lenz's I, 5 and 6. Although Brecht combines these two scenes, the dialogue of Lenz's I, 5 is reduced by more than half, and only a few speeches of the Geheimrat are taken over into the latter portion of Scene 2.

In Scene 2 of the adaptation, Gustchen discusses with Fritz the distance that will separate them physically when he goes to Halle to study at the university. He is confident that even when apart they will remain united in their love for each other. As a token of this love, more imaginary than real, he gives her, appropriately enough, a collection of Klopstock's *Oden*. In place of a declaration of love, which neither quite dares to put into words, Fritz has Gustchen read aloud portions of several odes, via the charged emotions of which they can vicariously experience each other's affection.

Whereas Lenz has Gustchen pretend that she is Shakespeare's Juliet, and Fritz her Romeo, Brecht's having them read Klopstock serves the same function while also making fun of the — for Brecht's taste, excessive — artifical emotional outpourings of the German poet. The exchange of oaths of loyalty by the couple is exactly as in Lenz, except that Brecht adds Fritz's promise to return to Gustchen during the holidays. With each embrace, the couple becomes more and more passionate; the *Modellbuch* photographs of the Berliner Ensemble production of the play show Fritz and Gustchen only a moment away from consummating their love when the Geheimrat enters. Their cries of surprise, which seemed rather exaggerated in Lenz's play, now are in keeping with their actions.

The Geheimrat reprimands Fritz in a manner quite the opposite of the way he speaks to him in Lenz's play. In the adaptation, his brutally authoritative reprimand effectively sobers the couple. The lovers are no longer allowed to embrace affectionately before parting, as in the model, but, observing social decorum, Fritz must merely bow to Gustchen, while she curtsies to him. The flexible, progressive attitude of Lenz's Geheimrat and the enlightened values for which he stands are distorted and reshaped by Brecht into everything that Lenz opposes in the powerful nobility, i.e., the repressive, tradition-bound behavior of a feudal aristocracy.

Lenz's II, 3 provides the setting and some of the action for Brecht's Scene 6 in which more than half of the dialogue of Lenz's scene is deleted. As in the model, so too in Scene 6 of the adaptation, Fritz's role remains that of an observer. His appearance, while aiding to further the exposition of the Pätus subplot, develops the action of the Fritz subplot only to the extent that the length of his absence from Gustchen and his feelings toward her are indicated.

In the adaptation, the action, polemic thrusts and dialogue of Scene 9, which takes up both subplots, are all Brecht's invention. Only the initial action of the scene and Fritz's decision at its center actually concern the Fritz subplot. The young von Berg has received a letter from Gustchen, in which she includes portions of two odes by Klopstock. Pleased by the apparent constancy of his cousin's love, Fritz reads the quotations to Pätus.

In the context of Brecht's play, the excerpts from the odes have decidedly erotic implications. Gustchen uses literature now not merely to declare her love, but to indicate her emotional, if not physical, experiences with Läuffer in Insterburg.

Also, the philosophical riddle posed by Pätus indicates to the spectator that what has recently happened between Jungfer Rehhaar and Bollwerk, can happen, or may already have occurred, between Gustchen and Läuffer. Fritz, however, has no grounds for doubting Gustchen's fidelity. He gives Pätus his holiday travel-money, apparently in the spirit of friendship, so that his friend may pay the fee for Jungfer Rehhaar's abortion. Thereupon Fritz mentions his fears, hinting, in as many words, that should he return to Insterburg during the Easter holidays, it might be difficult for him to avoid sexual involvement with Gustchen, in view of her rather passionate references to Rousseau's heroine of *La Nouvelle Héloïse:* "In den Osterferien wirst du eine kühnere Julie wiederfinden!" (GW VI, 2360).

Fritz insists that Pätus accept the money; in return for the favor, he would like Pätus to introduce him to Kant's ideas during the holidays. Brecht's suggestion that Fritz is becoming a devotee of the philosopher is without consequence for the remaining action in the Fritz subplot. Rather, the suggestion serves more the subsequent dialogue of the Pätus subplot and the characterization of Pätus.

Like Scenes 6 and 9, Scene 15 serves the portrayal of the action in both subplots. Only the central portion of Scene 15 deals with the Fritz subplot. This portion condenses the episode of Seiffenblase's letter to Fritz as it occurs in Lenz's V, 6. In Brecht's Scene 15, the concluding segment of the action in Lenz's V, 6 is replaced by new material.

The strand of the Fritz subplot in the adaptation is resumed with Fritz's account to Pätus of the ominous feelings he has about Gustchen's welfare toward the end of his six-months visit to Italy. After a hurried return to Germany, he stops in Halle, only to find a letter from a certain Seiffenblase waiting for him. Rather than read it himself, he brings it to Pätus.

In Lenz's subplot, Seiffenblase represents the snobbish aristocrat who is malevolent and useless, and ostensibly encouraged to be so by private tutors. He is an enemy of Pätus and attempts to make Jungfer Rehaar his mistress in Königsberg; prevented by Fritz's father, the Geheimrat, from seducing her, he takes his revenge on the gullible Fritz by writing a letter to him, stating only that Gustchen has been raped by the Major's tutor and that she and her father have drowned themselves.

In both Lenz's drama and Brecht's adaptation, the recourse to the device of the letter is a weakness in developing the action. The dramaturgical purpose of the letter is, of course, to make Fritz think the worst and return to Insterburg so that the subplot may be concluded. Lenz goes to perhaps excessive lengths to motivate and develop Fritz's return, for most of the action in stages three and four, and the initial part in stage five of the subplot prepare Fritz's decision to return to Insterburg. (As discussed earlier, Lenz defends in the essay "Von Shakespeares Hamlet" his belief that a protagonist's motivation should and may be shown at length.) Omitting these stages and then revising so radically what is left of Lenz's subplot, Brecht has only one fairly plausible recourse in dealing with the dramaturgically very effective and amusing letter. He makes its writer, Seiffenblase, a neighbor of the Geheimrat. As in Lenz's episode of Seiffenblase's letter, Fritz collapses briefly at the news of Gustchen's death. He takes leave of Pätus and Karoline to return speedily to Insterburg.

In Scene 16, the conclusion of the action in the Fritz subplot is reached. The scene owes only the idea of the reunion of the lovers, as well as a few scraps of dialogue to Lenz's V, 11 and 12. During the initial portion of Brechts's Scene 16, the Geheimrat and the Major with his family are celebrating St. Nicholas's Day. The two Berg brothers sadistically discuss the letter which Läuffer has sent to the Major. Their laughter at his castration is cut short by the entry of the maid; she breathlessly reports that Fritz has returned, surprised and overjoyed to find Gustchen alive.

Fritz enters and explains why he is willing to marry Gustchen; he relates with sincere and naive belief the story of Jungfer Rehhaar's affair with Bollwerk. His idealistic and noble attitude toward adversity also enables him to accept Gustchen's child by Läuffer as his own. The sentimental reunion is parodied by Brecht and ends with all characters happily drinking a toast to the couple and the child, while the Majorin, playing a popular melody on her spinet, sings a text appropriate to the season.

The parodied "happy end" of the subplot in Lenz's drama also concludes the play. However, the final action of Brecht's Fritz subplot in Scene 16 does not conclude the adaptation. The final thrust of the action in Lenz's subplot is the progressive stand taken by Fritz who, like his father, supports public education rather than private tutors. The Fritz subplot in the adaptation ends with no such social message, but with a tableau, a false idyll. The Geheimrat and the Major pretend to be sociable toward their servants, even though they are moved to scorn and laughter concerning Läuffer's castration, and Fritz believes that he has accepted reality and understood Gustchen's behavior.

The Pätus Subplot

In the adaptation, most of the action in Scenes 6, 9 and 15 takes up the Pätus subplot. The exposition and initial incidents in Scene 6 prepare for the complications in the rising action in Scene 9; the actual climax of the events there is indicated briefly in the entr'acte but occurs off-stage. A narrative anti-climax best describes the nature of the incidents in Scene 15.

Brecht's Pätus subplot owes little to Lenz's drama. Portions of four episodes in Lenz's II, 3 form the basis for the events in Brecht's Scene 6; but the action, dialogue and character portrayal in this scene have been extensively revised. Scene 9 is *entirely* the invention of the adaptor. The entr'acte is found only in the adaptation. The action in Brecht's Scene 15, where it concerns the Pätus subplot, is also wholly new. Hence, most of stage two, and all of stages three, four, and five of the action in Lenz's subplot are omitted in the adaptation.

The loudmouthed, inconsiderate Pätus of Lenz's II, 3 becomes a meek and retiring Pätus in Brecht's Scene 6. In the adaptation, Bollwerk is present from the outset of this scene and dominates the action in his role as a foil to Pätus. In the corresponding scene of the model, Bollwerk's role is far less significant; also, he appears on stage only toward the end of the scene.

Pätus is as impoverished in the adaptation as he is in Lenz's drama and is unable in either play to redeem his one frock coat from the pawnbroker. The lack of a coat is as important in the adaptation as in Lenz's play. Without proper attire, Pätus cannot appear in public and woo his beloved Jungfer Rehhaar. He compensates for his insolvency and his inability to visit his sweetheart by concentrating exclusively on the philosophy of Immanuel Kant. As noted earlier, Pätus's abiding interest in Kant and the considerable complications caused by it are all Brecht's invention, and are foreign to Lenz's drama. In Brecht's play, Pätus the devotee of an unpopular philosopher, rather than the blow-hard Pätus without a coat, becomes the comic axis of this scene. Whereas in Lenz's play, it is Pätus who verbally abuses Frau Blitzer, the landlady, in his violent demands for afternoon coffee, in the adaptation it is Bollwerk, the opportunist and "freeloader," who dominates the action.

Some of the complications caused by the introduction of Pätus's interest in Kant may be listed here. In the adaptation, Frau Blitzer has a larger role in the exposition than in Lenz's drama. She informs Fritz that Pätus has failed his licentiate's examination in philosophy for the fourth successive year. Pätus attributes his failure to pass his exams to the antipathy of his major professor toward Kant. Intending to prove that Kant, rather than Professor Wolff, is unworthy of the name of philosopher, Bollwerk reads a passage from Kant's treatise *Zum ewigen Frieden* where war is condemned as the activity of barbarians.[58] Fritz disagrees politely with Bollwerk's denigration of Kant, but Bollwerk insists that in any sphere of life belligerent behavior is necessary if one is to attain one's ends. He illustrates his point by stating that Frau Blitzer would serve him barley coffee instead of real coffee if he were not to brutalize her. He adds that Pätus does not pass the examinations that Wolff sets, simply because he defends Kant's view that wars of aggression are crimes against mankind.

As a sign of his steadfast beliefs, Pätus has carved "Nein" into Frau Blitzer's table top. He maintains that his "no" is a refusal to betray his position, and in a larger sense, a condemnation of the German trait to let oneself be exploited, to serve gladly as cannon fodder.

Fritz notes quietly that Frau Blitzer does indeed serve barley coffee, thereby tacitly contradicting Bollwerk's assertion about the necessity of bellicose behavior. Embarrassed, Bollwerk rages and stamps about, causing Frau Blitzer to rush in from her room below. Pätus innocently bears the full blast of her anger, especially when she discovers that her coffee service has been thrown (by Bollwerk!) out of the window, and her table disfigured by the carving. Bollwerk again intimidates her, driving her out of the room with his powerful voice and domineering manner.

When he announces later that he intends to see Lessing's comedy *Minna von Barnhelm*, Fritz accompanies him. Before they leave, Bollwerk indicates that he knows Jungfer Rehhaar, Pätus's sweetheart, and will introduce Fritz to her, especially since Pätus cannot publicly do so himself. If we note that Bollwerk's conversation reveals a preoccupation with sexual gratification, this last reference to Jungfer Rehhaar should portend disappointment for Pätus.

Scene 9 of the adaptation represents a wavering of Pätus's philosophical idealism. Bollwerk has seduced Jungfer Rehhaar, but the gullible Pätus is told that in making love they thought only of him. He justifies the validity of such vicarious experience in philosophical terms, maintaining almost consistently his belief in the idea that spiritual union between loved ones is more important than a physical union between one of the lovers and a third person. Further, his philosophical ideal of duty and his concept of morality dependent on that ideal convince him that *he* is ethically responsible for Jungfer Rehhaar's pregnancy. According to her wish, he promises to pay for her abortion.

Fritz is deeply moved by what he considers the nobility of Pätus's reaction to Jungfer Rehhaar's plight and offers his insolvent friend the sum he requires. Pätus accepts the money and agrees with Fritz's assurance that to

---

[58] The selection in GW VI, 2351 may be found in Kant, *Werke* (Leipzig. Insel, 1922), V, 675–76.

learn more about Kant's "revolutionary" ideas is a worthier action than to visit his Gustchen.

At this point, Bollwerk and Jungfer Rehhaar enter. Bollwerk's brutally cynical request for the abortion money meets with Pätus's ridiculously gallant compliance. The girl's honest amazement at the kindness (and blindness) of Pätus is expressed in an unhappily vulgar remark which indicates — to the spectator but not to Pätus — that she is hardly the sincere, sweet young lady that Pätus believes her to be: "Sie sind sehr gütig, gnädiger Herr Pätus. Wo Sie doch selber nichts dadurch gehabt haben!" (GW VI, 2361). When she and Bollwerk have left, Pätus searches for a certain passage in a volume of Kant and informs Fritz in complete seriousness that by giving him the money so selflessly, Fritz has just put Kant's Categorical Imperative into practice.

During the brief pantomime-like representation in Brecht's entr'acte, which is entirely new, the spectator notes that Pätus marries a certain Karoline the following spring. There is no surprise in this fact by itself; the surprise comes in Scene 15, which is the anti-climax to the action witnessed previously.

In Scene 15, as in Scene 9, it is characteristic of the initial action that a protagonist reads excerpts from a work of literature, summarizes past events and explains them to a friend. Only toward the middle of each scene does anything actually happen on stage. In Scene 15, Pätus recounts to his visitor, Fritz, the reasons which led him to marry Karoline. At first, he offers Fritz Kant's rather cerebral, legalistically interpreted definition of marriage. Brecht vulgarizes the excerpt, taken verbatim from Kant's *Eherecht,* by making a few minor changes in the text. Apparently, Pätus finally preferred to obtain a job and get married, rather than defend the unpopular ideas of Kant and repeatedly fail his licentiate examination. Accordingly, he renounced Kant publicly, and paid lip service to the idea that war is not to be condemned. His thesis defended the supposedly popular belief that wars are not caused by the very specific actions of particular men but mysteriously "break out" by themselves.

Pätus finds Fritz's questions about his personal life uncomfortable; he changes the subject by asking Fritz about his recent Italian journey. He reads Seiffenblase's letter and, noting that the young von Berg (in turn) considers himself morally responsible for Gustchen's misfortune, attempts to alleviate his distress by giving him his own rather coarse view of woman's sexual nature, but he drops the subject when his wife enters.

Brecht uses the language and behavior characteristic of the lower middle class or *Spießer* for the dialogue between Pätus and Karoline. The couple's view of coffee as a palliative for all ills is ignored by Fritz who leaves brusquely for Insterburg in mourning. The change wrought in Pätus by his newly found materialistic attitude to war, love, and life is made amply clear in his unfeeling request to Karoline to forget Fritz's worries and join him instead at the warm stove. Such is the conclusion of the Pätus subplot.

CHAPTER III

CHARACTERS AND POLEMICS IN THE
MODEL AND THE ADAPTATION
THE MAIN CHARACTERS: LÄUFFER AND WENZESLAUS

> The ethical man of letters is impressed by the tension between society as it is
> and by society as, according to his view, it ought to be. He is a social critic;
> he reveals, preaches, accuses, and is dominated by a tendency to cutting satire.
> — Ernest K. Bramsted, *Aristocracy and the Middle Classes in Germany — Social
> Types in German Literature* (Chicago: Univ. of Chicago P., 1964), pp. 4-5

The dissimilarity in the sociological views of Lenz and Brecht accounts
largely for the often radical changes in characterization in the *Hofmeister*
adaptation. To a great extent, Lenz believes that man can display freedom
of will in spite of the dictates of his sensuous nature and the pressures of
material conditions. The figures of the Privy Councillor and Fritz von Berg
are cases in point. Because Lenz believes in the freedom of will, and hopes
that his idealism can promote social change, he advocates reform of the
system.

Brecht, on the other hand, totally rejects, it would seem, all belief in
freedom of will and such idealism because he wishes to portray in the
Hofmeister a society in which oppressive conditions on all levels of existence will neither permit freedom nor tolerate reform. (It should be noted
that my statements concerning Brecht's polemics in the *Hofmeister* are made
from a detached, objective view in order to explain his often radical changes
in the *Bearbeitung.*) Precisely because the depicted situations admit neither
of these, Brecht implies that stout resistance is the only answer to an intoler
able system. And because he wishes to preach the necessity of such resistance he delineates character according to one or other of these views:
Either existing society creates and maintains conditions incompatible with
the dignity and rights of man, or the protagonist (Läuffer, Pätus) is such a
coward that he tolerates, or even supports, the system which degrades him.

Lenz does not simplifiy for the sake of argument, as does Brecht. The
Storm and Stress author does not divide all of society into the oppressors
and the oppressed. Despite the fact that his Läuffer is sadly abused by the
landed aristocracy, Lenz differentiates between various levels of the aristocracy and shows that the tutor is not entirely a victim of social and
economic circumstances but possesses a freedom of choice which he does not
have the courage to exercise. It is this freedom of choice, this belief that
the individual can shape his own worthwhile destiny — as opposed to the
view in Brecht's *Hofmeister* that the intellectual is not only too meek, but
is also actually quite powerless to determine his own existence — that

distinguishes, to a limited extent, the two writers and the characterization and motivation of their *dramatis personae*.

Lenz endows two of the major characters in the *Hofmeister*, namely, the Geheimrat and Fritz, with the rational and progressive spirit which informed such thinkers of the Enlightenment as Immanuel Kant.[1] In II, 1 of the play, Lenz's Geheimrat states in a discussion with Pastor Läuffer what is tantamount to belief in an enlightened ideal, i.e., the perfectibility of man. In this scene, certain arguments of the Geheimrat may indeed reflect the conviction of the time, if not of Lenz,[2] that men must first attain a certain measure of perfection within themselves and in their actions before they can seek to make society more perfect. Lenz depicts society in a time of change, advancing toward more complete social realization of humanitarian ideals than in the past:

GEH. RATH: . . . Was soll Dein Sohn werden, sag mir einmahl?

MAJOR: Was er . . . Soldat soll er werden; ein Kerl, wie ich gewesen bin.

GEH. RATH: Das letzte laß nur weg, lieber Bruder; unsere Kinder sollen und müssen das nicht werden, was wir waren: die Zeiten ändern sich, Sitten, Umstände, alles . . .

MAJOR: Potz hundert! wenn er Major wird, und ein braver Kerl wie ich, und dem König so redlich dient als ich!

------

[1] In his recently published dissertation [(*Jacob Michael Reinhold Lenz — Moralist und Aufklärer* (Bad Homburg v.d.H.: Gehlen, 1970)] Ottomar Rudolf discusses Lenz's relationship to the thought of the age: "*Der Hofmeister* [von Lenz], der in vielen Teilen zu der Denkrichtung der Aufklärung gehört, entwickelt aus dem Innern eine Dynamik des Sittlichen, eine Liebe zur Wahrhaftigkeit. Lenz hält, und das möchten wir mit Nachdruck sagen, an der aufklärerischen Entwicklung fest. Während die meisten Stürmer und Dränger den Intellektualismus bekämpfen, will Lenz das Gesunde an der Aufklärung erhalten, beim schärfsten Angriff auf die kulturellen Schäden, die die Aufklärung auslöste. Er versucht die Ideen der Aufklärung mit seinem neuen Menschheitsideal, dem Gefühlsbetonten, mit dem Subjektivierungsstreben, von Rousseau übernommen, zu vereinigen. Er sucht eine Brücke zwischen den beiden Richtungen." (pp. 162—163)

[2] Lenz gave us his own views on the *Hofmeister* in the second of the "Briefe über die Moralität der Leiden des jungen Werthers." He states: "Man hat mir allerley moralische Entzwecke [sic] und philosophische Sätze bey einigen meiner Komödien angedichtet, man hat sich den Kopf zerbrochen, ob ich wirklich den Hofmeisterstand für so gefährlich in der Republick halte, man hat nicht bedacht, daß ich nur ein bedingtes Gemählde geben wollte von Sachen wie sie da sind und die Philosophie des geheimen Raths nur in seiner Individualität ihren Grund hatte." (2. Brief). Quoted in Richard Daunicht, ed., *J. M. R. Lenz—Gesammelte Werke*, (München: Fink, 1967), Band I, p. 394.

Hans Mayer offers a slightly divergent view: "Sein [Lenzens] reformatorisch gemeintes Stück bedeutet Aufklärung, kennt den Rousseau, steht in der Nachbarschaft Pestalozzis. Darum ist der Geheimrat von Berg bei Lenz gleichsam der Sprecher des Autors; er ist der Raisonneur und aufgeklärte adlige Philanthrop. . . . Lenz strebte gleich so vielen deutschen bürgerlichen Künstlern und Reformern zum bürgerlich-feudalen Kompromiß. Auch bei ihm vertrat der Geheimrat als adliger Aufklärer die bürgerlichen Forderungen." Cf. *Bertolt Brecht und die Tradition* (Pfullingen: Neske, 1961), pp. 57—58.

GEH. RATH: Ganz gut, aber nach funfzig [sic] Jahren haben wir vielleicht
einen andern König und eine andere Art ihm zu dienem ...

(D I, 42)

Also, he seeks to prove that if men (Fritz and most father figures in the
Hofmeister) courageously use their energy and reason, show love, tolerance
and forgiveness, and strive to realize worthwhile ambitions, they can enjoy
personal fulfillment while also contributing to other people's happiness and
improving society's institutions.[3]

Lenz's conservative figures, such as the ascetic Wenzeslaus and the belligerent Major with their reactionary views on the Church and State, are necessary counterparts to the enlightened, benevolent, and forward-moving
figures of the Geheimrat and his son. The contrast between the ideologies
of these dissimilar figures as well as the egalitarian spirit between Fritz and
Pätus reflect Lenz's belief that the social structure should no longer be
based on outdated, often insuperable, and unjustly maintained *a priori* dis-
tinctions between men. Lenz also points to a future in which he hopes that
society will be founded on the belief in the equal social worth of all individuals and the unrestricted opportunity for each man to achieve his full
potential. These ideas are of paramount importance in assessing the character of Lenz's protagonists.

Because Lenz believes in man's freedom of will, it is his practice[4] not to
manipulate his characters like marionettes, dangling helplessly from the
threads of economic misery, as is the case with Läuffer and Pätus in Brecht's
Hofmeister.

----

[3] Taken together, the unselfish and responsible actions of the father figures, as
well as those of Pätus and Fritz in Lenz's *Hofmeister,* exemplify the very idealistic view that the author had of Christian charity. Ottomar Rudolf sums up
the ethical questions posed in Lenz's drama in this way: "Im *Hofmeister* wird
die Moral zur Wissenschaft des Lebens. Die ethische Frage wird wieder wie in
den Nachahmungen des Plautus als sittliche Forderung gelöst, ganz anders [sic]
in den kraftstrotzenden, zeitgenössischen Dramen seiner Freunde. Liebe, Güte,
Wahrhaftigkeit und Mäßigkeit sind auch hier die Grundantriebe Lenzischer
Morallehre .. Die Liebe, nicht so sehr in weltlicher Form, sondern die christ-
liche Nächstenliebe wird neben der Tugend des Maßhaltens zur treibenden
Kraft .. Im Namen der christlichen Liebe kämpft Lenz gegen den bornierten
Klassenunterschied, gegen ein veraltetes Gesetz, eine verstaubte Konvention und
eine seichte Moral." Cf. Rudolf, p. 174.
[4] If one subscribes to Albrecht Schöne's interpretation of Lenz's *Hofmeister* as a
drama of prodigal sons, the question of the autonomy of the dramatic personages, i.e., their independence of the author, may be subject to discussion. Cf.
Albrecht Schöne, "Wiederholung der exemplarischen Begebenheit — Jakob Michael Reinhold Lenz," in *Säkularisation als sprachbildende Kraft — Studien zur
Dichtung deutscher Pfarrersöhne* in *Palaestra,* vol. 226 (Göttingen: Vandenhoeck
und Ruprecht, 1958), pp. 80, 83, and 87.

The Läuffer of Lenz and Brecht:
Polarized Concepts of Characterization

Lenz's idealistic views on individual freedom and the liberal forces that should be at work in class society can be effectively illustrated by comparing the character and values of his Läuffer to those of his counterpart in Brecht's adaptation. In Lenz's *Hofmeister*, Läuffer is a man who belongs neither to the conservative nor to the liberal groups which are discussed above. The tutor scorns the views of the former faction without having the strength and courage to adopt the ideas of the latter. Because he is a man without firm principles, he works against his personal happiness, fails to use his freedom of will and neglects the development of his intellectual potential. At the university, he is frivolous rather than serious: "Wenigstens hab' ich in Leipzig keinen Ball ausgelassen, und wohl über die funfzehn [sic] Tanzmeister in meinem Leben gehabt." (DI, 43) Later, attracted by Gustchen, he practices self-indulgence rather than self-discipline; and ultimately confronted with the (erroneous) belief that she and her father have died because of his actions, he emasculates himself, confusing self-punishment with self-improvement.

Lenz takes care to demonstrate that Läuffer's situation is, to a certain extent, of his own making. To be sure, he also shows that Läuffer's decisions are often determined by a rigidly authoritarian society — and this is very much the case in Brecht's adaptation. Lenz is particularly critical of the weak stand of the middle class against the nobility, and the same is true to an even greater degree in the adaptation. Lenz's Läuffer does not continue his university studies because his father, who could pay his son's fees, does not choose to do so. Therefore, Lenz holds the class and economic structure of society only partly responsible for what Läuffer decides to do. He indicates consistently in the play, however, that Läuffer himself is to be accounted responsible for all that he does; his character determines his actions. This belief underlies the characterization of all the protagonists in Lenz's *Hofmeister*.

As observed above, Lenz feels that man must attain a measure of perfection within himself before he can seek to better society. Therefore, Lenz depicts a society in which such individual freedom of development is possible. Brecht seems to reverse the priorities. He omits or radically alters the polemic thrusts of the original drama and makes them consistent with his Marxist view of class relationships in the period treated by the play. The characterization of his *dramatis personae* proceeds from the Marxist view of the historical class struggle. Brecht adapts the *Hofmeister* in the conviction that a more perfect society must be created before the individual can possibly enjoy the freedom to better himself. In order to show this, Brecht removes all traces of the incipient flux and the progressive spirit of society as Lenz portrays them. Also, Brecht fairly and correctly stresses the fact that the social structure of the time was rigid[5] and that the feudal aristocracy ruthlessly defended all the privileges to which tradition had long accustomed them. This is indeed a vivid feature of the adaptation.

Lenz has diverse didactic intentions in the *Hofmeister*. Brecht tones down Lenz's strong criticism of the private tutor and satirizes the German schoolmaster and educational system instead. Lenz tries to demonstrate the need for public education by showing the shortcomings and dangers of private tutorship. He is equally interested in criticizing specific practices of the nobility and in portraying (in the figures of the Geheimrat and Fritz) exemplary, i.e., positive, constructive individuals whom all aristocrats should emulate. Lenz gives an example of the ideal role that he wishes the aristocracy to assume in society. Lenz also criticizes the middle class in the figures of the narrow-minded conservatives and lickspittles among the lay preachers and the clergy, such as Wenzeslaus and Pastor Läuffer.

Lenz is highly critical of these classes in his dramas *Die Soldaten* (1776) and *Der neue Menoza* (1774) and wishes, in his art, to hold up a mirror to reflect all that is wrong with society. He explains, in a letter of July 1775 to Sophie von La Roche, why he portrays society so realistically and so critically:

> ... in meinen künftigen [Stücken, e.g., *Die Soldaten*] sollen auch keine solche [sic] Schandtaten [wie im *Hofmeister* und in dem *Neuen Menoza*] mehr vorkommen. Doch bitte ich Sie sehr, zu bedenken, gnädige Frau! daß mein Publikum das ganze Volck ist; daß ich den Pöbel so wenig ausschließen kann, als Personen von Geschmack und Erziehung, und daß der gemeine Mann mit der Häßlichkeit seiner Regungen des Lasters, nicht so bekannt ist, sondern ihm anschaulich gemacht werden muß, wo sie hinausführen. Auch sind dergleichen wirklich in der Natur [d.h., Gesellschaft]; leider können sie nur in der Vorstellung nicht gefallen, und sollen's auch nicht. Ich will aber nichts, als dem Verderbniß der Sitten entgegen arbeiten, das von den glänzenden zu den niedrigen Ständen hinab schleicht, und wogegen diese die Hülfsmittel nicht haben können, als jene.[6]

In both *Die Soldaten* and *Der neue Menoza*, the morals of the nobility, as represented by Graf Desportes and Graf Camäleon, are severely condemned, in the former play by Gräfin la Roche, in the latter by Prinz Tandi. (Significantly, both of these critics are of noble birth.) The approximate counterpart of Seiffenblase *(Der Hofmeister)* is Desportes *(Die Soldaten)*, who is

---

[5] Describing the Weimar of 1775, W. H. Bruford notes the general historical value of Karl von Lyncker's memoirs which "... rescued from oblivion many features of everyday life before the French Revolution, when everyone knew and accepted his place in society, and from week to week and from year to year little ever occurred to break the long-established routine of the different social classes." Cf. *Culture and Society in Classical Weimar* (Cambridge: U. P., 1962), p. 59, p. 442. Cf. also *Am Weimarischen Hofe unter Amalien und Karl August*, Erinnerungen von Karl Freiherr von Lyncker, hrsg. von Marie Scheller (Berlin, 1962).

[6] *Briefe von und an J. M. R. Lenz*, hrsg. von Karl Freye und Wolfgang Stammler (Leipzig: Wolff, 1918), vol. I, no. 57.

both an aristocrat and an officer. He and his class are shown to be the terror of the middle class in *Die Soldaten.*

But Lenz also examines the middle class and finds them wanting in moral fibre and unable to assert their rights or maintain their human dignity. Father Wesener in *Die Soldaten* has neither the courage nor the wisdom to forbid Desportes to court Marie. He sacrifices his daughter's honor and happiness to his vanity, i.e., his hopes to marry her to the nobleman Desportes. Nor does Eisenhardt, the army chaplain in *Die Soldaten,* as a representative of the clergy, have the courage to defend his convictions about the depravity of the soldier, i.e., officer. Rather than interfere when matters become serious, he remarks, for example: "Lassen Sie mich aus dem Spiel, ich bitte Sie." (II, 2)

Much of the criticism that Lenz aims at the institution of the family in *Der Hofmeister* deplores the harshness of the various father figures, including the Major, Old Pätus, and Pastor Läuffer. Finally, Lenz's play takes up a topical issue of some Storm and Stress dramatic works and, in defiance of established moral thinking on the subject, boldly makes a plea for the acceptance and defense of the unwed mother and her child.[7]

In contrast to Lenz's varied intentions, Brecht's critical concern in the adaptation is more ideological; he intensifies the social differences and depicts the bondage of the intellectual and the schoolmaster in a stereotyped society, whose economic and class system efficiently and ruthlessly prevents any real personal freedom of choice or action. In Brecht's view, the inwardness and moral idealism of the intelligentsia of recent German history discouraged serious political activity. Brecht portrays in the *Hofmeister* an intelligentsia unwilling and too cowardly to make the personal and material sacrifices necessary to resist those authorities who control freedom of thought and the distribution of wealth. Accordingly, Brecht portrays Lenz's Läuffer not as someone who chooses foolishly to become a tutor rather than pursue his studies, but as the thoroughly helpless victim of feudal rulers whose penchant for war creates such economic deprivation among the members of the lower middle class that they can exercise no autonomy in their personal, social or financial affairs.

Because, at times, Brecht alters the motives for Läuffer's action and makes them social rather than personal, and at other times economic and biological rather than moral and psychological, Läuffer appears as an individual without freedom of choice. This determinism, combined with the

---

[7] Gert Mattenklott discusses briefly the radical nature of Lenz's plea. Cf. *Melancholie in der Dramatik des Sturm und Drang* (Stuttgart: Metzler, 1968), p. 131 and note 23. Discussing Lenz's views on the position of women in the Storm and Stress era, Ottomar Rudolf remarks: "Lenz kämpft für die freie Gefühlsentscheidung der Frau, übt Kritik an der Erziehung der Frau, dem verderblichen Einfluß sentimentaler Bücher auf diese. Vor allem aber ergreift er Partei für die Gestalt des gefallenen Mädchens, ein dem Sturm und Drang eigenes Problem." Cf. *J. M. R. Lenz,* p. 161.

fact that Läuffer must act within the limits of an extremely rigid social order tends to detract from Läuffer's credibility as an independent dramatic character.

There are various alternatives open to Läuffer in Lenz's play, should he decide not to remain a private tutor; there are none in the adaptation. In Lenz's work, Läuffer's self-emasculation is shown as an act motivated by strong psychological forces, and neither social pressures nor material needs directly influence his decision to castrate himself. In Brecht's adaptation, Läuffer mutilates himself — not without the irony of the author — because his professional and economic situation seems, to him at least, to allow no other solution.

The fact that Läuffer's character is greatly changed in the adaptation, whereas his actions remain essentially the same, points to the issue central to this discussion of Brecht's dramaturgical practice and political thought. The decisions made by the oppressed individual in Brecht's adaptation are determined neither by his character nor by his moral principles, but by the dictates of natural law, such as the sex drive, or by the economic and class structure of society. These behavioristic and mechanical formulae, as shown in the adaptation, permit Brecht to manipulate and group his protagonists into two well-defined camps; these are the exploited and the exploiters, or, in other words, the anti-heroes, who are forced to conform, and the villains, who force them to do so.

Läuffer, the Major and the Geheimrat

As I am concerned with the new emphases and the changes present in Brecht's portrayal of Läuffer, it is particularly rewarding to examine, scene by scene, his relationship to other important figures in the adaptation. This method effectively contributes to a thorough discussion of the specific details of the changes in the characterization and Brecht's intentions behind them.

In I, 1 of Lenz's *Hofmeister,* Läuffer is portrayed as a hostile, conceited and rather unambitious person who prefers not to become a clergyman because he feels he is too young, too good-looking and too sophisticated to renounce the pleasurable kind of life he has led until now. On account of his frivolity, he has lost his father's financial support for continuing his university studies. Unwilling to remedy his lack of academic qualifications, and consequently also unfit to obtain a position as public school teacher, Läuffer is eager, however, to settle for a job as private tutor.

Significantly, Läuffer fails to see that his failure to make the most of his restricted opportunities stems from faults within himself. He attributes his misfortune to the parsimoniousness of his father and to the animosity of the Geheimrat. The young man hopes to compensate for his deficiencies by doing all he can to please his social superiors.

The Major, in I, 2 of Lenz's play, is deceived by Läuffer's show of politeness and deference, whereas the Geheimrat rightly suspects that Läuffer's obsequious behavior is a mask to conceal lacunae in his educational background and pedagogical fitness. The Geheimrat believes that it is especially due to these deficiencies that Läuffer is willing to subordinate himself without reservation.

We get to know the Läuffer of Lenz's drama via his direct self-characterization in the opening monologue of I, 1. Here, Lenz emphasizes not the social conditions, as does Brecht later on, but the individual's character, what that individual thinks of himself, and what others think of him. By contrast, in Brecht's Scene 1, which combines the first two scenes of Lenz's drama, the slant is reversed. Brecht purposefully modifies the reasons for Läuffer's becoming a private tutor. In the adaptation, the Major's references to an economic depression in the wake of the Seven Years' War clearly indicate that Läuffer cannot continue his university studies for financial reasons beyond his control. His father continues to supply financial support, but it proves insufficient in this period of inflation and hardship: "Seines Vaters Beutel hat für die Schlußexamina nicht gelangt," explains the Geheimrat. (GW VI, 2335) Therefore, Läuffer has no choice but to leave the university without his degree and seek a job. The only position which his father can obtain for him is the thankless job as private tutor. Läuffer is thus made to appear the unfortunate victim of the age.

In Scene 1 of Brecht's adaptation, we become acquainted with Läuffer, for the most part, only indirectly via the dialogue between the Major and the Geheimrat. Their talk, devoted mainly to the young man, stresses his abject material condition and his function as tutor; his character is not mentioned specifically until near the end of their conversation, and then only in passing by the Geheimrat. Neither of the aristocrats respects Läuffer as a person or as a potential teacher. To the Major he is just "der verhungerte Kerl" (GW VI, 2335) who keeps crossing his path. Brecht intends the Geheimrat's term of contempt for Läuffer, "der Speichellecker" (GW VI, 2335), to increase the spectator's consciousness of the social gulf between the two classes in question. Of course, with such a crude epithet Brecht not only typifies Läuffer but also demonstrates the antagonist-protagonist polarization vividly. In their remarks about Läuffer the Major and the Geheimrat also characterize themselves.

The dominant impression that the aristocrats have of Läuffer as a teacher is that he will be a possibly adequate "tool;" he is regarded as a mere servant. The Major disinterestedly suggests that Läuffer "mag vielleicht dienen so gut wie ein anderer" (GW VI, 2335) and conceives of his pedagogical duties as an uninspiring mechanical task: "er soll ihm [Leopold] die Wissenschaften und Manieren eintrichtern." (GW VI, 2335)

In the Major's view, Läuffer's most important qualification is neither his academic background nor his ready servility; nor is it an irreproachable character or reputation, which the Geheimrat snobbishly seems to consider desirable. It is really the cheapness of his services which makes him an attractive candidate.[8]

Läuffer's function in Brecht's Scene 1 is sociological in nature. The tutor lurks in the background, preparing to greet the two aristocrats conspicuously, and possibly engage them in conversation. His on-stage position is — as in Lenz's drama — a visual symbol of his role in society. He is, and will always remain, an insignificant figure in the background. Läuffer's polite bows are not acknowledged by either aristocrat. A part of the action, such overt disregard for Läuffer reveals the social gulf that separates the aristocracy from the middle class. Läuffer's repeated genuflexions exaggerate his inferior social rank; his curse, "der Teufel hol' euch, Flegel" (GW VI, 2335) belies his gesture of subordination and respect. The fact that his curse is barely audible and is uttered only during the last bow is a further illustration of his hypocrisy. (This instance of contradictory actions performed simultaneously by the same figure is also a good example of Brecht's love of dialectic argument.) Läuffer appears to consider the aristocracy as the scourge of the middle class. Indeed, it seems that Brecht endows him with an acute sense of class consciousness and class struggle.

In any case, this first scene leaves us with the situation typical of Läuffer. He is always a desperate man in an impasse. He can act only as conditions and the aristocracy permit. Whereas in Scene 1 he depends on the nobility only for his material support, in Scene 17 he is at their mercy and totally bound over to them. The extent of his development as a spineless servant and *Mitläufer* is amply shown by the difference between his behavior in Scene 1 and Scene 17. In the end, his words of hatred for the nobility become enthusiastic expressions of respect, brimming with obsequiousness and gratitude.

If the noteworthy feature of Läuffer's character and behavior in Brecht's Scene 1 is servility, this readiness to subordinate himself to the demands of the nobility is increasingly made his most striking trait in the remaining scenes of the adapted drama.

Läuffer and the Majorin

Lenz's text of I, 3 is retained almost verbatim in Scene 3 of the adaptation; here Brecht pays particular attention to the episode of the two dances. Whereas Lenz's Läuffer executes only a few steps of the minuet and *pas de deux* before the Majorin, who is sitting on a couch, Brecht expands the episode and has Läuffer vigorously perform a series of measures from each dance for her. In the adaptation, she is seated at her "commandpost," the

---

[8] Brecht emphasizes this point later on in the notes to Scene 3 of the adaptation: Der Schlußsatz der Majorin enthält die Antwort auf die Frage, warum Läuffer nicht ... entlassen wird; er ist billig." (GW XVII, 1225)

spinet, where she plays the melodies to which he should dance. Brecht makes Läuffer acutely aware that his immediate future depends on obeying the Majorin, no matter how excessive her demands. The adaptor elaborates and exaggerates this episode because he wants to show the degree to which Läuffer will force himself to submit to the abuse of the nobility in order to secure a position as tutor.

In his notes to the stage version of the *Hofmeister*, Brecht writes that Läuffer is portrayed in the minuets as a man conscious of his great strength, anxious to suppress this strength and place himself meekly at the service of his employers. The poetic and artistic moments of the choreography notwithstanding, Brecht also wishes Läuffer's dancing to be understood as a "tödlichen Existenzkampf," as indicated in his *Regiebuch*, BBA 539/18.

Whereas only two dances are mentioned in the dialogue of the stage play and the printed text, what Brecht writes in the note "Das aufsässige Menuett" indicates that Läuffer was requested to perform a third dance but avoided doing so by trying to appeal to the sensual nature of the Majorin:

Danach [nach dem Pas] steht er allerdings in völliger Erschöpfung. Die Majorin jedoch, angeregt, spielt ihm gnädig ein Menuett vor.... Läuffer, nach kurzer Selbstüberwindung, geht mit weiten federnden Schritten, sich unaufhörlich den Schweiß vom Gesicht wischend, zum Spinett hinter, wo er einen tiefen tierischen Laut des Entzückens ausstößt und sich gierig über die fleischige Hand der Majorin beugt. (GW XVII, 1250)

Kissing her hand is not only a concrete gesture of Läuffer's masochistic pleasure in self-abasement and his acceptance of her superior will; it is also a sign of the savage animal instinct in him lurking beneath the surface and impatient for release. Brecht hints at this in BBA 539/18. The second sentence of a scribbled stage direction there contains the germ of the excerpt noted above: "Nun ein großer (langer) Gang auf die Majorin zu, als auf die *Frau* [sic]."

The fact that Brecht's Läuffer appeals to the erotic instinct in the Majorin is brought out further in Scene 3 by the following action. When he learns that she also likes to sing, Läuffer tries to flatter her even before she has sung a note. He senses that she is particularly vain and fawns on her, clumsily exaggerating his compliments (as in Lenz) and kissing her hand again. Both authors intend this behavior to illustrate how easily Läuffer dons the mask of the lickspittle. His attentions are apparently not unwelcome, for, according to Brecht's notes to the play (GW XVII, 1224—25), the bored Majorin flirtatiously offers him her hand to kiss again, even after reprimanding him in French for having already dared to do so! This liberty that he takes with the Majorin also serves to illustrate the social gulf between her and Läuffer. Both Lenz and Brecht wish to create the temporary impression that this gulf is lessened by Läuffer's forwardness. Such an impression must be given in order that Läuffer's humiliation may appear all the more complete when he is banished from the salon a moment later for presuming to interrupt and contradict Graf Wermuth.

Läuffer and the Young Girls

In Scene 4 of the adaptation, Brecht intensifies Lenz's portrayal of the tutor's sensual and servile nature. The girls at the skating rink attest to his sexual appeal indirectly in their giggling and chatter. That he is physically attractive is also obvious from his accomplished skating. Indeed, his physique, as well as his sexual frustration, have not gone unnoticed in the town of Insterburg, for he is·now the subject of gossip, especially since he propositioned one of the local "prostitutes" and was rejected by her. Despite their unwillingness to do so, the girls at the rink ignore him. Brecht attacks society here by implying that Läuffer is the victim of middle class reserve which dictates that decent girls who value their reputation do not associate with strange, lonely men.

Läuffer's inferior position in society is further made visually clear in pantomime when he stumbles on his skates and falls at the feet of the awkward Leopold. Wherever Läuffer is associated with members of the aristocracy, he is abased — in this case, in the literal sense of the word, with a humor reminiscent of Shakespeare's punning.

Läuffer, Leopold, and the Major

Intensifying Lenz's depiction of the animosity which Läuffer bears toward the nobility, Brecht shows the tutor's hatred of them in a short new episode in Scene 5 of the adaptation. Leopold sees in his tutor only another servant to be scorned. Because Läuffer possesses neither pedagogical principles nor self-respect, he accepts Leopold's abuse and stifles his anger. This is amply demonstrated in the ensuing encounter with the Major. In addition, Läuffer reveals that he neither possesses a very accurate knowledge of Prussian history nor feels patriotic toward Frederick II. The Major reproaches him, giving a lecture at the same time:

> Der Aufsatz über den Heldenkönig, den ich da lese, ist schlampig, daß ichs nur sag. Bei der Aufzählung der Feinde, die Er auf sich genommen hat, ist vergessen, daß Er nicht nur die Sachsen, die Österreicher, die Franzosen und die Russen herausgefordert hat, sondern daß Er auch noch mit den Briten eine deutliche Sprache gesprochen hat. Es kommt so nicht heraus, wie Er vor dem Untergang gestanden ist — und so nichts von der Glorie. (GW VI, 2344)

The passage is typical of the new dialogue added in this scene. By exaggerating the Major's respect for the glory and heroism of war, the adaptor renders this eulogy of Frederick II ridiculous, and expands on character traits already present but not stressed in Lenz's drama. Such a technique is common to the interpolated passages about war which are found throughout the adaptation.

The tutor's unenthusiastic attitude to war also stresses the class differences between him and his employer. As the young man owes neither wealth nor rank to Frederick, he sees the monarch and his war of territorial aggrandizement in a very different light from the Major.

Läuffer's cringing before the Major is illustrated in the adaptation, as in Lenz's play, by the tutor's spineless acceptance of a lower salary and additional instructional duties. The Major is made to appear particularly grasping because he exploits Läuffer's compelling situation to the fullest. Brecht further intensifies Läuffer's lack of pride here by adding slightly to his part in the dialogue. The tutor now agrees with the Major and responds twice with the military "Jawohl." (GW VI, 2346) Hearing that his plea for a horse might be granted, Läuffer bows with simulated deference, mouthing "O gnädigster Herr Major" (GW VI, 2346), a term totally inconsistent with the real character and coarse behavior of his employer.

Hypocritical, yet unsuspecting, Läuffer possesses a remarkable ability to accept humiliation and exploitation without complaint. As the Major quickly perceives, Läuffer lacks the self-respect necessary to take a stand and protest against the excessive demands made of him. He also knows that the tutor will accept any kind of degradation because he has no other opportunities for employment.

Läuffer and Gustchen

In II, 2 of his *Hofmeister,* Lenz suggests that Läuffer has developed a sincere, somewhat adolescent romantic interest in his pupil, Gustchen, and that she welcomes his lessons. She appreciates the presence of someone who is kind to her, considering the spiteful treatment and neglect she experiences from her mother. She uses the opportunity of his visits to flirt with him, but in a manner which can be described only as innocent and hesitant, in contrast to the provocative behavior of Gustchen in the adapted drama.

Brecht retains Lenz's II, 2 almost word for word in Scene 7 of the adaptation. He quite alters the relationship and character of the two young people, however, by placing Lenz's II, 2 in a different context: The first portion of Brecht's Scene 7 consists of about twenty-five lines of new dialogue in which Gustchen tries to recite her catechism; Lenz's II, 2 then forms the latter half of the scene.

This new episode shows that Läuffer suffers intensely from sexual frustration as a result of his forced association with a young but unavailable woman in Insterburg. Gustchen is well aware of this frustration, for she is endowed with a vibrant sensuality herself. The adaptor's consistent principles of vulgarization of sentiment and his stress on the biological as well as sociological aspects of human relationships are strikingly demonstrated here. Annoyed that he is mocked as a teacher and teased as a man, Läuffer exhibits here a dwindling ability to control his contradictory feelings for Gustchen. He yearns for her as a sexually desirable female but cannot repress his rising antagonism toward her for being his social superior.

In the new dialogue at the beginning of Brecht's Scene 7, Gustchen is supposed to recite Luther's Catechism[9] to Läuffer. As recited by Gustchen, it is no longer a solemn, sincere declaration of faith, and has nothing to do with religious belief. Gustchen is not stating her faith, but is teasing her tutor. She plays with him, cleverly stumbling over fragments of the text precisely at those points where the word "Leib" or a form of it occurs. Läuffer sees himself forced to assist her memory and must unwillingly remind himself of his physical desire for her:

GUSTCHEN: Ich glaube, daß mich Gott geschaffen hat.
LÄUFFER: Hätt ers doch nicht! *Hilft ihr aus:* Samt...
GUSTCHEN: Samt allen Kreaturen...
LÄUFFER: Mir Leib...
GUSTCHEN: Mir Leib und Seele...
LÄUFFER: Auch Leib...
GUSTCHEN: Augen, Ohren und alle Glieder, Vernunft und alle Sinne gegeben hat...
LÄUFFER: Und noch...
GUSTCHEN: Und noch erhält. Dazu Kleider und Schuh, Essen und Trinken, Haus und Hof, Weib und Kind, Äcker, Vieh und alle Güter...
LÄUFFER: Mit aller Notdurft und...
GUSTCHEN: Nahrung...
LÄUFFER: Des Leibs...
GUSTCHEN: Und Lebens...
LÄUFFER: Leiblich und täglich...
GUSTCHEN: Versorget. Wider alle Fährlichkeit beschirmt und vor allem übel...
LÄUFFER: Bewahret...

(GW VI, 2353—2354)

---

[9] Brecht's parody of familiar literature is not confined merely to the works ironized in the adaptation. There can be a concatenation of literary works suggested, as evident from Gustchen's exclamation "Klopstock!" Cf. Chapter IV, notes 10—14. Brecht's mockery of the Catechism might well have been suggested by *Buddenbrooks.* A comparison of the two passages lends credence to this suggestion. In Thomas Mann's novel, grandfather Johann Buddenbrook has asked little Toni to recite her Catechism; she does, at first hesitantly, but then quite fluently. Her recitation is, however, a subject of harmless good humor for the old man: "Er lachte vor Vergnügen, sich über den Katechismus mokieren zu können.." Mann's irony could have stimulated Brecht to use the Catechism in a manner opposite to Toni's recitation; whereas Gustchen falters, Toni hurries:

Wenn man im Gange war, dachte sie, war es ein
Gefühl, wie wenn man im Winter auf dem kleinen
Handschlitten mit den Brüdern 'den Jerusalemsberg'
hinunterfuhr: es vergingen einem geradezu die
Gedanken dabei, und man konnte nicht einhalten,
wenn man auch wollte.

Cf. Thomas Mann, *Buddenbrooks — Verfall einer Familie* (Stockholm: Fischer, 1951) Stockholmer Gesamtausgabe, vol. I, pp. 9—10.

The emphasis is transferred from the spiritual to the physical. Forms of the word *Leib* occur in final, i.e., stressed position in five of the fragmentary lines; Brecht has substituted the word *leiblich* for *reichlich;* also, the stress which Gustchen places on the words *Glieder* and *Sinne* serves to intensify her already unashamed and unabashed exhibition of sensual longing. The fact that Läuffer attempts to restrain his own physical urges by slapping the palm of his hand with a ruler reveals to what an extent Gustchen's behavior has aroused his desire. (The motif is repeated later in Scene 14a of the adaptation, when Läuffer's sexual yearning for Lise is stimulated by her naive flirtation with him.)

The quarrel between Läuffer and Gustchen toward the end of the original flirtation episode of Lenz's II, 2 must be re-interpreted in the adaptation in the light of the introductory episode of the Catechism. Now Brecht's Gustchen shamelessly plays hot and cold with Läuffer and as much as suggests that she would enjoy being seduced. Läuffer's reaction to Gustchen's unambiguous and challenging remark: "Es ist das einzige, was ich mit Lusssttt tue,"[10] is to substitute his hatred of the nobility for his desire to possess her: He feels that he dare not declare his desire for her and reacts angrily. His outburst, taken almost verbatim from Lenz, reads as an attempt to save himself from temptation by pretending to misunderstand Gustchen's words:

Oder Sie nehmen einen Zeichenlehrer. Überhaupt würde ich Ihren Herrn Vater bitten, den Gegenstand Ihres Abscheues, Ihres Hasses, Ihrer ganzen Grausamkeit von Ihnen zu entfernen. Ich sehe doch, daß es Ihnen auf die Länge unausstehlich wird, von mir Unterricht anzunehmen. (GW VI, 2355)

His final rejoinder, "Sie foltern mich" (GW VI, 2355), is no longer the remark of a man who felt that his affections were being trifled with, as in Lenz's drama, but the agonized outcry of a slave who dares not fall victim both to the desire and the opportunity to seduce his master's daughter. To take advantage of her and overstep class boundaries in addition, he fears would cost him his job and his life.

Whereas Lenz suggests in II, 2 and II, 5 that Läuffer takes a possibly romantic interest in Gustchen, Brecht vulgarizes and parodies the sentimental moments of the original play. This is true for Scene 7 as well as for Scene 10.[11] Here Läuffer argues that the Major is solely responsible for

---

[10] Cf. GW VI, 2355 and GW XVII, 1229.

[11] Brecht's Scene 10 is based on Lenz's II, 5. Compare Lenz's II, 5 of the first printing of the *Hofmeister* [published in 1774 by Weygand in Leipzig and reproduced in Richard Daunicht's *J. M. R. Lenz-Gesammelte Werke*, (München: Fink, 1967), vol. I, pp. 39–121] with II, 5 of the manuscript of 1772. This latter is presently in the "Depot Tübingen der ehemaligen Preußischen Staatsbibliothek Berlin" and is reproduced in Britta Titel and Hellmut Haug's *J. M. R. Lenz-Werke und Schriften*, (Stuttgart: Goverts, 1967), vol. II, pp. 720–721. In II, 5 of the manuscript of 1772, Läuffer and Gustchen *are* in love with each other.

Gustchen's seduction and reminds us that the officer has lowered his salary, forced him to teach Gustchen and unwittingly refused him access to the Königsberg brothels. Brecht is introducing a problem here not found in the corresponding scene in Lenz's drama, namely, that of moral guilt.[12] (Brecht is also ironically suggesting that Läuffer's "immoral" behavior is solely the result of economic misery.) The tutor refuses to blame himself at all for seducing Gustchen, and in all seriousness attributes his sexual aggressivity to over-indulgence in the rich foods of the Major's table. Brecht rejects the traditional Christian concepts of morality and substitutes the biological determinism of natural law. Läuffer remarks: "Soll ich mir da ein Gewissen daraus machen, daß ich mich nicht bezähmt? Sicherlich, ich werde zu üppig verköstigt für einen Sklaven." (GW VI, 2362)

Apparently, ethics are irrelevant where there are grounds for resentment of social inequities. Sentiment has become cynicism, and Läuffer's anxious concern for his precarious position takes precedence over Gustchen's romantic idealism. The tutor rejects her ravings about Shakespeare's Romeo, sharing neither her belief in romantic passions nor her escapist admiration for idealistic and tragic heroes. By causing Läuffer to behave in this way, Brecht suggests that the tutor rejects for economic and social reasons the art form (tragedy) which reflects and glorifies the values of a superior class. Whereas Lenz's Läuffer, unsentimental and coarse, is too realistic to accept such nonsense: "Ich bin nicht Romeo, ich bin Läuffer, wenns beliebt." (GW VI, 2363).

Läuffer also cannot indulge in romantic illusion because he is too anxious about the Major's predictably violent reaction to the inevitable discovery of his affair with Gustchen. The hilarious and anti-romantic moment of Läuffer's mention of Abälard in Lenz's drama is retained in Brecht's adaptation, but is expanded to tell what actually happened to the priest. Reverting to a tutor-pupil relationship with Gustchen, Läuffer commands her to summarize the punishment of Abälard in Rousseau's novel *La Nouvelle Héloïse*. Whereupon she responds pedantically as though her answer had been rehearsed:

> Als es ruchbar wurde, daß Abälard und seine Heloise sich insgeheim verehelicht hatten, ließ ihr Oheim, Monsignore Fulbert, Canonicus in Paris, ihn durch Häscher ergreifen und seines Geschlechts berauben. (GW VI, 2363)

The digression also stresses the social gulf between Läuffer and Gustchen: The tutor's recollection of Abälard's castration reveals his anxiety for his own safety. He knows that if apprehended for having seduced a nobleman's daughter, a mere servant can expect no mercy from the father.[13]

---

[12] But it may be argued that later, in V, 3, Lenz makes Läuffer's sense of moral guilt responsible for the decision to emasculate himself.

[13] The dilemma of a lover who belongs to a social level inferior to that of his beloved is traditionally used in literature to portray a certain irreconcilability

In II, 1 of Lenz's drama, the conversation between the Geheimrat and Pastor Läuffer centers on the Privy Councillor's interest in educational reform; Läuffer himself is not present. Two episodes in this scene are of particular interest. Firstly, Pastor Läuffer attempts to persuade the Geheimrat to pay Läuffer a supplemental salary in return for tutoring his younger son, Karl von Berg. The Privy Councillor refuses sympathetically, urges Läuffer to quit the Major's service, and offers him a sum of money out of his own pocket instead. Brecht omits this episode from Scene 8 because it shows the Geheimrat as an honest and generous man and thereby casts a favorable light on the aristocracy in general.

In the second of these episodes, Lenz's Pastor Läuffer asks the Geheimrat to read the tutor's desperate letter in which the young man pleads for assistance in order to obtain a horse from the Major for trips to Königsberg. The purpose of the trips was not specified. The Privy Councillor is being kind in the truest sense of the word here by refusing to help Läuffer get the horse; he reasons that the tutor will, in the long run, be better served by being encouraged to give up his position and improve his academic qualifications.

In Brecht's Scene 8, however, Läuffer is now present; he silently follows his father's fruitless discussion with the aristocrat, and in desperation finally puts forward his request for the horse. One may ask: "Why does Brecht find it necessary for Läuffer to be present during Scene 8 of the adaptation?" The adaptor wishes to show how spineless the tutor — and his father, and thus the middle class — really are. The young man listens to the insults directed at his patient father and tolerates the scorn heaped on himself without taking offense or registering the slightest protest. He has even less pride and self-respect than his father, for the latter departs when at last he perceives that nothing but abuse can be expected from the Geheimrat. Läuffer stays to plead almost on his knees for the horse, only to be quashed by the spiteful and vulgar taunts of the aristocrat: "Ihn sticht

---

of the social classes. In Scene 9 of the folkplay *Puntila und sein Knecht Matti*, Brecht uses this motif and resolves in ironic comedy what makes Läuffer's comic situation in *Der Hofmeister* desperately serious. The chauffeur, Matti, is asked to consider marrying Eva, the estate owner's daughter, but she fails the tests which he sets her. Immediately following this "examination," the mortal dangers of a union between members of unlike classes are told of in a ballad sung by the Communist Surkkala, "Es lebt eine Gräfin in schwedischem Land:"

> Es war eine Lieb zwischen Füchsin und Hahn
> "Oh, Goldener, liebst du mich auch?"
> Und fein war der Abend, doch dann kam die Früh
> Kam die Früh, kam die Früh:
> All seine Federn, sie hängen im Strauch.
>   GW IV, 1694

der Hafer? ... Mein Bruder bekommt für seine Ökonomie nicht Ackergäule, und da will Er von ihm einen Gaul für Seine Ausschweifungen!" (GW VI, 2357)

The tutor is no longer characterized as a man who has the opportunity to better his position, as in Lenz's drama. Brecht deletes the just admonitions of the Geheimrat that the tutor should quit the Major's service and return to university. As already indicated in my discussion of Scenes 1 and 6 of the adaptation, Läuffer and the middle class are consistently made to appear as victims of unfavorable economic conditions in the wake of the Seven Year's War. Accordingly, Läuffer now has no choice but to stay with the Major and accept his terms.

The second episode of Lenz's II, 1 — concerning Läuffer's written plea for the horse — is amplified in the adaptation in order to show the power of the biological: Läuffer is aware not only that he is the victim of economic depression, he also knows that he is the helpless prey of his sexual appetite. Whereas Lenz subtly indicates, by means of Läuffer's letter, that the tutor might wish to visit the Königsberg brothels, Brecht crudely construes the hint as a fact. Of course, Läuffer's plight is unfortunate and his treatment abominable. On the other hand, his repeated plea for the horse and his transparent explanation are so hilarious that he appears as a ridiculous, comic figure. Also, his agonized outcry (with the amusingly archaic spelling of the adjectival noun) "Gnädiger Herr ..., es könnte zu etwas Schröcklichem kommen..." (GW VI, 2357) is comic for the spectator while it is most serious for the tutor. It is a humorous situation because it seems a foregone conclusion that he must seduce Gustchen. Läuffer trembles because the power of natural law assumes the menacing visage of inexorable fate.

In Scene 8, as in every scene of Brecht's adaptation, the tutor becomes an ideological marionette, now dangling grotesquely, now deftly manipulated by the strings of economic and biological determinism. Under such circumstances, the spectator is unable to believe in Läuffer's independence as a dramatic character, i.e., that he is an individual in his own right. In fact, from the beginning of Brecht's play, the spectator is encouraged to think of Läuffer as controlled by forces against which he is powerless. As the speaker of the prologue, Läuffer recites and gesticulates in time with the rhythm of a music box. (GW XVII, 1222) This same music was also played between each scene (with the exception of 13, 14a, 14b, and 14c) in the Berliner Ensemble production.

Läuffer and Wenzeslaus:
Prototypes "der Teutschen Misere"

Radical changes in Lenz's characterization of Läuffer and Wenzeslaus are particularly striking in Scene 12 of the adaptation. Here Läuffer and Wenzeslaus appear quite unlike their counterparts in the corresponding three scenes of Lenz's drama (III, 2 and 4, IV, 3) which Brecht combines. As we shall see, the adaptor understands the two teachers as symbols of the traditional German schoolmaster.

One means whereby Brecht changes the characters of the protagonists is to omit sections of dialogue and even whole episodes from Lenz's drama. Generally, the omitted passages show redeeming or mitigating qualities in a person's nature and contribute to portraying a more rounded and sympathetic character than is suitable for Brecht's purposes. Particular character traits which the adaptor wishes to appear predominant are also emphasized by the addition of new dialogue which focuses attention on them.

In Lenz's III, 2 and 4, Läuffer for example, does not display the fawning and cringing now so characteristic of his behavior in Brecht's Scene 12. In Lenz's drama, the tutor remains generally taciturn and subdued during most of these two scenes. His almost complete silence may be due to amazement at the torrent of words which Wenzeslaus blithely directs at him. At no time does he perform any services for the old ascetic. In Lenz's text there are no indications to the contrary that Läuffer tries to be anything but polite and self-effacing. He has no need to act otherwise, for his host is quite different from the Wenzeslaus in Scene 12 of Brecht's play.

In Lenz's drama, Wenzeslaus is, by and large, a caricature of a village schoolmaster. The old bachelor is obviously pleased to have someone present whom he can impress with his honest and sincere dedication to teaching. The schoolmaster's criticism of the profession of private tutors occurs in several of his lengthy digressions, during which he moralizes about whatever topic comes to mind. His criticism is couched in gentle humor to render the facts less harsh; his insights are meant well, for he seeks to convince his charge — perhaps as a spokesman for the former private tutor, Lenz, himself — that tutoring is an idle, uninspiring profession. Although kind, Wenzeslaus is pedantic and excessively moralistic. His sermonizing about good and evil appears sincere. His ethical values, while puritan and conventional, encourage the ascetic life and service to God through works for mankind's benefit.

Lenz regards Wenzeslaus sympathetically in these first two scenes, particularly when it is a question of establishing that the schoolmaster has an independent mind and seeks the welfare of his students by encouraging the development of their critical intelligence. The old teacher is convincingly portrayed as an idealist, interested not in monetary rewards but in the satisfaction that comes from a good conscience and the responsible fulfillment of his teaching duties. To be sure, Lenz makes fun of Wenzeslaus, the bachelor and the teacher, mocking here and there his ridiculous ideas about tobacco and its soporific effect on the sexual urges.

Lenz endows the aging master with a predominantly wholesome character. Towards the close of II, 4, for instance, Lenz has him speak his mind about Läuffer's pedagogical qualifications. Wenzeslaus believes that hard work is both virtuous and necessary if the former tutor is to improve his mind and his Latin. Wenzeslaus encourages him to study for his own edification during the day and to help him in clerical matters at night. Lenz's schoolmaster sees in Läuffer a possible successor — not just a cheap helper, as does Brecht. Lenz presents a convincing case that Wenzeslaus's offer to employ the young man is well intentioned and unselfish, i.e., without hind-thoughts of exploiting him.

How does Brecht characterize Läuffer and Wenzeslaus in the portions of Lenz's scenes that he takes over? The changed character of Läuffer is not revealed at all via the dialogue retained almost verbatim from Lenz's drama, but by the tutor's behavior in response to new speeches of Wenzeslaus. Läuffer now plays opposite a much more perspicacious Wenzeslaus and demonstrates throughout the entire scene how thoroughly anxious he is to please his protector. Brecht adds no new speeches to the tutor's part in the dialogue until the Major's intrusion in the latter portion of Scene 12, yet he wants Läuffer's excessively obsequious nature to manifest itself in action. Accordingly, he makes Wenzeslaus a far shrewder judge of character than does Lenz.

At the beginning of Scene 12, Wenzeslaus immediately suspects the obsequious lackey in Läuffer. Although there are no apparent reasons for his suspicions, he suddenly puts the refugee tutor to the test by imperiously commanding: "Reich Er mir doch das Sandbüchslein;" (GW VI, 2368) "Leg Er mir doch die Blätter dort hinüber!" (GW VI, 2368) "Reich Er mir noch einmal das Sandbüchslein!" (GW VI, 2369) Läuffer's immediate and unprotesting compliance with the old man's demands indicates in pantomimic, and thus excessively demonstrative, form that the tutor is indeed a spineless creature who will serve whatever master orders him about.[14]

Egon Monk made a number of notes about the Berliner Ensemble's performance of the play which illustrate the intended effect and the then desirable interpretation of Brecht's textual additions. Monk remarks in these notes that in Scene 12, Läuffer is being examined for the second time as to his fitness as a servant:

---

[14] If we see Brecht's dramatic work as a unity, then his Läuffer is, in principle, really the slightly more intellectual brother of the "Panzerreiter" in *Der kaukasische Kreidekreis* who serve each successive ruler (and judge) with the same unquestioning, unfeeling, bestial devotion. In the *Kreidekreis*, Azdak appropriately calls the courtroom soldiers "Hunde," and "Mithunde." (GW V, 2094—95) The image shows that, in his view, the soldiers epitomize the unthinking, blind collaborators among the military class, who, by allying themselves with whichever ruler usurps power, prevent the political revolution of the masses, whom they should support instead of brutalizing. Because these soldiers are useful, they are never punished for their criminal acts; they need have no ethical values; they must merely follow orders obediently. Brecht would likely agree that it is appropriate to draw the parallel that Läuffer is intellectually to the Major and Wenzeslaus what the soldiers in the *Kaukasischer Kreidekreis* are politically to each successive ruler: The enemies of enlightened justice and mass revolution.

Erst nachdem sich Läuffer den Schweiß von der Stirn gewischt und zweimal laut gestöhnt hat, setzt Wenzeslaus sein Verhör fort. Ein Verhör ist es und es hat, was den Ernst der Lage für Läuffer betrifft, große Ähnlichkeit mit dem der Majorin aus der dritten Szene. (BBA 2062/26)

Monk sums up the "official" conception of Läuffer's character as follows: "Läuffer in seiner Zwangslage tut alles, seine Anstelligkeit zu zeigen. Eifer und Demut bestimmen seine Haltung bis zum Engagement am Schluß der Szene." (BBA 2062/26)

Concerning the first of Wenzeslaus's orders, Monk recorded an apt comment by Brecht, who assessed the reason for Wenzeslaus's behavior as the following: "In ihm [Wenzeslaus] erwacht der potentielle Arbeitgeber (Brecht)." (BBA 2062/26) Is the adapted Wenzeslaus really "der potentielle Arbeitgeber" that Brecht calls him? Indeed, he is from the outset of Scene 12. Now, there is a sound dramaturgical reason why Brecht extensively changes the character of the old schoolmaster in the adapted portions of III, 2 and 4, which constitute the initial episodes of Scene 12. Lenz's IV, 3 — which forms the last episodes of Scene 12 — originally took place an entire year after III, 2 and 4. During this year, Wenzeslaus came to regard Läuffer as a kind of personal slave-servant. On account of this attitude, Brecht had to alter the character of the aging master in the earlier episodes of Scene 12 in order to make it consistent later on in the adaptation with the portrayal of Wenzeslaus as a selfish autocrat. In subsequent episodes, Brecht shows that the schoolmaster hypocritically exploits Läuffer in the name of moral good, while cowardly serving the very nobility he despises.

It would be wrong to interpret Lenz's Wenzeslaus as a cynic. It is not convincing to regard his old schoolmaster's moralistic exhortations to Läuffer as deceptive double talk, the purpose of which is to secure an admiring and credulous servant. That Brecht intended us to think this of *his* Wenzeslaus is occasionally true when moral good is discussed; it is always true that the old man hankers after an admiring and credulous servant.

Has Wenzeslaus really become a cynic in Brecht's adaptation? He has indeed. There are various reasons for the schoolmaster's brave defense of Läuffer on the occasion of Graf Wermuth's rude intrusion in Scene 12 of the adaptation. We should remember, however, that few motives of Lenz's protagonists are retained in Brecht's version of the drama. In the original play, Wenzeslaus is intoxicated with his importance as a teacher and easily repulses the surprised aristocrat with a torrent of words. Also, the schoolmaster emphasizes that he is proud of the clearly emerging rights and independence of the middle class and will stand up for that he believes in. An additional motive for his defense of the tutor may simply have been human charity.

These reasons must be seen in a new light in the adaptation: Brecht's village schoolmaster is most anxious to secure Läuffer's services for his own ends because he suspects the fugitive in the tutor. The old man is no longer disinterested, permitting Läuffer to catch his breath and consider his next move; instead, he puts Läuffer to work immediately and orders: "... helfen Sie mir beim Liniieren, daß Sie Ihr Abendbrot verdienen, das hilft der Moral." (GW VI, 2370) Also, Wenzeslaus now gives the impression that he is without human charity. And significantly, it is no longer emphasized that he is proud to be a member of the middle class. His subsequent exploitation of Läuffer goes unnoticed by the tutor, for with his guilty conscience, he accepts most readily the "moral" justifications which the schoolmaster facilely and ironically invents for the tasks that he assigns.

Although Lenz's Wenzeslaus tends to moralize with obvious relish, he does appear sincere. Because Brecht endows Wenzeslaus with selfish motives, those moralizing passages which are retained in the adaptation appear strikingly cynical, for the new Wenzeslaus's purposes are transparent. For example, in a passage which Brecht takes almost verbatim from Lenz's drama, Wenzeslaus admonishes Läuffer:

> Aber wenn der Schulmeister Wenzeslaus seine Wurst ißt, so hilft ihm *das gute Gewissen* verdauen, und wenn der Herr Mandel Fasan mit der Champignonsauce aß, so stieß ihm *sein Gewissen* jeden *Bissen,* den er hinabschluckte, mit der *Moral* wieder in den Hals zurück. (My italics: GW VI, 2370)

Monk notes that Maurer, the actor who played the role of Wenzeslaus in the 1950 Berliner Ensemble production of the *Hofmeister* succeeded in giving the impression that Wenzeslaus is indeed cynical:

> Er [Maurer] wollte damit [der Überreichung der Arbeitsutensilien] zeigen, daß sich Wenzeslaus nicht nur für heute abend zurückzieht, sondern für immer. Der Schulmeister hat einen Sklaven für die niedrigen Verrichtungen gefunden und kann sich in Zukunft ganz auf das Geistige konzentrieren. (BBA 2062/31)

In Lenz's II, 4, Wenzeslaus talks harmlessly of being a free and independent teacher, who does his work for the sake of his pupils in the honest belief that his real reward will come from God:

> ... *es ist nun einmal so; und damit muß man zufrieden seyn:* bin ich doch auch mein eigner Herr, und hat kein Mensch mich zu schikanieren, da ich alle Tage weiß, daß ich mehr thu als ich soll. (My italics; D I, 82)

In the adaptation, Brecht deletes this passage and all mention elsewhere of Wenzeslaus as an independent teacher who develops the critical intellect of his pupils.

Concerning the italicized portion in the above excerpt, it is unacceptable to Brecht that Lenz's Wenzeslaus sees social conditions as unalterable, possibly even ordained by God. Committed to revolution, in theory at least, the adaptor can hardly retain this defeatist Lutheran ethic upheld so staunchly by Wenzeslaus. Brecht's Wenzeslaus lamely justifies his heavy work load as schoolteacher by claiming — in Lenz's words — "Gottes Lohn hab ich dafür, ein gutes Gewissen!" (GW VI, 2371) But this shows Wenzeslaus in a new light; for Brecht, the old man is "brain-washed," believing in the Christian promise.

Actually, Brecht's rather perverse Wenzeslaus proudly sees the real reward and justification for his work in educating pupils in his own image, inculcating in them a slave-mentality which will make of them as obedient and usable servants of the aristocracy as he is himself. He angrily tongue-lashes Läuffer in an entirely new passage of eleven lines interpolated between portions of the text taken from Lenz:

> Weiß Er denn überhaupt, was das heißt: Lehrer sein? *Stolziert schrecklich auf und ab.* Ich bilde Menschen nach meinem Ebenbilde. Teutsche Hermanne! Gesunde Geister in gesundem Körper, nicht so welsche Affen. Er mag wohl sagen: halb Geistesriesen, halb gute Untertanen? Was ist das? Untertänige Riesen oder riesige Untertanen? Immer sternenwärts, aber: dreimal wehe, wenn Er gegen den Stachel lökt! (GW VI, 2371)

The ironic presentation of such a grotesque conception of a pedagogue's duties causes the adapted Wenzeslaus to appear a somewhat mediocre intellectual lackey who — *plus royal que les royalistes* — proclaims loftily that the function of schooling must be to provide the ruling class with servants to achieve their grandiose ambitions for them.

These statements by the schoolmaster contradict the picture that we have of the Wenzeslaus of Lenz and even the Wenzeslaus of those portions of Brecht's Scene 12 immediately preceding and following this episode. The schoolmaster's spirited stand early in Scene 12 against Graf Wermuth and, in a later episode, against the assembled aristocrats is now inconsistent with his professed ideal of "subordinate giants or giant subordinates." Why does the old man suddenly seem to step out of character? Brecht intends this contradiction for various reasons; Wenzeslaus, the educator who slavishly teaches the values and propaganda of the ruling class, is supposed to be a representative "der Teutschen Misere." (GW VI, 2333) The exaggerated, comic manner in which Wenzeslaus idealistically explains his professional goals clashes with the tragic implications that his words have for his own and humanity's destiny.

The new passage in which Wenzeslaus reproaches Läuffer and instructs him in the real duties of a German pedagogue parodies not only Genesis, Chapter I, verses 26—28, but particularly Goethe's passionate cry of revolt and defiance in the poem "Prometheus," written in 1774. In fact, Brecht's Wenzeslaus is the exact opposite of Goethe's rebel. Prometheus exclaims:

> Hiert sitz' ich, forme Menschen
> Nach meinem Bilde,
> Ein Geschlecht, das mir gleich sei,
> Zu leiden, zu weinen,
> Zu geniessen und zu freuen sich,
> Und dein nicht zu achten,
> Wie ich!

Before berating Läuffer, Wenzeslaus appeared to relish his own power and seemed proud of the growing independence of the middle class. Now, he casts that independence to the winds. In contrast to the mythical Prometheus in Goethe's poem, Brecht's Wenzeslaus now stands drably there, neither as god, nor artist, nor creator, but as a perverse lackey and thoroughly reliable collaborator of repressive feudal aristocrats. As such, he will characterizes himself well in his manner of speaking: He is the reverse of what he claims to be and strikes us as a ridiculously inept architect of "Teutsche Hermanne." His professed belief: "Gesunde Geister in gesundem Körper," is not Germanic but a translation from Juvenal. It is rather Wenzeslaus who is the "Welscher Affe," the imitator. The tragedy of the German schoolteacher is apparent: Half intellectual giant, half reliable subject. The expression: "Was ist das?" literally recalls the question and answer technique in Luther's Catechism; it introduces the explanation "Untertänige Riesen oder riesige Untertanen?" (GW VI, 2371) The figure of Wenzeslaus must rank among the most skillful of Brecht's caricatures.

Monk's record of the reaction to this episode during rehearsals is valuable, for it gives Brecht's frank assessment of the historical German schoolmaster and the far-reaching implications of his conception of the *deutsche Misere*:

Nach dem gebrüllten: "Weiß er denn überhaupt, was das heißt, Lehrer sein?" beginnt Wenzeslaus im Zimmer herumzumarschieren. (Maurer meinte zunächst, er könne den Marsch nicht in der von uns geforderten übertriebenen Art bringen, weil das den Schulmeister zu einer Karikatur mache, und es sei doch tragisches und komisches gemischt in dieser Figur. Er fürchte, daß das Resultat dann unmenschlich sei, und Wenzeslaus solle doch bei aller Skurrilität ein Mensch bleiben. Brecht antwortete sinngemäß, daß er, Maurer, Recht habe, wenn er das komische nicht überwiegen lassen wolle, daß aber der Marsch, den der Schulmeister hier in der Dorfschule bei Insterburg beginne, erst bei Stalingrad zum Stehen gebracht worden sei, und das mache eine übertriebene Darstellung unerläßlich. Wenn die Komik Wenzeslaus die eines Unmenschen sei, könne auch ruhig gelacht werden, auch über Hitler habe man lachen können.) (BBA 2062/33—34)

The fact that Brecht spoke about Wenzeslaus in this light necessitates examining the extent to which the schoolmaster is responsible for the intellectual castration which Läuffer undergoes during the course of Scenes 12, 14 and 17. In Scene 12 of the adaptation, shortly before the Major's armed intrusion, a significant piece of dialogue is interpolated between portions of Lenz's original text:

Mit dem Hofmeisterspielen ist es ja nun wohl aus, junger Herr, so ohne Zeugnis. Und auf eine Stelle in der Dorfschule kann Er da auch nicht hoffen, wo jetzo der König doch nach seinem Krieg die invaliden Unteroffiziers zu Lehrern anstellt, ja, ja.[15] (GW VI, 2372)

---

[15] With the reference to Frederick's installing invalid officers as teachers, Brecht continues to exorcise the spectre of the military tradition in the classroom: Prussian discipline and obedience, harsh, conservative and incompetent teachers.

Agreed, the tutor is told quite bluntly that because of his past errors and present economic conditions, he cannot hope to find private or public employment, but he has really known this for some time already. Wenzeslaus is simply preparing the ground to make his offer of a job seem like a gift from Divine Providence.

In Lenz's drama, when Wenzeslaus offers Läuffer a job, he attempts to improve the tutor's knowledge of Latin and quite sincerely cautions him that diligence is the prerequisite for becoming his eventual successor. In Brecht's adaptation, the artful Wenzeslaus does neither; he prefers to keep Läuffer as an ignorant subordinate, for he has tested him and found an ingenuous and willing worker in him. Because of the new context of the original passages which Brecht takes over from Lenz, the schoolmaster's remarks now smack of self-interest. The remark by Wenzeslaus about Läuffer's faulty knowledge of Latin now must appear but a wile to enhance the offer of the menial clerical duties foisted off on the unsuspecting tutor.

In order for us to be convinced that Läuffer sincerely regards Wenzeslaus as his benefactor, we must conceive of him as totally naive. Mork's remarks indicate that this was actually Brecht's intention:

> Läuffer sieht in Wenzeslaus nur den Wohltäter. Wenn er hört, daß er engagiert ist, springt er freudig auf, dienert, zieht den Rock aus, hängt ihn über den Stuhl und scheint fest entschlossen, noch einmal so schnell weiterzuarbeiten. (BBA 2062/34)

What a contrast there is later in Scene 12 of the adaptation between Läuffer's attitude to Wenzeslaus and the attitude of the schoolmaster to his protégé! After the attack by the Major, Läuffer is, however, so preoccupied with his inner thoughts and his gunshot wound that he fails to note his "benefactor's" lack of concern for his welfare. In order to appreciate how insensitive Wenzeslaus is in Brecht's drama, we should first examine the corresponding episode in Lenz.

Desirous of keeping his cheap assistant, Wenzeslaus, in IV, 3 of Lenz's drama, sees only the captive worker in Läuffer, rather than a loyal fellow human being in pain. The old schoolmaster gives the impression of being quite unsympathetic towards Läuffer's injury. Confronted by the armed intruders, his verbal defense of the wounded tutor smacks of self-interest and pedantic indignation. After all, Läuffer has performed the unpleasant duties for him for a whole year, and now it seems that the tutor may be unable to continue. The old man quickly runs off to fetch a surgeon, but only to protect his "investment" in Läuffer, as it were.

To an even greater extent, Brecht's Wenzeslaus pathologically disregards the distress of his newly found[16] assistant. This is an important exaggeration in Brecht's characterization of the schoolmaster. Let us consider two reasons

---

[16] In the adaptation, the episode of Läuffer's being shot occurs on the same day that he fled from the Major's house, and not a year later, as in Lenz's play.

for Wenzeslaus's failure to symathize with Läuffer. Firstly, the schoolmaster in Brecht's adaptation is particularly angry at the apparent loss of his "collaborator" because his plans for retiring from menial duties of his office seem ruined. The second reason concerns his character as well as Brecht's theme "der Teutschen Misere." Wenzeslaus, infatuated with his imagined importance as the divine-like creator of "riesige Untertanen" so argues the point about the inviolability of his rights to privacy that he completely loses sight of the need to attend to the wounded Läuffer. Although it is a comic moment to see[17] the garrulous old schoolmaster berating the Geheimrat for the armed intrusion and standing opposite him, the body of Läuffer between them on the floor, it is equally a tragic occasion: Wenzeslaus is so totally committed to the abstract idea (his rights) that he ignores the urgency of actual reality (the wounded Läuffer).

This shortsightedness concerning human and social problems, as well as the preference for the abstraction were already observed in Brecht's Scene 12 in the case of Wenzeslaus's embarrassed attitude toward his salary. In this regard Monk noted a pertinent comment by the adaptor: "Das war dumm gefragt, Herr Mandel." [gesprochen von Wenzeslaus] 'Einen Deutschen fragt man nicht nach dem Lohn. Auf das Ideelle soll Läuffer achten, die Materie erhält sich selbst ([sagte] Brecht).' " (BBA 2062/33) Brecht seems to be saying here that the German educator (Wenzeslaus) does not care to think of the distressing reality of his situation (his low wages) which he is powerless to change for the better; he has therefore come to prefer the compensation afforded by idealistic thought (Wenzeslaus's "Promethean calling"), for he can thereby justify the unfortunate material situation in which he finds himself.

This alarming lack of human and social sympathy referred to above — Wenzeslaus's ignoring the wounded Läuffer — is a particularly apt example of Brecht's conception "Der Teutschen Misere" which he makes into one of the chief thrusts of his version of the play. According to Brecht, the theory-bound German intellectual has, throughout the last two centuries, ignored, to his own and society's detriment, the importance of real and energetic commitment to social and political issues. This apparently traditional preference of the German intellectual for idealistic philosophy and literature rather than for social engagement becomes — as we shall see in Chapter IV — the central consideration in Brecht's ironic portrayal of Kantian philosophy and its defender, the student Pätus.

It is also a tragicomic moment when in Scene 12 of the adaptation, Wenzeslaus, ignoring the Geheimrat's plea to fetch a surgeon, races out of the schoolhouse in order to sound the alarm: "Ei was! Wenn Ihr Wunden macht, so mögt Ihr sie heilen, Straßenräuber. Ich lauf nicht nach dem Gevatter Schöpsen, ich lauf die Sturmglock läuten! Ab" (GW VI, 2373)

---

[17] Cf. Berliner Ensemble *Modellbuch* photographs of the 1950 *Hofmeister* production and the notes to the adaptation, GW XVII, 1234.

Now, Wenzeslaus's professed aim in leaving — to sound the alarm — does get him offstage. His absence is a dramaturgical necessity, for if he were present during the ensuing action, he would hardly permit the Major to threaten Läuffer with torture, nor would he tolerate Läuffer's bitter aside in front of Lise: "Wo bleibt meine vita sexualis?" (GW VI, 2374) But why does Wenzeslaus leave to sound the alarm? Whom is he going to warn? What does he intend? Is his remark merely an excuse to avoid further confrontation with the aristocrats?

In Lenz's IV, 3, Wenzeslaus does leave, but in order to fetch the surgeon. However, Brecht omits the entire comic episode with Barber Schöpsen. Are Wenzeslaus's rebellious actions and remarks in this scene of the adaptation to be taken seriously? Actually, they are empty threats, merely the product of anger and bravado. Possibly, Brecht conceives of the schoolteacher in this potentially critical situation as an effusive but impotent revolutionary. A spark of rebellion is there, it flares up only to flicker weakly and be extinguished as quickly as it was ignited. Wenzeslaus has subordinated his mind too long to the values of the aristocracy to be able to sustain his anger and give it revolutionary purpose.

In adapting the *Hofmeister*, Brecht omits from Scene 12 the latter half of Lenz's IV, 3. The deletion in necessary because the passage contains statements by Läuffer which reveal noble qualities in his character. Also, its comic episode of Barber Schöpsen's greed is unproductive in further developments of the main plot and is, accordingly, replaced by an intentionally melodramatic episode introducing Lise, the pretty, young ward of Wenzeslaus.

It is important to consider the omitted portions of this scene in Lenz's play, where Läuffer tries to dissuade the excited Wenzeslaus from taking legal steps to prosecute the Major for the armed intrusion. Magnanimously, Läuffer exclaims: "Ich bitt Euch, seyd ruhig. Ich habe weit weniger bekommen, als meine Thaten werth waren." (D I, 89) If Brecht retained such a statement in Scene 12 of the adaptation, it would be quite inconsistent with Läuffer's abiding hatred of the aristocracy. Also, later on, toward the end of Lenz's IV, 3, Läuffer unselfishly hands over to Wenzeslaus the large sum of money which the Geheimrat generously leaves for damages and the tutor's surgical expenses.[18] This concluding portion of Lenz's scene shows that Läuffer has some good qualities after all. The tutor recognizes his failings here and charitably pardons the shooting as a justifiable punishment

---

[18] In Brecht's adaptation, Läuffer receives much less money from the Geheimrat, and, it would seem, does not give it to Wenzeslaus. In Lenz's drama, Wenzeslaus immediately softens his extreme but amusing verbal denunciation of the aristocrats when he sees the large sum that the Geheimrat has left behind. Because Brecht already shows in Scene 12 that Wenzeslaus avoids a serious confrontation with the aristocrats, it is unnecessary to show, as does Lenz, that the schoolmaster can be bribed to keep quiet. The new Wenzeslaus has a sense of mission which he finds far more sustaining than the possession of money.

for having sorely wounded the Major's paternal pride and ruined his family's honor. These positive traits are totally unacceptable to Brecht because, if retained in the adaptation, they would detract from the carefully fashioned, one-sided portrayal of the tutor as a despicable sycophant.

Whereas Lenz indicates that Läuffer can be unselfish and considerate, Brecht shows him to be selfish and unsympathetic in Scene 12. In Lenz's IV, 3, it is clear that Läuffer feels guilty for having wronged the Major by seducing Gustchen. As noted above, Lenz's tutor appears repentant and accepts the wound as just punishment for what he conceives of as misdeeds. When asked where Gustchen has fled to, he replies briefly but politely. Thus, the original Läuffer gives the impression of being a free individual who, in accepting the responsibility for his actions, supports the status quo and conventional morality.

Brceht seeks to give quite the opposite impression of Läuffer in the portion of Lenz's episode taken over in Scene 12. The new Läuffer is neither a free individual nor does he accept the traditional ethics and structure of society. In his responses to the questions and threats of the hostile Major, the tutor appears equally hostile. He feels neither regret nor guilt for having seduced Gustchen and wronged the Major. A new speech in Läuffer's part of the dialogue reflects his selfish, unsympathetic and amoral view of what has happened: "Was hat das Pferd damit zu schaffen! Wo bleibt meine vita sexualis?" (GW VI, 2374) Brecht argues seriously here that Läuffer has done nothing wrong; seducing Gustchen was merely a foolish mistake. The adaptor claims that the real culprit is not Läuffer, but biological determinism which creates sexual appetites that have to be satisfied, come what may. Hence the Major is equally to blame, to the extent that he unwittingly denied Läuffer the opportunity to satisfy those appetites elsewhere.

"Elsewhere" almost becomes Wenzeslaus's schoolroom in Scene 14a of the adaptation. The initial portion of this scene [up to the third entrance of Lise into Läuffer's room "Lise tritt noch einmal ein" (GW VI, 2378)] represents entirely new dialogue which makes clear to the spectator that Läuffer has, in the interim, become a very moral person. This new material precedes an amended and shortened version of the first half of Lenz's V, 10. In the original drama, Läuffer castrates himself just after V, 1. Therefore, his subsequent and persistently serious interest in Lise in V, 10 appears grotesque as well as ridiculous. In contrast, in Brecht's adaptation, the castration does not occur until after the end of Scene 14b. The tutor's interest in Lise in Scene 14a therefore, takes on a significance not present in the model. Läuffer's courting of Lise in Scene 14a shows the beginning of his violent and hilarious conflict between inclination and duty, which, in the self-emasculation in Scene 14b, culminates in his successful and savage suppression of his personality as well as the loss of his independence as an individual.

Throughout Scene 14a, Läuffer remains as constitutionally helpless before the onslaught of his sexual urges as he appeared previously in the adaptation. More than a year has passed, however, between his hiring in Scene

12 and Lise's tempting him in Scene 14a. During this interval, Läuffer's character has so changed that it is now impossible to observe in him the self-seeking, discontented tutor of old. He has been quietly constrained by his mentor-employer Wenzeslaus to forget his former amoral ideas about sex, work, and class inequities. The schoolmaster has gradually and cunningly remade the tutor in his own image, endowing him with his own conservative and excessively puritan attitudes.

Very early in their relationship, Wenzeslaus counts on converting and dominating Läuffer with the power of his moral teachings, when he exclaims in Scene 12 of the adaptation: "Ich wette, nur noch ein paar Tage mit dem alten Wenzeslaus zusammen, und ich will Euch nach meiner Hand ziehen, daß Ihr Euch selber nicht mehr kennen sollt." (GW VI, 2372) His words — taken almost verbatim from Lenz's drama — have certainly come true in Scene 14a.

Like the new Wenzeslaus, Läuffer now sees in the sexual urges, or "die bösen Begierden" (GW VI, 2371), as the schoolmaster considers them, only an evil, corruptive influence. Although the tutor may still be a physical weakling in the presence of desire, he has become — for Wenzeslaus — a moral giant in his ability to suppress such natural yet apparently wicked feelings. Indeed, the tutor is soon disgusted to discover that in addition to admiring the simple beauty of Lise, he also desires her sexually: "Was entdeck ich? Dieses unschuldsvolle Wesen. Dieser Engel der Freundlichkeit, und ich, in wenigen Minuten eine Beute der verabscheuungswürdigsten Regungen? Woher dieser Orkan im Innern...?" (GW VI, 2377) Wenzeslaus's moral teachings have made Läuffer so perverse that the tutor is now utterly revolted by his naturally human and healthy male reaction to Lise's equally natural but naive female interest in him. Believing that sexual desire can be effectively suppressed by "right" moral thinking and dutiful attention to his assigned tasks, Läuffer views himself as an ungrateful and even profane monster:

> Von ihr eine unschuldige Handreichung, und von mir, zum Dank, eine fleischliche Regung! Und unter dem Dach meines Wohltäters, im Anblick der Gegenstände, des Stuhls hier, des Bettes dort, mit denen seine Menschenliebe mich umgab! Dies ihm, der mir erste lehrte, was lehren heißt! Kann ich Ungeheuer mich niemals verbessern? (GW VI, 2377—78)

The tutor has "bettered" himself so much that, totally unlike his former self, he now respects the necessity of hard work and self-subordination:

> Zu den Schulheften Mandel! *Er arbeitet weiter.* Rechtschreibung, Rechtlebung. Wohin gehen wir mit den Orkanen in der Brust? ... Schreib Zensuren, du, entdecke Schreibfehler, der du deine Augen nicht bändigen kannst, daß sie nicht sehen, was das Brusttüchlein verhüllt! (GW VI, 2378)

Brecht's ironic treatment of the conflict between inclination and duty in Läuffer makes of the tutor a tragicomic figure. The young man has become such a fervent disciple of Wenzeslaus that he even uses epithets characteristic of the schoolmaster's speech to prick his already overburdened conscience: "Schurke ohne Zeugnis und Zukunft!" (GW VI, 2378)

In the latter half of Scene 14a, taken mainly from Lenz's V, 10, the new statements that Brecht adds to Läuffer's part in the dialogue are intended to stress the tutor's sexual aggressiveness. Brecht wishes to create at the close of Scene 14a a situation comparable to that of Läuffer at the end of Scene 10. The tutor must discover that the demands of his private life are incompatible with the demands of his employer. For example, whereas Lenz's Läuffer merely asks Lise about her previous experience with men, Brecht's Läuffer cross-examines her, and then, when he asks her to marry him, he slaps himself with the ruler ["... gibt sich Tatzen mit dem Lineal..." (GW VI, 2379)] in the attempt to curb his passion. In the original drama, after the tutor learns she would gladly marry him, the stage direction for Läuffer reads: "... will ihr die Hand küssen..." and "... küßt sie..." (D I, 112—113) In the adaptation, Brecht substitues violent actions: "Läuffer stürzt sich auf sie, küßt ihre Hand..." and "... stürzt sich auf sie und reißt sie an sich." (GW VI, 2379)

Significantly, Brecht omits altogether from the adopted passages of Lenz all mention of Läuffer's spiritual attraction to Lise and his sincere affection for her. Since the new Läuffer no longer has an opportunity to defend himself or explain his actions, the result is, of course, an increased emphasis on his sexual frustration. Brecht further stresses the power of the biological urges by substituting the word "Sinn" for Lenz's expression "Herz" in the statement: "Er [Läuffer] hat deinen [Lises] unschuldigen Sinn verführt (GW VI, 2380) Clearly, the adapter prefers a term with more physical than psychological connotations because he does not wish to attribute any importance to spiritual bonds between people, as does Lenz.

The original Läuffer does not possess the exaggerated willingness to subordinate himself to Wenzeslaus that the adapted figure has. Nor is the original Läuffer made to appear such a spineless weakling by unreservedly espousing the schoolmaster's moral philosophy. In order to make these changes credible, Brecht also has to alter aspects of the personality of Lenz's Wenzeslaus. In V, 10, of the original drama, the schoolmaster is far less of a moral tyrant than Brecht's figure. Whereas Lenz's figure argues on traditional Christian — but very pedantic — moral grounds that Läuffer has sinned in caressing Lise, Brecht's Wenzeslaus mercilessly condemns the tutor as an incorrigible rapist. In the notes to the adaptation, Brecht actually uses the term "Vergewaltiger." (GW XVII, 1247)

The fact that in the adaptation Wenzeslaus bids Läuffer leave his house because of this alarming display of interest in Lise, points to apparent inconsistencies in the characterization of the schoolmaster. Does he want to lose Läuffer? Why is he so prudish and moralistic? Why does he choose to ignore Läuffer's earnest intentions? Does Wenzeslaus prefer that Läuffer and Lise do not marry, so that he does not lose his servant-girl in addition to the tutor? The only convincing reason for the manner and action of the schoolmaster here is really dramaturgical. Läuffer is reminded of his abject material condition and his lack of credentials, and is banished so that he has no choice but to castrate himself in the following scene!

All of Scene 14b is new material which Brecht adds to display the terrible conflict that rages in Läuffer's mind. The tutor is most poetic and articulate in his anguish. Brecht is highly successful in portraying the agitated inner life of his protagonist in this scene. It cannot fail to strike one, however, that Läuffer's sudden use of poetic diction such as "schaffender Weltgeist" (GW 2381), while reminiscent of Storm and Stress aulogies of *Genie*, Rousseau and Nature, is quite inconsistent with his use of language elsewhere. If Läuffer's sensitivity has not been greatly blunted by the brutal Major or the tyrannical Wenzeslaus, it is surprising to discover now that he can not only register poetic feeling after all but can — like Goethe's Tasso — express himself so well in his suffering.

Läuffer gives voice to his conflict in a dramatic monologue, which is unique in the adaptation. The original drama does not stand as model in any way for this scene. Lenz, it would seem, is loath to attempt the portrayal of Läuffer's consciousness at the time of the tutor's decision to castrate himself. V, 1 of the original drama must, therefore, be regarded as the author's explanation of Läuffer's mental and spiritual state, as we shall see shortly.

The reasons for the tutor's self-emasculation in the original drama are purely personal. Läuffer's decision is made in private and with no conscious forethought as to the consequences, beneficial or detrimental, for himself or for society. The reverse is true of Brecht's figure. In Lenz's play, Läuffer castrates himself in an uncontrollable fit of despair after he has (erroneously) learned, to his shame and horror, that Gustchen and the Major have perished in the village pond. In the opinion of Läuffer in Lenz's *Hofmeister,* mutilating himself is an act of atonement for the bitter sufferings and the ghastly suicides that he believes he has caused. He takes this drastic action to punish himself in what he thinks is a just and moral way.

In the adaptation, Brecht so manipulates the situation and the character of Läuffer that the tutor has virtually no choice but to castrate himself. Wenzeslaus has too often cracked the whip of moral righteousness, he has dwelt too pointedly on the tutor's lack of material security for him to rebel now and seek self-fulfillment on his own terms or die in the effort.

As Brecht remarks in the short paragraph "Die Selbstentmannung" in his notes to the *Hofmeister,* (GW XVII, 1235), the Berliner Ensemble, in adapting the drama, was concerned less with the concrete situation or Läuffer's ghastly solution to his economic and social dilemma, than with raising the tenor of Scene 14 to a poetic and hence, symbolic plane. Läuffer's decision in favor of his professional rather than his private life has actually been long in the making, for he has slowly extirpated his own ideas during the year he spent as Wenzeslaus's assistant.

This is evidenced particularly by the tutor's excessively moral condemnation of the — formerly prized — natural man in himself: "Du willst Menschlein erziehen nach deinem Ebenbild? Beschau dich im Spiegel und schaudere.. Wächter, wo ist dein Wächter?" (GW VI, 2381) Läuffer's intellectual castration really precedes his physical self-emasculation. The physical act is but a symbolic indication of the thoroughness of the intellectual mutilation he has practiced for so long as Wenzeslaus's "collaborator."

Läuffer speaks of himself in Brecht's Scene 14b in the same manner that the schoolmaster has previously spoken to him; the tutor actually believes his own words: "Du [Läuffer] kannst nicht hintreten nach deinem Fehltritt: unglücklicher Mann [Wenzeslaus], unglücklich, weil Ihr mir vertraut habt, gebt mir Eure geschändete Schutzbefohlene [Lise] jetzt in die Ehe. Du [Läuffer] kannst sie vernichten, aber nicht nähren." (GW VI, 2381) Later, when talking apologetically to Wenzeslaus in Scene 14c the tutor reveals, in another statement deprecating himself, the disastrous extent to which he has destroyed his own self-respect: "Ich hoff, Ihr gönnt mir noch ein paar Tag unter Eurem geschändeten Dach." (GW VI, 2382)

Figuratively, Läuffer's emasculation is also to be understood as the loss of his identity as an individual. The renunciation of individuality, whether constrained or voluntary, is a problem which occupies Brecht in one dramatic work after another, long before his adaptation of Lenz's *Hofmeister*. Perhaps the most striking instances of this problem in the adaptor's earlier works are the figure of the brainwashed coolie, Galy Gay, in *Mann ist Mann* and the depersonalized activists in *Die Maßnahme*.

In *Mann ist Mann,* one thinks of both Sergeant Fairchild and Galy Gay. Both men decide to give up their identity as private individuals in order to devote themselves entirely to their roles in the army. Like Läuffer, Sergeant Fairchild finds that his sexual urges distract him from the fulfillment of his official duties. Accordingly, the Sergeant castrates himself so that he can retain without interruption his public identity as "der Blutige Fünfer." (GW I, 354—55) In contrast, Galy Gay's transformation is an intellectual rather than a physical process. For the sake of material gain he willingly pretends to be someone other than himself. He agrees to impersonate the machine-gunner Jeraiah Jip at roll call. Later, the fear of death — he believes that in his capacity as Galy Gay he has been executed — constrains him to continue pretending that he is Jeraiah Jip. After his execution he gives a funeral oration for himself, noting:

> Und ich, der eine ich und der andere ich
> Werden gebraucht und sind also brauchbar.
> Und hab ich nicht angesehen diesen Elefanten
> Drück ich ein Auge zu, was mich betrifft
> Und lege ab, was unbeliebt an mir, und bin
> Da angenehm. (GW I, 361)

At this point in the action, however, Galy Gay is not yet completely willing to admit that he is Jeraiah Jip, even though he refrains from calling himself Galy Gay. It is the ghastly sight of Sergeant Fairchild castrating himself that encourages Galy Gay to renounce once and for all his original name and identity. Galy Gay exclaims in horror: "Dieser Herr hat wegen seinem [sic] Namen etwas sehr Blutiges mit sich gemacht. Er hat sich eben sein Geschlecht weggeschossen!" (GW I, 369)

On this occasion, Galy Gay affirms his resolve to forget his former self and henceforth, to be as others would have him be: Jeraiah Jip or "die menschliche Kampfmaschine." (GW I, 376) The continuity of one's real self, being true to one's principles, is less important than remaining alive and finding an acceptable function within society; this is as true for Herr Egge in the Keuner story "Maßnahmen gegen die Gewalt" (GW XII, 375—376) as it is for Galy Gay, who rejoices:

> Das ist ein großes Glück für mich, daß ich das gesehen habe: jetzt sehe ich, wohin diese Hartnäckigkeit [sich selbst sein zu wollen] führt, und wie blutig es ist, wenn ein Mann nie mit sich zufrieden ist und so viel Aufhebens aus seinem Namen macht! (GW I, 369)

From now on, Galy Gay, like Herr Egge and the castrated Läuffer, behaves exactly as those who control society would have him behave. He obliterates within himself all independence of thought so that he may be the automaton of his superiors.

In contrast, the renunciation of personal identity is treated as a purely abstract and absolutely humorless process in Brecht's tragedy about Marxist ideology,[19] *Die Maßnahme*. Here, the Young Comrade symbolically dons a mask to signify his wish no longer to be an individual with personal and humanitarian motives; he and his fellow activists term the process "unsere Gesichter auslöschen." (GW II, 636) They are told:

> Dann seid ihr nicht mehr ihr selber, du nicht mehr Karl Schmitt aus Berlin, du nicht mehr Anna Kjersk aus Kasan und du nicht mehr Peter Sawitsch aus Moskau, sondern allesamt ohne Namen und Mutter, leere Blätter, auf welche die Revolution ihre Anweisung schreibt. (GW II, 637)

In this didactic piece, the extinguishing of one's personality amounts to total self-denial or complete dehumanization. Denying his humanitarian feelings, however becomes problematical for the Young Comrade. He finds that "Individualism and idealism are inexcusably regressive postures in a world where all value is collective"[20] and must agree to his liquidation by his fellow activists, who have no difficulty in suppressing their former identity. Like Galy Gay, the activists are constrained to become inhuman,

---

[19] Cf. R. Grimm, "Ideologische Tragödie und Tragödie der Ideologie. Versuch über ein Lehrstück," *Zeitschrift für deutsche Philologie*, LXXVII (1959), 394ff.

[20] Max Spalter, *brecht's tradition* (Baltimore: Johns Hopkins Press, 1967), p. 180.

as it were, in their suppression of the more gentle human emotions. Läuffer, too, is forced by necessity to develop into a ruthless and thoroughly reliable teacher who will educate pupils to be as dehumanized as himself. The process has ultimately the same result in both plays: Individuals enthusiastically support a society which does not allow their existence as genuine human beings with the right to seek self-fulfillment.

Whereas the tutor in Lenz's *Hofmeister* reveals that his motives for the emasculation were "Reue, Verzweiflung" (D I, 101), Brecht alters the explanation to „Reue ... Sorgen um meinen Beruf." (GW VI, 2382) The psychological determinant is replaced by equally compelling sociological constraints. The dialogue following these words of Läuffer in Scene 14c is entirely new material, written in order to spell out and mock grimly the tutor's utter mental and physical prostration before the ruling powers in society. In contrast, Lenz understands Läuffer's physical castration as symbolic less of the tutor's intellectual state than of the inhuman treatment and abuse he receives from the aristocracy and the middle class, too. Art also imitates life, for Lenz models the fate of Läuffer on that of a young tutor known to him in East Prussia.

It is clear that Lenz is imposing his own moral censure on Läuffer by having him castrate himself. The tutor's action is a desperate resolve to atone for his sins and lead an ascetic life, as his last words in V, 3 indicate:

O Unschuld, welch' eine Perle bist du! Seit ich dich verloren, that ich Schritt auf Schritt in der Leidenschaft und endigte mit Verzweiflung. Möchte dieser Letzte mich nicht zum Tode führen, vielleicht könnt' ich itzt wieder anfangen zu leben und zum Wenzeslaus wiedergeboren werden. (D I, 102)

Lenz vigorously condemns the irresponsible behavior of men toward women n *Der Hofmeister, Der neue Menoza* and *Die Soldaten.* In his excessively noralistic view it would seem that a man's taking advantage of a woman should be punished most severely, as the fates of Läuffer, Camälon *(Meno-za),* and Desportes *(Soldaten)* indicate.

Toward the end of Scene 14c, Brecht alters and widens the scope of Lenz's censorship of the morals of the unfortunate class of private tutors .o include universal condemnation of all German intellectuals, philosophers and teachers who subordinated their minds to the authorities of their time.

Whereas Lenz makes Wenzeslaus a lay-preacher and ironically has him extol Läuffer's self-emasculation as an act which fits him to become an exemplary churchman, Brecht, equally ironically, alters the career to that of pedagogue. Lenz's text reads: "Das ist die Bahn, auf der Ihr [Läuffer] eine Leuchte der *Kirche,* ein Stern echter Größe, ein *Kirchenvater selber* werden könnt. Ich beglückwünsche euch ... mein *geistlicher* Sohn." (D I, 101, my italics) Brecht simply substitutes "Schulwelt" for "Kirche," "der Pädagogik" for "ein Kirchenvater selber," and "geistiger" for "geistlicher." (GW VI, 2382)

In Brecht's adaptation, Wenzeslaus regards Läuffer as made in his own image, particularly after adressing him as "mein geistiger Sohn." Therefore, there is a double irony in the schoolmaster's praise of the tutor's deed, what he says to the tutor applies to himself surely as much as it does to Läuffer:

> Wer sollte Lehrer werden können, wenn nicht jetzt Ihr? Von allen habt Ihr die höchste Qualifikation! Habt Ihr nicht die Aufsässigkeit in Euch für ewig vernichtet, der Pflicht alles untergeordnet? Kein Privatleben kann Euch fürder noch abhalten, Menschen zu formen nach Eurem Ebenbilde. (GW VI, 2382—83)

When he reproaches Läuffer in Scene 12 of the adaptation, Wenzeslaus makes it quite clear that he entertains no thought of rebellion against the nobility; he conceives it as his duty toward the aristocracy to produce "untertänige Riesen oder riesige Untertanen." (GW VI, 2371) Nor does the old schoolmaster enjoy any private life, as is amply demonstrated by the account of his long daily work-schedule and his disgust for "die bösen Begierden." (GW VI, 2371)

Lenz's Wenzeslaus considers the necessary qualifications for a teacher to be a broad knowledge of the Latin classics and Christian moral philosophy. Such a view encourages one to consider the old man sincere and wholesome, albeit conservative. In contrast, Brecht's Wenzeslaus appears a monster when he praises Läuffer's physical and mental ruin as desirable qualities in an educator.

Whereas Brecht's Wenzeslaus conceives of duty only in terms of an inferior's intellectual, social and political subordination to his feudal rulers — the noble classes and the King of Prussia — Lenz's Wenzeslaus entertains a Kantian concept of duty by which he understands duty to be not what he owes to others but what he owes to himself, if he is to maintain his dignity and self-respect as a representative of the species man. Specifically, the schoolmaster in Lenz's drama holds it to be his duty to do more than he should in encouraging the critical intellect of his pupils. As is to be expected, the changed context and Brecht's use of the word "Pflicht" and "pflichtschuldigst" (GW VI, 2382—83) in Scene 14c contribute to a grotesque misrepresentation of Kant's concept of duty toward mankind as represented in oneself.

Toward the close of Scene 14c, Brecht uses the technique of the letter, a device which Lenz often employs in the *Hofmeister,* to introduce a turn in the action. Läuffer's letter to the Major is a convenient dramaturgical way of informing the spectator of the tutor's new and radically different attitude toward the nobility and the Prussian monarch:

> ... und hoffe ich, Sie werden mir ein Zeugnis gnädigst nicht versagen, damit ich meinen Beruf wieder ausüben kann. Um so mehr, gnädigster Herr Major, als ich auch im übrigen mich pflichtschuldigst bemühen werde, in allem, ich schreibe in allem, immer das zu tun und zu lehren, was gewünscht wird, zu meinem und aller Besten ... Empfangen Sie ... Dero alleruntertänigster Diener ...Nachschrift: Und ich verspreche auch, unseres Heldenkönigs Martyrium immer ohne Weglassung zu lehren. (GW VI, 2383)

In his efforts to find a remunerative position, Läuffer's obsequious behavior toward his superiors makes him a distant cousin of another teacher, Galilei, in Brecht's play *Leben des Galilei,* the first version of which was written more than a decade before the *Hofmeister* adaptation. In Scene 3 of *Leben des Galilei,* after he has discovered that the planet Jupiter has four moons revolving about it, Galilei decides to write a flattering and obsequiously worded letter to the Grand Duke of Florence, Lorenzo di Medici, requesting a position for himself as court mathematician. He comments to his assistant Sagredo about this letter:

> Ich frage mich, ob er [mein Brief] unterwürfig genug ist, nicht zu formell, als ob es mir doch an echter Ergebenheit fehlte. Einen zurückhaltenden Brief könnte jemand schreiben, der sich das Verdienst erworben hätte, den Aristoteles zu beweisen, nicht ich. *Ein Mann wie ich kann nur auf dem Bauch kriechend in eine halbwegs würdige Stellung kommen.* Und du weißt, ich verachte Leute, deren Gehirn nicht fähig ist, ihren Magen zu füllen. (GW III, 1259, my italics)

Läuffer, too, knows he must "crawl" in order to find position and preferment. Although Galilei uses the conventional manner of supplication in his letter, his words there are as insincere as his devotion. For him, however, using the Grand Duke is merely a dishonest means to an honest end: Proving the Copernican theory of the universe to be true. Galilei's letter resembles somewhat that of Läuffer in the terminology and spirit of self-subordination;[21] the end of the scientist's message reads:

> Ich [Galilei] aber bringe mich Euch [Lorenzo di Medici] in Erinnerung als einen aus der Zahl der treuesten und ergebensten Diener, der sich zur höchsten Ehre anrechnet, als Euer Untertan geboren zu sein. (GW III, 1261)

The exaggerations in the conventional, precious diction of Läuffer's letter to the Major (GW VI, 2383) notwithstanding, the language is typical of that used by German (as well as other European) writers great and small in their letters to equals and superiors during the age of absolutism — the age of revolution and republican thinking in France and America.[22] Brecht

---

[21] As Brecht was engaged in producing *Leben des Galilei* for the Berliner Ensemble at the time of his death, it is possible that he might have written or revised Galilei's letter to the Grand Duke in the light of Läuffer's humble letter to the Major in the *Hofmeister* adaptation. It was noted earlier, for example, that Brecht would borrow ideas and motifs used in his earlier plays. At one time, he thought of using the epilogue from *Der gute Mensch von Sezuan* as the epilogue to *Der Hofmeister.*

[22] Compare, for example, the ending of Goethe's letter of October 18, 1829, to the King of Bavaria:
   In reinster Verehrung mit unverbrüchlicher
   Dankbarkeit lebenswierig [sic] verharrend
   Weimar, den 18. Oktober 1829

chooses, however, to take the epistolary convention seriously and intends the once popular expressions of politeness and loyalty to be understood literally rather than figuratively. He implies ironically, therefore, that the German philosophers, teachers and intellectuals of the past who supported this convention had, by their *de facto* adoption of the popular formulae of self-subordination, abdicated all responsibility to themselves and society as individuals and free intellectual beings, and were consequently as docile and submissive servants as Läuffer.

While the caricatures and exaggerations in Brecht's Scene 14c, particularly in the latter part, are intended to be comic, the tragedy of the situation, as the adaptor sees it, is that Wenzeslaus and Läuffer, symbolically representing the German schoolteacher of the past two hundred years, have literally made a virtue out of a pernicious vice: The subordination and prostitution of their minds. Brecht sincerely believes it to have been a tragedy for Germany that in the process of practicing such virtue, the potentially powerful class represented by Wenzeslaus and Läuffer cowardly refused to resist injustice and failed to exercise their rights to independence and freedom of expression. They thereby prolonged the duration of the conditions which made their prostration necessary in the first place.

As mentioned earlier, the figure of the cowardly teacher has long been a favorite one in Brecht's work. Before adapting Lenz's *Hofmeister,* Brecht provided a more or less contemporary example of such spineless educators in "Der Spitzel," Scene 10 of the collection *Furcht und Elend des Dritten Reiches,* written about 1938. There, Studienrat Karl Furcke (Furcht!) anxiously explains his dilemma to his even more anxious and cowardly wife:

> Ich bin ja bereit, alles zu lehren, was sie [die Nazis] gelehrt haben wollen, aber was wollen sie gelehrt haben? Wenn ich das immer wüßte! Was weiß ich, wie sie wollen, daß Bismark gewesen sein soll! Wenn sie so langsam die neuen Schulbücher herausbringen...! (GW III, 1143)

The parallel to Läuffer is striking, indeed. This is the kind of teacher to which Brecht was referring in the epilogue of the *Hofmeister:*

> Denn ihr saht die Misere im deutschen Land
> Und wie sich ein jeder damit abfand
> Vor hundert Jahr und vor zehn Jahr [.] (GW VI, 2394)

In Lenz's drama, the last meeting of Läuffer with the aristocrats is the occasion of their shooting him. Läuffer's fate thereafter is in his own hands. Presumably, he continues as Wenzeslaus's assistant after his marriage to Lise.

Ew. Königlichen Majestät
alleruntertänigster Diener
Johann Wolfgang von Goethe
See *Der Briefwechsel zwischen Schiller und Goethe* (Berlin: Deutsche Buch-Gemeinschaft, 1960), p. 6.

In Scenes 14 and 16 of Brecht's adaptation, however, it is made clear that the only way by which Läuffer can improve his lot is to win the favor of the nobility, specifically the Major and the Geheimrat. Their opinion of him both as a person and a servant has changed greatly from Scene 1. They now have his assurance that he will faithfully adapt his pedagogy to their aims.

Whereas elsewhere, Brecht conceives of Läuffer's kind as a "tame elephant,"[23] i.e., a traitor to his kind and class, he has the Geheimrat in Scene 16 consider him an ox and finds a Biblical proverb with striking imagery that aptly characterizes the tutor and his function: "Du sollst dem Ochsen, der da drischet — haha, dem Ochsen — nicht das Maul verbinden." (GW VI, 2388)[24] Whether Läuffer learns the aristocrats' real attitude to him or not, it can matter little to him that they have nothing but contempt for him and ridicule for his sufferings and grovelling.

It is characteristic of the changes which Brecht makes in adapting the *Hofmeister* that the issues which Lenz considers important for moral reasons Brecht now considers important for political reasons. An example of a more subtle kind of change of this type follows a brief sketch of a pertinent episode in Lenz's drama. Arguing about the sermon which he has just preached in the village church, Wenzeslaus explains to Läuffer in Lenz's drama that the corollary of an active Christian superstition is a stronger Christian faith among the lower classes. Lenz's Wenzeslaus also defends the necessity of superstition because, as a Christian, he supports the status quo and fears that confusion and violence would exist among the masses without a strong faith: "Nehmt dem Bauer seinen Teufel und er wird ein Teufel gegen seine Herrschaft werden, und ihr beweisen, daß es welche giebt. Aber wir wollen das bey Seite setzen." (D I, 110) As a moralist, Lenz emphasizes the desirability of keeping the faith because it not only encourages personal humility and decent, moral behavior, but it also influences one to keep the peace. Our Storm and Stress author sees, therefore, only benefits in the practice of Christian religion.

On the other hand, Brecht, omitting much of the context of these speeches of Wenzeslaus, makes the old man's argument about the necessity of superstition seem but an insignificant one, which is certainly not the case in Lenz. Although the quotation given above is retained verbatim in the adaptation, its context is not. The statement "Aber wir wollen das bey Seite setzen" (D I, 110 and GW VI, 2392), in its now abbreviated context, implies the reverse of what the words themselves say. Brecht invites the spectator to

---

[23] This expression is applied by Brecht to Sun in Scene 8 of *Der gute Mensch von Sezuan*. Cf. the "Lied vom achten Elefanten" in which the tame elephant is mentioned: GW IV, 1582—83.

[24] This proverb from the Epistles of St. Paul has been discussed by Barbara A. Woods in "A Man of Two Minds," *German Quarterly*, XLII (1969), 44—45. Cf. Also her article, "The Function of Proverbs in Brecht," *Monatshefte* LXI (1969), 49—57.

consider whether Wenzeslaus might not have touched upon a key issue, a possible solution to the conditions of the age: Abolish Lutheran Protestantism and its "pernicious" moral order and, with these two, the feudal order as well. Brecht's Wenzeslaus is quite unaware that here he "... [spricht] ein großes Wort gelassen aus."[25]

Brecht's change of emphasis from the moral to the political brings out the fact that both characters in the adaptation are hopelessly shortsighted when it comes to the very political matters which should actually concern them most. Läuffer, who has been private tutor, Wenzeslaus's "collaborator" and "Kollege" (GW VI, 2391 and D I, 108), is well suited to become a *Mitläufer* in the fullest sense of the word and its recent connotations: „Und ich bins gewiß, die Herren zu Insterburg werden mir, so wie ich vor ihnen stehe, eine gute Stell verschaffen, so daß ich mein Eheweib ernähren kann." (GW VI, 2393)

Contrary to Brecht's expectation, the audience at the first performance of *Mutter Courage und ihre Kinder* in Zürich in 1941 failed to note the pessimism of his message in the play, i.e., that Mother Courage has not learned and never will learn that in the end she cannot profit from war. Läuffer's optimism that things will get better, like the faith of Mother Courage in war, is without a solid foundation. The tutor has not learned the truth about his adversary, for as Lenz's Geheimrat warns:

> Noch nie hat ein Edelmann einen Hofmeister angenommen, wo er ihm nicht hinter eine Allee von acht neun Sklavenjahren ein schön Gemählde von Beförderung gestellt hat und wenn Ihr acht Jahr gegangen waret, so macht' ers wie Laban und rückte das Bild um noch einmal so weit vorwärts. (D I, 55)

Taking his cue from such a description of the unscrupulous among the aristocrats, Brecht presents, as we shall see in the following chapter, a very different view of the Geheimrat and the Major than Lenz.

---

[25] Cf. Goethe's *Iphigenie auf Tauris*, Thoas to Iphigenie, line 307.

CHAPTER IV

CHARACTERS AND POLEMICS IN THE MODEL
AND THE ADAPTATION: SECONDARY CHARACTERS

Da ist das Moment des "Versagens" der deutschen Klassik, dieses mehr oder
weniger freiwillige Erstellt-Euch der großen bürgerlichen Karyatiden, die ange-
sichts des revolutionären Sodoms zu Salzsäulen erstarren. Die bedeutenden realistischen Anfänge müssen wieder etabliert werden. Die Unterdrückung Lenzens
durch die Literaturgeschichte muß man aufzeigen. Das Theater muß zurückgehen
zu diesem Punkt, um vorwärtszukommen, d.h. um einen realistischen Stil der
großen Gegenstände zu erarbeiten — haben wir doch den großen Stil eben nur
für die idealistischen Werke überliefert bekommen! Dann ist da das Lehrer-
problem des "Hofmeisters" als Teil der deutschen Misere, . . . es wird einfach
ganz realistisch . . . die Selbstentmannung der Intellektuellen, die zu dieser Zeit
mehr oder weniger alle, also als Kaste in den Lehrerberuf gedrängt waren, an
einem Exempel in Fleisch und Blut vorgeführt, . . .
— Bertolt Brecht, letter of March 25, 1950 quoted in Hans Mayer, *Bertolt Brecht
und die Tradition* (Pfullingen: Neske, 1961), p. 56

The Aristocrats

The Reinterpretation of Character: Theoretical Considerations

The character and actions of the Geheimrat von Berg and his brother, the
Major, have been grossly distorted in Brecht's adaptation. The characterization of the Geheimrat in Lenz's drama reflects that author's respect and
admiration for him as a dramatic personage, an individual, and a representative of the aristocracy. In contrast, the portrayal of the Privy Councillor in the adaptation is in black and white. Here, the Geheimrat, has
become a stereotype villain whose actions and attitudes are the subject of
Brecht's moral condemnation. The adaptor depicts the Geheimrat in the
context of a social system which favors only the nobility with privileges
while totally disenfranchising the middle and lower classes. The Storm and
Stress author, however, is sympathetic to certain strata of the aristocracy
which are enlightened; he is also critical of other levels which are rather
conservative, such as the landed aristocracy as represented by the Major,
or the lower court nobility, as represented by Graf Wermuth. Whereas Lenz
is far more dissatisfied with the middle class than with the nobility, Brecht
condemns both classes without reservation.

Brecht's Marxist convictions allow him only a narrow Mephistophelian,
i.e., nihilistic view of established society. It is as if God were asking Brecht
instead of the devil in the scene "Prolog im Himmel" in Goethe's *Faust I:*

DER HERR: Hast du mir weiter nichts zu sagen?
Kommst du nur immer anzuklagen?
Ist auf der Erde ewig dir nichts recht?

MEPHISTOPHELES: Nein, Herr! Ich find es dort, wie immer,
herzlich schlecht.
Die Menschen dauern mich in ihren
Jammertagen, . . . (lines 293—297)

In the eyes of Brecht-Mephisto, all aspects of the established order need radical change. In contrast, Lenz's social criticism in *Der Hofmeister* is never as purely negative and one-sided as is Brecht's.

Lenz's Geheimrat is an idealized figure. He is the leader in education, ethics, and human relations. He tries to stimulate the middle class to emulate his behavior and implement his ideas for their own and society's benefit. The Privy Councillor is a wholly constructive figure who offers sensible proposals for far-reaching reforms in these important areas of universal concern. He is unique among the aristocrats. Because his counterpart in the adaptation finds nothing at all wrong with the structure of society, he proposes no reforms and mocks the faults of such representatives of the middle class as Läuffer and his pastor-father. Whereas Lenz's Geheimrat is accessible, fair, and polite to all, Brecht's figure remains aloof, contemptuous, and thoroughly insulting in his relations with the middle class and with his servants. Nevertheless, of the two portrayals of the Privy Councillor, that of Brecht tends to be the more convincing, i.e., the more probable in a historical sense. This is so because Brecht no longer conceives of him as a unique figure but as a typical representative of the aristocracy.

If we derive Brecht's (negativistic) theory of adapting the figure of the Geheimrat, or of the Major for that matter, from his practice in the new version of the *Hofmeister,* we see that he consistently employs the principles of brutalization of the characters and vulgarization of their sentiments. The adaptor's aim is to distort wherever Lenz was critical and to discredit wherever Lenz sought to praise or to idealize. Brecht succeeds in causing the Geheimrat and the Major to appear brutal, coarse, and insensitive in the following ways. Wherever possible the adaptor omits all mention by Lenz of any admirable or noble qualities in these figures. On some occasions, the adaptor singles out and exaggerates a personality trait already present in the original character. Brecht strikes out the redeeming, purely *personal Gestus* or characteristic quality of a protagonist in order the better to emphasize the relevance of that figure's *social* attitudes. Brecht's manner of recasting personalities can be described as pragmatic rather than imaginative, for wherever Lenz conceives of his characters in psychological terms, Brecht — as is well known — reshapes them in sociological terms. Whereas Lenz's Major and Geheimrat confide in each other or speak in asides about what disturbs them, Brecht's figures are devoid of all inner life. They do not suffer from any gnawing spiritual and emotional disturbances which interfere with their thoughts or trouble their lives.

Sometimes Brecht rewrites a scene or merely adds dialogue when it is a question of alienating all sympathy of the spectator from the Geheimrat and the Major. Invariably, these additions to the text introduce a new and despicable character trait or emphasize it if already present. Also, such additions may function to present ironically the characters' biased views about controversial topics. The result is a preposterously one-sided characterization.

When Brecht wishes the spectator to become *emotionally* incensed at the nobles' callous treatment of their social inferiors, their treatment is exaggerated in scene after scene. It would be untenable for a Marxist to claim that Brecht wants to encourage the spectator's rational thought and mature, informed reflection concerning the brutality of the Geheimrat or the Major. Because the onlooker can sympathize neither with the aristocrats nor with the middle class, he is manipulated into condemning the system which produced these classes.

The Privy Councillor and the Major

Having examined various theoretical considerations underlying Brecht's character "remodelling," we can now consider specific examples of the changes made in the two protagonists under discussion. But in order to do so we shall need to see first how these figures are portrayed in Lenz's drama before we assess Brecht's changes and the reasons for them.

Lenz portrays the Geheimrat as an experienced, progressive, and enlightened educator in I, 1 and 2 of the *Hofmeister*. The Privy Councillor is a perceptive judge of character, for he seriously questions Läuffer's academic fitness and maturity. As he has the welfare of the public at heart, he refuses to appoint the young man as a teacher in the town school of Insterburg.

The Geheimrat in Lenz's drama can sanction neither his brother's short-sighted educational plans for Leopold, nor the (then popular) practice among the nobility of hiring a private tutor for one's children rather than sending them to public school along with the sons of the middle class. The Privy Councillor sincerely doubts the quality of instruction that can be given by even the most learned private tutor. He considers Läuffer to be "ein galonirter Müßiggänger, unterstützt von einer eitlen Patronin [the Major's wife]." (D I, 42) Here, the Geheimrat purposely insults his brother in the hope that he will be shocked into listening more to him and less to the Majorin. Unfortunately, he underestimates the Major's stubborn pride and consequently finds him unwilling to discuss the matter further.

The Geheimrat's serious reservations about the wisdom of the Major's decision to employ Läuffer reflect one of the main educational reforms suggested in Lenz's play. The Privy Councillor desires to improve the system of public education by supporting it rather than private tutors. The Major snobbishly believes, however, that a child of the nobility who associates with commoners will become little better than a commoner himself. The Major seems to be as conservative as his brother is progressive, for he thinks that if his son emulates his own military career, is loyal to the King, and has a smattering of court manners, this will be education enough.

In Scene 1 of the adaptation, Brecht's Geheimrat and Major bear little resemblance to their counterparts in the corresponding scenes of Lenz's drama. The entire scene has been rewritten. Now the brothers are openly contemptuous of the tutor, not because of his inadequate training — it is adequate enough for the Major's purpose, which his brother now sanctions — but because of his inferior social position.

The Geheimrat is no longer a forward-looking and enlightened educator at all. In fact, he has no interest in education, either public or private! The fact that Brecht drops this central concern of the original figure has the consequence that the Privy Councillor no longer works for social reform as in Lenz's drama. On the contrary, Brecht chooses to depict both brothers as feudal barons owing allegiance only to Frederick II of Prussia.

In the adaptation, Brecht transforms both the Geheimrat and the Major into superficial and unquestioning supporters of the status quo. The Privy Councillor, concerned about the image of his family and his class, now worries whether Läuffer's morals might give rise to gossip or scandal. Unlike the financially hardpressed Major, the Geheimrat believes that an aristocrat owes it to his class to spend more money by sending his son to university than to hire a tutor. Brecht indicates that the Major's main concern is to help his monarch defray the expenses of the Seven Years' War. Throughout the adaptation, Brecht shows that the officer spends most of his time worrying about his finances and doing the menial work on his farm himself. The fact that Brecht stresses helping to pay the cost of this war as the Major's preoccupation is less preposterous than historically realistic. In his discussion of conditions which prevailed in Prussia after the Seven Years' War, a recent historian notes:

> The same Spartan discipline that ruled in the Prussian army was made the basis of the life and occupations of the entire aristocracy. They were under the constant supervision of the crown and had to pay dearly for belonging to a caste whose special privileges were outweighed by the heavy burdens they had to carry in the service of their government.[1]

In Lenz's drama and in the adaptation, the Major is shown in situations where his qualities — or lack of them — as an educator can be exhibited. In I, 4 of Lenz's drama, the Major displays a number of qualities which disqualify him from being an effective pedagogue. Lenz disapproves vigorously of retired officers becoming full-time teachers, as was a common practice in his day. The Major is totally incapable of teaching his son anything but fear. Lenz indicates that there are good reasons why the Major

---

[1] Kurt F. Reinhardt, *Germany — 2000 Years* (N. Y.: Ungar, 1961), vol. I, p. 319.

is so impatient and short-tempered with Leopold. The officer merely transfers his intense hatred of his wife to the boy and "lets off steam" by criticizing him mercilessly, administering physical punishment, and threatening extreme violence. The officer is not only disappointed that he has such a weak good-for-nothing as a son, he also resents his wife's coddling the boy while expressly neglecting Gustchen. Also, the Major, a battle-hardened officer, is accustomed to demanding the strictest discipline and meting out harsh treatment to his subordinates. There is little wonder that he should treat his son like a new recruit.

Lenz does not, however, portray this Prussian officer as all blood and thunder; he endows the Major with a quality which renders him more human, namely his great love for his daughter. The grandiose plans he entertains for her marriage attest to his exaggerated opinion of her beauty as well as to his rather egoistic social ambitions. Lenz creates in the officer a character almost Shakespearean in his subjectivity, in so far as the Major has the makings of a man who can and will cause himself great suffering; everything he does is done to excess. As Lenz shows later on in the drama, not even grief can soften his explosive temper or drain his furious energy.

In Scene 5 of the adaptation, Brecht adopts most aspects of Lenz's characterization of this figure, but makes two significant changes in emphasis. In becoming a focus for Brecht's anti-militarism, the Major is made to appear much more the Prussian officer than in Lenz's play. Eight lines of dialogue are added to the Major's part in the adaptation;[2] in the new passage, the Major reproaches Läuffer for his lack of attention to military detail in Leopold's essay about Frederick the Great and the Seven Years' War. The Major also suspects that the tutor lacks the appropriate reverence for the monarch.

According to Elisabeth Hauptmann,[3] Brecht used to recall in their conversations the chauvinistic attitude some of his Augsburg schoolteachers had toward the nation's history, which they allegedly conceived of as a record of wars fought by Germans. As a schoolboy, Brecht was expected to be able to describe in detail the wars of the German states and be proud of German militarism. The interpolated passage referred to above mocks those teachers and arm-chair heroes of his youth[4] who expected war to be spoken of in as glowing terms as the Major uses.

The second significant change in the characterization of the Major concerns his relationship to his daughter, Gustchen. The adaptor either deletes or shortens the Major's long digressions in Lenz's play concerning how much

---

[2] Cf. GW VI, 2344.

[3] In my interviews with her on February 4 and 6, 1970.

[4] When the First World War broke out, Brecht recorded his disagreement with his teachers' glorification of war in an ironic school essay called „Dulce et decorum est, pro patria mori." His radically pacifist stand touched off a storm of indignation among his instructors, and almost got him expelled. Cf. Martin Esslin, *Brecht — The Man and his Work* (N. Y.: Double Day Anchor, 1961), p. 6.

his daughter means to him; Brecht also omits all mention of the officer's plans for her marriage. Actually, Brecht deletes almost all of the four scenes in the original drama in which the Major so takes to heart the loss of his daughter's health and vivaciousness that he becomes psychologically distraught, and subsequently, physically ill. Indeed, in Lenz's drama, the Major's mind is so affected by his grief that he even considers (IV, 1) joining the Russian army to fight the Turks;[5] on another occasion (III, 1), he raves about giving up his whole existence as a nobleman and officer in order to become a simple peasant-farmer and forget his sorrows and the evils of society in nature, à la Rousseau.

Because Brecht deletes this tearful and exaggerated melancholy which was so popular in the sentimental novel and drama before and during Storm and Stress, the Major appears much less fatherly and less affectionate in the adaptation than he does in Lenz's play. The omission of the Major's melancholia and paternal tenderness precludes in the adaptation the relief or softening of the short temper and brutality he displays in the original drama. As a result, he now possesses only the harsh and insensitive traits of a Prussian officer — in the popular conception — to the exclusion of all redeeming qualities. In short, the doting father is replaced by the militarist.

The chief focus of Lenz's lengthy and important II, 1 is to depict the altruistic Geheimrat as a man whose democratic ideas about school reform place him in the first rank of educators. As a person too, the Privy Councillor is portrayed as most sympathetic and scrupulously honest. He has no qualms about telling the Pastor that Läuffer is useless as a teacher, and that he, the Pastor, is an indifferent father:

> ... Ihr Sohn [sollte] Gott danken, wenn ihn nur der Major beym Kopf nähm' und aus dem Hause würfe. Was soll er da ... ? Wollen Sie ein Vater für Ihr Kind seyn und schliessen so Augen, Mund und Ohren für seine ganze Glückseligkeit zu? (D I, 53)

Because Brecht omits this and other well-meant speeches of the aristocrat, the new figure of the Geheimrat appears totally callous toward Läuffer, uncritical of the Major, and disinterested in the Pastor's duties as a father.

Lenz's Geheimrat is not only of noble birth, he also thinks and acts nobly. His argument with the Pastor reflects Kantian concepts of the spiritual nobility and ethical duty of man. Referring to the servile tutor, the aristocrat remarks:

> Mögen die Elenden, die Ihre Ideen nicht zu höherer Glückseligkeit zu erheben wissen, als zu essen und zu trinken, mögen die sich im Keficht zu Tode füttern lassen, aber ein Gelehrter, ein Mensch, der den Adel seiner Seele fühlt, der den Tod nicht so scheuen sollt' als eine Handlung, die wider seine Grundsätze läuft.... (D I, 54)

---

[5] Compare the intentions of Werner (I, 12) and even Tellheim (V, 1) in Lessing's *Minna von Barnhelm!*

This passage, too, is absent in Scene 8 of the adaptation. In fact, Brecht retains *only* those speeches of the Geheimrat which contain unmitigated criticism of the tutor and his father. Significantly, the Privy Councillor's exhortation in Lenz's drama: "Laßt den Burschen was lernen, daß er dem Staat nützen kann" (D I, 54) is also absent in Brecht's Scene 8, as are the severe criticisms of Lenz's Geheimrat concerning Läuffer, who fails to devote "seine Kräfte und seinen Verstand dem allgemeinen Besten." (D I, 54)

Lenz's aristocrat is not afraid to point out to Pastor Läuffer the vain and tyrannical practices of some members of the nobility and the slavish nature of the middle classes:

> Ihr beklagt Euch so viel übern Adel und über seinen Stolz, die Leute sähn Hofmeister wie Domestiken an, Narren! Was sind sie denn anders? Stehen sie nicht in Lohn und Brod bey ihnen wie jene? Aber wer heißt euch [sic] Domestiken werden, wenn Ihr was gelernt habt, und einem starrköpfischen Edelmann zinsbar werden, der sein Tage von seinen Hausgenossen nichts anders gewohnt war als sklavische Unterwürfigkeit? (D I, 55)

To retain such passages in the adaptation would have detracted from Brecht's depiction of the Geheimrat as haughty, spiteful, and uncritical. Also, Lenz's Privy Councillor implies that Läuffer — and the middle class generally — have the free will and the opportunity to better themselves, if they so desire. As we have seen, Brecht, on the other hand, wishes to create the firm impression that economic conditions and a feudal arictocracy prevent Läuffer and his kind from exercising their free will.

Brecht utterly falsifies Lenz's portrayal of the Geheimrat as a keen critic of the nobility. The adapted figure is no longer the sincere, progressive educator who, in making the school system democratic, would also do away with class differences. The following significant passage, in which Lenz's Privy Councillor advances his program for school reform, is also missing in Scene 8 of the adaptation:

> Würde der Edelmann nicht von Euch in der Grille gestärkt, einen kleinen Hof anzulegen, wo er als Monarch oben auf dem Thron sitzt, und ihm Hofmeister und Mamsell und ein ganzer Wisch von Tagdieben huldigen, so würd' er seine Jungen in die öffentliche Schule thun müssen; er würde das Geld, von dem er jetzt seinen Sohn zum hochadlichen Dummkopf aufzieht, zum Fond der Schule schlagen: davon könnten denn gescheidte Leute salarirt werden und alles würde seinen guten Gang gehn; das Studentchen müste [sic] was lernen, um bey einer solchen Anstalt brauchbar zu werden, und das junge Herrchen, anstatt seine Faullenzerey... künstlich und manierlich zu verstecken, würde seinen Kopf anstrengen müssen, um es den bürgerlichen Jungen zuvorzuthun, wenn es sich doch von ihnen unterscheiden will. (D I, 56—57)

Indeed, in Scene 8 of the adaptation, Brecht's Geheimrat is concerned only with expressing an undisguised scorn for tutors who accept their status as menials. The aristocrat no longer emphasizes the importance of the public school's influence in Fritz's education, as is the case in Lenz's drama. Rather, he claims: "Die paar Prinzipien, die er braucht, daß er sich treu philosophisch im Leben verhält, die hat er von mir gehört, da waren einige

Tischgespräche genug." (GW VI, 2357) Such a comment illustrates not only the Geheimrat's limited and inimical views on education, it also shows his exaggerated (and mistaken) idea of the importance of reason in his son's actions.

The Geheimrat in II, 1 of Lenz's drama learns from a letter handed to him by the Pastor that Läuffer is desperate to leave Heidelbrunn — the Major's country estate — where he has been kept isolated for a whole year. Apparently, the horse which the Major has promised the tutor for trips to Königsberg is always denied. As Lenz's Geheimrat is a man of good taste, he does not speculate aloud about Läuffer's possible reasons for wishing to travel to Königsberg. In response to the letter, the Privy Councillor shows little sympathy but suggests sensibly and fairly: "Je nun, laß ihn quittiren; warum ist er ein Narr und bleibt da?" (D I, 58)

In Scene 8 of the adaptation, Läuffer now confronts the Geheimrat personally, and repeatedly begs him to influence the Major to keep his promise concerning the animal. Brecht's Privy Councillor has not the slightest intention of helping Läuffer to a horse, nor of advising him to quit the Major's service. He realizes only too well why the tutor wishes to ride to Königsberg and mocks him cruelly with a vulgar taunt: "Ihn sticht wohl der Hafer?" (GW VI, 2357) Not content with depicting the Geheimrat as devoid of all human kindness, Brecht emphasizes his hostility and selfish materialism in a final brutal retort: "Mein Bruder bekommt für seine Ökonomie nicht Ackergäule, und da will Er von ihm einen Gaul für seine Ausschweifungen!" (GW VI, 2357) In Lenz's drama, however, the Geheimrat generously adds out of his own pocket a sum of money to Läuffer's salary in order to make up the amount that the Major has subtracted.

In all scenes of the adaptation, Brecht has destroyed all resemblance of the Geheimrat to Lenz's figure. The friendly smile of the respected and enlightened aristocrat has become the coarse sneer of the feared and inaccessible boor. The original Privy Councillor's sympathy for Läuffer has now become scorn; the nobleman's belief in the freedom of man and the desirability of reforming society have disappeared in the adaptation behind the dark cloud of feudal thinking and the determination to retain the status quo.

As mentioned briefly above, Brecht conceives of the Major rather simplistically as a brutal Prussian officer who not only glorifies war and Frederick II, but also unquestioningly devotes all his energy to farming in order to help defray the King's horrendously large military expenses. This rather one-sided portrayal of the Major as an exploited feudal lord receives special attention in Scene 11 of the adaptation.

Brecht's method here is to substitute materialistic and political motives for the Major's actions wherever Lenz shows that psychological and personal reasons are responsible for the officer's behavior. In Scene 11 of the adaptation, a number of new speeches are found in the conversations which the Majorin has with her husband and Graf Wermuth. These innovations in the dialogue emphasize the Major's preoccupation with the Seven Years'

War and its cost. The Majorin exclaims, for example: "Der Major kennt seit dem Krieg nichts mehr außer seiner leidigen Ökonomie." (GW VI, 2365)

In Lenz's drama, the Majorin is inclined to attribute her husband's insomnia and his neglect of her to emotional or psychological disturbances. She relates indiscreetly to Graf Wermuth:

> ...da ist er [der Major] mitten in der Nacht aus dem Bett' aufgesprungen und hat sich ... auf die Knie niedergeworfen und an die Brust geschlagen und geschluchst und geheult, daß mir zu grauen anfieng. Ich hab ihn aber nicht fragen mögen, was gehen mich seine Narrheiten an? Mag er Pietist oder Quacker werden. (D I, 68)

Whereas in Lenz's drama, the Major's behavior during his insomnia apparently points to a sense of profound personal and religious guilt, the behavior of Brecht's figure is motivated only by very tangible material concerns. The above passage from Lenz is adapted slightly in Scene 11 to read: "...da ist er mitten in der Nacht aus dem Bett aufgesprungen und hat sich ... an die Rechnungsbücher gemacht. Er hat im Schreibzimmer drunten gestöhnt, daß mir zu grauen anfing...." (GW VI, 2365) This amusing example of Brecht's changes in the dialogue illustrates well his preference for the material to the abstract or the conscious to the subconscious when adapting a character along sociological rather than psychological lines.

In the adaptation, the Majorin and Graf Wermuth fail to grasp fully the real reason why the Major works so hard. This is so because Brecht wishes the Major himself to spell out his real motives in unmistakable terms, addressed more perhaps to today's theater audience than to the play's other characters: "Meiner Treu, du vergißt, Frau, daß ein Krieg bezahlt sein muß." (GW VI, 2366) Such a remark is intended to raise questions in the spectator: "Paid by whom? For what gains?"[6]

Brecht's desire to portray the material and political considerations underlying a protagonist's behavior causes the Major, for example, to appear far less human and sympathetic than in Lenz's drama. Although Brecht combines II, 6 and III, 1 of the original drama to make up the scene under discussion, he omits the long passages in the initial half of Lenz's III, 1 where the Major weeps, deploring Gustchen's loss of health and vivacity. Brecht considers that the deletion of all the passages in which Lenz's Major expresses concern for Gustchen's condition is necessary in order to "dehumanize" this character. Accordingly, the adaptor shifts the stress from the warmth of the Major's personal interests to the impersonality of his material obligations.[7]

---

[6] Ideally, Brecht would have the spectator react similarly to his well-educated worker, as depicted in the critical poem "Fragen eines lesenden Arbeiters." Cf. GW IX, 656—657.

[7] There is, of course, another reason why the adaptor omits the passages where the Major is concerned for his daughter's health. Brecht wishes to vulgarize Lenz's (critical) portrayal of Gustchen and her unhealthy interest in tragic and senti-

In our discussion of Brecht's adaptation so far, we have noted that the Major and the Geheimrat deliberately behave brutally toward the middle class. The two aristocrats always appear constitutionally unsympathetic to members of other classes; i.e., Brecht argues that because the Major and the Geheimrat are aristocrats, they can display only hatred and scorn for their social inferiors. These aspects of their behavior are particularly emphasized in Scene 12 of the adaptation when the Major, accompanied by the Geheimrat and Graf Wermuth, shoots Läuffer. Brecht conceives of the shooting as an act of cold-blooded revenge.

In contrast, the Storm and Stress author takes pains to indicate clearly that the Major's judgment is clouded by his violent temper.[8] In Lenz's IV, 3, the Major does indeed shoot Läuffer but is apparently unaware at the time of what he is doing. At the retort of the pistol, the officer awakes as if from a dream, exclaiming: "Was? ist er [Läuffer] todt? *schlägt sich vors Gesicht.* Was hab' ich gethan? Kann Er mir keine Nachricht mehr von meiner Tochter geben?" (D I, 88) Nevertheless, Lenz's Major shows absolutely no sympathy for Läuffer; in the officer's opinion, the tutor is first and last a servant and never a human being. Lenz hereby criticizes those among the nobility who, with armed might, abuse the privacy and freedoms of the middle class. The Major's gesture and comment of surprise: "Was hab' ich gethan?", does tend, however, to lessen the gravity of his offense. In Scene 12 of the adaptation, Brecht omits both the stage direction and the Major's question from Lenz's dialogue. Consequently, the Major appears to be fully conscious of his actions.

Brecht's conception of the Major tends toward the grotesque. A new speech added to the Major's part in the dialogue causes that officer to appear like a medieval torturer: "Und jetzt zu Ihm [Läuffer]! Und wenn wir glühende Zangen ansetzen sollten." (GW VI, 2371) Even before Brecht adds this savage trait to the Major's character, he has deleted that grief-stricken and very human outcry of the officer in Lenz's scene where he despairs of finding his daughter and seems to prefer death to life: "Laßt ihn [Läuffer] liegen und kommt bis ans Ende der Welt. Ich muß meine Tochter wiederhaben, und wenn nicht in diesem Leben, doch in jener Welt...." (D I, 89)

Whereas Lenz's Geheimrat sympathizes with Läuffer's distress and actually dresses the tutor's wound himself, Brecht's Privy Councillor seems quite detached, displaying a callous disregard for the unfortunate young man. The

---

mental literature. In Scenes 10 and 11 of the adaptation, Gustchen is in perfect health. She is no longer the pining adolescent romantic that she was in Lenz's drama; on the contrary, Brecht emphasizes (mainly for humorous reasons) the physical. Her keen sensuality as well as her awakend sexual interest in Läuffer are far too strong for imaginative literature to have any deleterious influence on her health and thoughts.

[8] The choleric Odoardo of Lessing's tragedy *Emilia Galotti* may well have been a model for Lenz's Major in this respect.

adaptor changes the original stage direction which describes the Geheimrat's action as "bemüht, Läuffern zu verbinden" (D I, 88) to "winkt einem Bedienten, Läuffer zu verbinden." (GW VI, 2373)

The adapted figure of the Privy Councillor possesses here as also in Scene 13 the habit of ordering servants right and left to perform all manner of menial and distasteful tasks, a habit that Brecht wrote of with scorn in one of the late *Svendborger Gedichte,* "Verjagt mit gutem Grund."[9] Lenz's Geheimrat apologizes for the Major's having shot Läuffer: "Es thut uns genug" (D I, 89), but Brecht's protagonist has no sympathy at all; he only fears the scandal: "Meinen Fritz schick ich nach Italien, er darfs gar nicht erfahren." (GW VI, 2373)

Lenz's Privy Councillor is extremely generous when, assuming the moral and financial responsibility for his distraught brother's action, he leaves money behind for the tutor's surgical expenses:

Lassen Sie [Läuffer] sich davon kuriren, und bedenken Sie, daß Sie meinen Bruder weit gefährlicher verwundet haben, als er Sie. Es ist ein Bankozettel drin, geben Sie Acht drauf und machen ihn sich zu Nutz so gut Sie können. (D I, 89)

In the adaptation, the last sentence of this remark is deleted. The retained portion of the Geheimrat's statement becomes a hypocritical, moralistic reproach; his giving money to Läuffer takes on the aspect of a bribe to silence the tutor's protests. Gone is all indication of that somewhat idealized human charity so characteristic of Lenz's Privy Councillor.

Because the motivation of Brecht's characters is not the same as in Lenz's play, the language of the play — wherever it is retained verbatim — may no longer mean the same. For example, in Scene 13 of the adaptation, the Major pardons Gustchen and uses exactly the same expressions as in Lenz's drama. But Brecht's Major is not pardoning the same thing as Lenz's figure. Gustchen's attempted suicide is not only faked, the girl also believes that she has done nothing morally wrong in encouraging Läuffer to seduce her. What has she done, then, that the Major should pardon? She has simply dealt a cruel blow to her father's pride in his family's social standing and made him an object of scorn in the eyes of his fellow aristocrats. Gustschen's plea for forgiveness is nothing more than a plea to be reinstated in the

---

[9]
Ich bin aufgewachsen als Sohn
Wohlhabender Leute. Meine Eltern haben mir
Einen Kragen umgebunden und mich erzogen
In den Gewohnheiten des Bedientwerdens
Und unterrichtet in der Kunst des Befehlens. Aber
Als ich erwachsen war und um mich sah
Gefielen mir die Leute meiner Klasse nicht
Nicht das Befehlen und nicht das Bedientwerden
Und ich verließ meine Klasse und gesellte mich
Zu den geringen Leuten.

GW IX, 721, lines 1—10

social hierarchy from which she has fallen. Because he pardons a social *faux pas* rather than the sins of a penitent daughter, the Major's display of apparent tenderness when taking Gustchen in his arms cannot be taken as seriously as it was in Lenz's drama.

As we have seen, the relationship of Brecht's Major to Gustchen is very different from the officer's relationship to her in Lenz's *Hofmeister*. Throughout the original play, the Major is depicted as a warm and loving father. Because he loves her so much, his personality and actions are affected by her seduction and disappearance. Lenz is concerned with showing that spiritual values can alter man's behavior. Brecht removes this emphasis altogether from the portrayal of the Major and develops the motif in Fritz instead. The change is especially evident in Scene 16 of the adaptation. But first what of the corresponding scene in Lenz's drama?

Here, in V, 12, Lenz portrays the surprising development that has taken place in the Major's personality since Gustchen and her child have been restored to him. Gone are the brutality, stubbornness, and masculine pride of the former Prussian Junker. In their place are humility, gentleness, and consideration for others. Lenz's Major gives the impression that he is truly delighted about Fritz's wish to marry Gustchen. He greets the young man with joyous surprise and gratitude: "Willst Du meine Tochter heyraten? — Gott segne Dich ... (drückt ihn [Fritz] immer an die Brust) ... Ich möchte Dich todt drücken — Daß du so großmüthig bist, daß Du so edel denkst — Iaß Du — mein Junge bist —" (D I, 119) He conceives of Fritz's resolve to marry Gustchen not only as a noble and generous personal act, but also as an act of God, which is made possible by his own sincere religious atonement for his foolishness:

> Meine Tochter hat Busse gethan und ich hab für meine Thorheiten und daß ich einem Bruder nicht folgen wollte, der das Ding besser verstund, auch Busse gethan; ihr zur Gesellschaft: und darum macht mich der liebe Gott auch ihr zur Gesellschaft mit glücklich. (D I, 120)

Lenz's emphasis on the Major's becoming religiously devout is appropriate in the last scenes of his drama, which show the reconciliation of prodigal sons with their fathers.

In contrast to Lenz, Brecht no longer portrays the Major as a doting father. Only snatches of the Major's speeches, as they occur in Lenz's dialogue, are found in Brecht's newly-written Scene 16. The adaptor is concerned here less with the figure of the Major than with the failure of Fritz to pierce the fog of his Kantian idealism and recognize Gustchen's behavior for what it really was. Major von Berg is still portrayed as the feudal aristocrat, but Brecht presents him as a cold, unsympathetic officer, almost completely indifferent to Gustchen and her child.

The manner in which Brecht's Major receives Fritz is tinged with ridicule and scorn: "Was, du willst sie heiraten? Dennoch?" (GW VI, 2389) Brecht "uses" the figure of the Major here not as a character in his ow right but merely as a foil to elicit Fritz's idealistic defense of Gustchen. The Major's almost contemptuous and incredulous questions make it clear that he is of the opinion: "Darüber kann kein Mann weg" — as was the Secretary in Hebbel's tragedy *Maria Magdalene* (II, 5). It is as though Brecht's officer disowns Gustchen, for he impersonally uses the pronoun "her" ("sie") to refer to her when he could have used her name. In contrast, the Major of Lenz's drama gave the impression that he was emotionally attached to Gustchen, for he used the words "meine Tochter."

Lenz's Major also admires Fritz's magnanimity. He can appreciate the young man's forgiving and considerate nature: "Siehst Du, dort ist das Kind. Bist ein Philosoph? Kannst alles vergessen? Ist Gustchen Dir noch schön genug?" (D I, 119) In the adaptation, the Major confronts Fritz suddenly with Gustchen's child as though to bring him to his senses and discourage his resolve: "Komm! *Führt ihn zum Kanapee.* Bist du ein Philosoph?" (GW VI, 2389) Lenz's use of the term "Philosoph" is wholesome; it signifies a person to whom spiritual values are a more noble concern than material values. But in the adaptation, the term carries an overtone of contempt, for the Major appears to conceive of a philosopher as a man who will overlook reality to spite himself. Thus, the Major behaves as a shallow, unsympathetic materialist in his denigration of Fritz's idealistic intentions, and seems totally lacking in paternal sentiment.

In all, Brecht offers a one-sided portrait of the Major. The spectator sees in him only the unfeeling Prussian officer, the economically harrassed estate owner, the negligent, hostile husband, and the scornful father whose social sensitivity smothers the paternal instinct. Brecht tries to be historically realistic even when exaggerating, whereas Lenz idealizes the Major in his relationship with Gustchen. Both authors advocate social change. Lenz finally sees the officer as an exemplary figure on a familial level, whereas Brecht widens the frame of reference and portrays him as a representative of a class which must be abolished.

F r i t z   v o n   B e r g

Brecht's Fritz: A Man without a Mission

In Lenz's drama, the character and social philosophy of Fritz von Berg undergo considerable development during the course of the play's action. Fritz matures quickly into a liberal and progressive thinker who takes it upon himself to encourage others to let reason guide them toward virtuous behavior. The naive, romantic adolescent of I, 5 in Lenz's *Hofmeister* ultimately becomes a thoughtful pragmatic member of society in V, 12. He is actually a Rationalist in the spirit of the philosopher Christian Wolff. It is this development in the character and social involvement of Lenz's figure which offers the key to understanding the very different portrayal of Fritz in the adaptation.

Significantly, Brecht's figure undergoes no development as an intellectual, moral, or social being. In the adapted drama, Fritz is as removed from society in Scene 16 as he is in Scene 2. He turns out to be the worst judge of character, he fails to understand or evaluate other people's motives, and he remains blind to the forces which determine how people live together.

In contrast, Lenz's Fritz ushers the aristocracy into a new age in which their class is an active, constructive influence in improving the relationships between social classes; his actions are marked by a wisdom and magnanimity of thought that place him ahead of his contemporaries. For Lenz, Fritz is, therefore, an exemplary figure who suggests reform in two areas of life: Publicly, in education and social relationships, and privately, within the family.

Brecht rejects the social structure portrayed in Lenz's drama. The nobility is depicted in the adaptation as callous and self-seeking. Hence, it would be illogical for the adaptor to show Fritz as a positive figure, who, worthy of emulation, strives even in his personal acts to work also for society's betterment.

To be sure, Lenz's Fritz seems a somewhat improbable character, and his later development toward maturity appears sudden and inconsistent with his character as observed earlier in the drama. The dénouement of the action, although clumsy and contrived, has to show that Fritz has become the responsible man. Of greatest importance to Lenz is the idea that the figure of Fritz should point the way to new and more humane relationships between the aristocracy and the middle class, between father and son, and between the sexes. Also, since Fritz is portrayed as a product of the not so popular public school, Lenz hopes that the young aristocrat's behavior and development will be regarded as arguments in favor of abolishing the often unfortunate practice of hiring private tutors.

Fritz is clearly the most important *constructive* figure in Lenz's *subplot,* if not in the play as a whole. It is Fritz's function to exemplify liberal and progressive ideas about education and social behavior which the dramatist wishes to popularize. Also, the young von Berg's abiding friendship with Pätus is the axis of the subplot in Lenz's drama.

None of this is true in Brecht's *Hofmeister.* Fritz von Berg's connections with Pätus now attest more to an unfortunate association than to a friendship founded on like interests. The adaptation offers only biting, often ridiculously exaggerated criticism of education and society in the past and contains no truly positive, constructive ideas pertinent to modern education or class society.

In the adapted drama, Fritz is reduced to being the dupe of those whom he trusts most. (Almost all the action concerning Fritz and his "friends" is entirely Brecht's invention; of the various common experiences of Fritz and Pätus in Lenz's drama only one single important incident — the episode of Seiffenblase's letter — is retained by Brecht.) In the adaptation, it seems that profound friendships, common human bonds, and values worth fighting for are no longer possible, as they were in Lenz's drama.

In contrast to Lenz, Brecht portrays eighteenth-century society as one in which there is no real spiritual and moral solidarity among men; in the adapted drama, there are only a middle class and an aristocracy pitted against each other. Brecht's characters are lone individuals who are set either against one another (Läuffer-Major-Wenzeslaus), or against a class (Läuffer versus the aristocracy). Some of Brecht's "loners" reveal themselves sooner or later as opportunists, for they seek only self-gratification (Bollwerk, Pätus); they are well aware that society has nothing to offer them if they do not take it by force or falsity.

In Lenz's drama, some individuals (Pätus, Old Pätus, Old Rehaar) want or need help to become "better" persons, i.e., ethically responsible, and thus more desirable members of society. This is not the case in the adaptation, where there are no rewards for "moral" or altruistic behavior. There are not even any obvious and universally accepted ideal values in the society that Brecht portrays. In contrast to the figures in Lenz's *Hofmeister,* not a single character in the adaptation shows that his actions are consonant with an ideal of self-perfection. The futility of virtue in class society is a constant theme in Brecht's drama, from *Trommeln in der Nacht* onward.

In Brecht's play, there is no longer anything exemplary about Fritz's actions. This is so for two reasons. The young von Berg's role is even more that of a passive observer than in Lenz's drama. Secondly, nothing really happens to him. Whereas the Storm and Stress author portrays Fritz as a moral leader in the thick of social issues, the Marxist conceives of the young aristocrat as a would-be "Kerl" — "... auch trägt er bereits ein Schillerhemd" (GW XVII, 1231) — who is as aimless as he is young. Fritz von Berg is little more than an ineffectual, unambitious adolescent almost totally preoccupied with his emotions or the victories and disappointments of his love for Gustchen as they exist in his imagination. He fails to develop or exhibit values of self-reliance and leadership because he experiences neither danger nor moments of crisis.

Fritz's Love for Gustchen

In I, 5 of Lenz's drama, the young Fritz exhibits no social consciousness. He is as much a dreamer here as his counterpart in Scene 16 of Brecht's adaptation. In the Storm and Stress play, the young man's attention is focussed only on his sweetheart Gustchen and their impending separation. Lenz suggests that Fritz's love for his cousin is more Platonic than real, i.e., erotic. The touching aspect to Fritz's youthful interest in Gustchen is its naive sincerity and unselfishness. His kissing Gustchen appears merely affectionate.

He feels that life should imitate art, for he imagines her as Juliet, himself as Romeo. There is even some substance to his fear that Graf Wermuth is a rival for Gustchen's hand; this anxiety adds to the poignancy of the romantic tragedy which he believes he is acting out. Speaking of Wermuth, Fritz notes: "Er wird ein Graf Paris für uns seyn." (D I, 49) Like true romantic lovers, both Gustchen and Fritz consider their love more as something to die for than to live for: "FRITZ: O ich kann mich auch erstechen . . ."[10] and "GUSTCHEN: . . . es giebt Schlaftrünke zum ewigen Schlaf." (D I, 49) Indeed, they resemble their counterparts in Shakespeare's tragedy in a number of ways.[11] The behavior of Lenz's Fritz calls to mind Romeo's words to Friar Lawrence: "Do thou but close our hands with holy words, / Then love-devouring death do what he dare, — / It is enough I may but call her mine." (II, 6)

Unlike the romantic lovers in Lenz's play, Fritz and Gustchen in Brecht's adaptation have none of the fatalism or the death wishes of Romeo and Juliet. To be sure, the adaptation retains Fritz's words of bravado and romantic exaggeration, but these were already clichés in Lenz's time, as for example: "Verlange mein Leben, meinen letzten Tropfen Bluts" and "Ich schwör' dir hunderttausend Eide." (GW VI, 2338)

In Scene 2 of the adaptation, Brecht's Fritz, like Lenz's figure, uses literature to say for him what he is too bashful to say outright himself. Although Fritz still takes his cue from famous lovers in literature, he conceives of his relationship to Gustchen in more intimate terms as her mate and lover. His affections, no longer shyly concealed, are modelled on the conjugal and erotic love of husband and wife as passionately described in

––––––––

[10] Gustchen is uncertain whether she should believe Fritz and claims he would be too cowardly to stab himself. Her reference to Gellert applies, specifically, to Christian Fürchtegott Gellert's poem "Der Selbstmord." These playful verses gently mock the exaggerated romantic sentiment of a desperate lover:

> Er [der Jüngling] reißt den Degen aus der Scheide,
> Und — O was kann verwegner seyn!
> Kurz, er besieht die Spitz und Schneide,
> Und steckt ihn langsam wieder ein.

C. F. Gellert, *Sämmtliche Schriften Erster Theil* (Leipzig: Weidmanns Erben, 1775), neue, verb. Auflage, p. 31.

[11] It is not the purpose here to determine Lenz's debt to Shakespeare nor which English edition(s), French or German translation(s) of the English poet Lenz may have known when writing his *Hofmeister*. It is interesting to note in passing, however, one of the several episodes from *Romeo and Juliet* which served as a model for episodes in Lenz's drama. The episode in Lenz's I, 5 in which Gustchen requests Fritz to swear that he loves her seems modelled closely on Juliet's lines in II, 2 of *Romeo and Juliet*:

JULIET: Dost thou love me? I know thou wilt say Ay;
         And I will take thy word: yet if thou swear'st
         Thou mayst prove false; at lovers' perjuries
         They say Jove laughs. O gentle Romeo,
         If thou dost love, pronounce it faithfully . . .
ROMEO: What shall I swear by?
JULIET: Do not swear at all;
         I hear some noise within; dear love adieu!

Klopstock's ode: "Hermann und Thusnelda".[12] The excerpts from the sentimental poet's odes presented in Scene 2 and Scene 9 of the adaptation depict powerful feelings which seek expression and immediate fulfillment.

There are strong reasons why Brecht generally does not care to portray Platonic or romantic love between the sexes; he considers that such relationships do not lend themselves to portraying the more important real conditions such as economic and social forces acting on men. Specifically, Brecht finds that Lenz portrayed the relationship of Fritz and Gustchen in an artificial manner because the erotic was strictly avoided.[13]

Brecht's frequent mockery of sincere sentiment as he finds it expressed in serious literature and in music contributes in large measure to making the adaptation into a memorable comedy. There is hardly a line in the dialogue which does not typify his ironic irreverence either for things Biblical, the heroic view of history, or the work of his own and Lenz's contemporaries.

In Scene 2 of the adaptation, Brecht's literary parody is far superior to the innocuous references to Shakespeare and Gellert in the corresponding scene of Lenz's play. Fritz's inwardness and preference for the spiritual over the physical is exemplified effectively in selections from Klopstock's odes. Gustchen joyfully calls out the name of the poet when Fritz presents her

------

[12] In the notes to the adaptation, Brecht refers the reader to a literary work which may have been the model for this episode in Scene 2: "Die Wahrnehmung, daß Menschen unter der Wirkung der Poesie zusammengebracht werden, ist selber poetisch. Die Verführung, die von der Lektüre eines Liebesgedichts ausgeht, wird in Dantes 'Inferno' im fünften Gesang meisterhaft beschrieben. Etwas von dieser Poesie, leicht verfremdet durch schwache Komik, sollte das Klopstocklesen der Liebenden haben."

GW XVII, 1241

In Laurence Binyon's translation, the particular passage to which Brecht refers, reads:

One day together, for pastime, we read
of Launcelot, and how Love held him in thrall.
We were alone, and without any dread.
Sometimes our eyes, at the word's secret call,
Met, and our cheeks a changing colour wore.
But it was one page only that did all.
When we read how that smile, so thirsted for,
Was kissed by such a lover, he that may
Never from me be separated more
All trembling kissed my mouth. The book I say
Was a Galahalt to us, and he beside
That wrote the book. We read no more that day.

Cf. *The Portable Dante* (New York: Viking Press, 1962) edited by Paolo Milano, p. 30, lines 127—138.

[13] The first sonnet in Brecht's "Studien" is entitled "Über die Gedichte des Dante auf die Beatrice." There, Brecht crudely mocks the love poem inspired by Platonic rather than physical love. See *Versuche* (Berlin: Aufbau, 1957), Heft 11, p. 81 or GW IX, 608.

with his verses. She is made to read aloud selected portions from certain odes where love and passion are celebrated, as for example: "Jene trunkene Lust, wenn die erweinete / Fast zu selige Stunde kommt, / Die dem Liebenden sagt, daß er geliebet wird!" (GW VI, 2337) In their new context, these selections function as unabashed statements of erotic desire:

> Ha, dort kömmt er mit Schweiss, mit Römerblute,
> Mit dem Staube der Schlacht bedeckt! So schön war
> Hermann niemals! So hats ihm
> Nie von dem Auge geflammt!
>
> Komm'! ich bebe vor Lust, reich' mir den Adler
> Und das triefende Schwert! komm', athm' und ruh' hier
> Aus in meiner Umarmung,
> Von der zu schrecklichen Schlacht. (GW VI, 2337)

Fritz must strike the spectator here as ridiculous: He hardly cuts a very dashing figure as a lover nor does he resemble at all Klopstock's idealized portrait of the fearless Germanic warrior of the days of Varus!

Klopstock is an obvious choice to exemplify Fritz's inwardness, for the poet's works helped usher into German Literature a vogue of unrestrained feeling, which became at times an intoxicated, breathless outpouring of highly aroused emotion and excessive sentiment.

It is possible that Brecht intends Gustchen's cry "Klopstock!" to remind the spectator of an equally passionate moment in a famous work where the spiritual union between lovers is described. One thinks of Lotte and Werther in Goethe's *Leiden des jungen Werthers* of 1774, a work which documents and holds up for caution the immoderate predilection of the age for excessively emotional and sentimental behavior. Werther's letter of the 16th of June records how Lotte:

> ... sah gen Himmel und auf mich, ich sah ihr Auge tränevoll, sie legte ihre Hand auf die meinige und sagte "Klopstock!" Ich erinnerte mich sogleich der herrlichen Ode, die ihr in Gedanken lag, und versank in dem Strome von Empfindungen, den sie in dieser Losung über mich ausgoss. Ich ertrug's nicht, neigte mich auf ihre Hand und küsste sie unter den wonnevollsten Tränen.[14]

In his notes to the *Hofmeister*, the adaptor seriously maintains that Fritz's attempt to seduce Gustchen is an involuntary act:

> Die Abschiedsszene hat zärtlich zu zeigen, wie der junge von Berg sein Bäschen, das mit in den Pavillon möchte, sich vom Leibe und an die Lektüre mit *ununterdrückbaren* Gefühlen erfüllt und er sie unter dem Eid aufs Bett wirft: ein Umweg über die Literatur! (GW XVII, 1224; italics mine)

---

14 The ode of which both Lotte and Werther are thinking is Klopstock's "Die Frühlingsfeier" of 1759.

We are supposed to understand Fritz as powerless in the grip of natural law, compelled to follow the promptings of his aroused sexual desire. Perhaps this physical demonstration of affection exemplifies what Brecht intends when he claims that the truth is concrete. (Of course, Brecht does not really believe in the romantic fiction of lovers who melt into each other's arms; he mocks it in the Pätus-Bollwerk-Rehhaar love triangle and elsewhere, as in the *Dreigroschenoper*. — The important theatrical aspect of the romantic seduction for Brecht is its poetic and artistic quality as a moment of beauty on stage.)[15] The fictions of romantic infatuations are simply out of place in the Marxist Brecht's unadorned depiction of traditional class society in which he sees the basic facts of life as sex and the struggle for survival and power.

In Lenz's *Hofmeister*, Fritz discovers that his threat of romantic suicide and his oaths of eternal loyalty to Gustchen have been overheard. Fritz is all that the Geheimrat calls him: Foolish, childish, and irrational. The youth is too young to dissimulate, too unacquainted with life to refrain from swearing that his love and loyalty are absolute, and too ready to believe that life can imitate the romantic tragedies so glowingly idealized in popular sentimental literature. The criticisms and insights provided by his father point toward the moral values and the ideal of rational behavior according to which Fritz will later develop during his long absence from Gustchen.

On the other hand, in Scene 2 of Brecht's adaptation, Fritz profits little from the criticism and mockery of his (quite different) father. The ironic observations of the Geheimrat about his son's love for Gustchen allow Fritz only submission to paternal domination and self-denial as acceptable alternative behavior. The Privy Councillor seems to be denying the validity of what Fritz has just personally experienced as the inexorable dictates of natural law — the bondage of the sexual urges: "Daß du [Fritz] ... die wahre Freiheit kapierst! Als welche die Menschen von den Tieren unterscheidet. Die Hengste und Stuten müssens, aber die Menschen sind frei, es nicht zu tun." (GW VI, 2338) If, as is shown in the later action of the adaptation, Fritz does follow his father's advice consistently, he really uses his reason and his "freedom" to cheat himself by not returning to see Gustchen during his holidays as promised.

The Mature Fritz in Lenz's Drama

In Lenz's drama, during the first year of his absence from Gustchen, Fritz is depicted as constant in his affection for his distant sweetheart; not only does he write letters to her, he also has avoided girls in Halle: "... ein Jahr

---

[15] Brecht discusses the poetic moments of Scene 2 of the adaptation in GW XVII, 1241.

in Halle und noch mit keinem Mädchen gesprochen. . . ." (D I, 60) He lives, it would seem, a reputable, less boisterous life than such student rowdies or *Kerls* as Pätus, for he has a room in a minister's home. Apparently the young aristocrat gives Frau Blitzer, Pätus's landlady, the impression of being orderly, self-disciplined and in possession of all the desirable middle-class virtues, for she believes that his influence would greatly improve Pätus's habits and his character: ". . . wenn doch der Herr von Berg zu uns einlogiren thäte. Ich weiß, daß Sie viel Gewalt über ihn haben: da könnte doch noch was ordentliches aus ihm werden, aber sonst wahrhaftig." (D I, 62)

Although Fritz — in Lenz's *Hofmeister* — attempts to correspond with Gustchen, the distractions of student life prove greater than his good intentions. Later, his imprisonment, his flight with Pätus from their creditors, and his university studies in Leipzig cause him to disregard his promise to return to Gustchen. But these crises and sobering experiences greatly contribute to building his character and molding strong moral values. The result is that Fritz matures into a man of sympathy and love for his fellows. (He stands by his friend Pätus, goes to jail in his stead, and believes in him when everyone else disowns him.) He becomes the advocate of rational, sober, responsible behavior. This is brought out in IV, 6 when he cautions Pätus: "Wir sind in den Jahren; wir sind auf der See, der Wind treibt uns, aber die Vernunft muß immer am Steuerruder bleiben, sonst jagen wir auf die erste beste Klippe und scheitern." (D I, 92) The financial and emotional scrapes of Pätus have taught Fritz that yielding to impulse eventually brings only unhappiness and debts: "Die Hamstern war eine Kokette, die aus Dir machte, was sie wollte . . . ." (D I, 92) Possessing a steadfast fraternal love for Pätus, Fritz sees the potential good in his friend and brings it to fruition by providing him with understanding, encouragement, and the opportunity to act honorably toward Old Rehaar and his daughter. Fritz also brings out the best in Bollwerk, inspiring him nobly to defend Pätus against the unscrupulous von Seiffenblase and his tutor.

The Fritz of Lenz's drama becomes an exemplary moral preceptor of his peers, a reflective, mature guide who masters his impetuosity and desire for self-gratification at the expense of others. On a larger scale, he becomes a link between the aristocracy and the middle class, for his greatest friendships are among commoners.

On his return to Insterburg and Gustchen, he comes as a penitent seeking the forgiveness of his father for having — so he believes — deceived Gustchen and caused her death. Instead, he finds that it is he himself who must prove his good will and love, for he is called upon to forgive Gustchen. He is prepared to do so because he acknowledges a coresponsibility for her fall and pardons the frailty of women and the impulsive nature of men. Lenz regards Fritz as the bringer of Christian love — for his father, for Gustchen, and for mankind — as symbolized by her illegitimate son. By marrying Gustchen and adopting her child as his own, Fritz postulates a new social ethic of forgiveness and advances society a step further toward humane toleration and acceptance of its members' weaknesses.

Turning now to Brecht's adaptation, one sees that in his Scene 6, as in Lenz's II, 3, Fritz's main dramaturgical function is still that of passive observer. (Brecht: "Fritz muß als der beobachtende Gast gespielt werden" GW XVII, 1227.) In the adapted drama, it is not the petty issues leading to the vociferous outbursts between Blitzer, Bollwerk, and Pätus that interest Fritz, but the opportunity to discover more about sex: "... die Physiologie nicht zu vergessen" (GW VI, 2349) and current idealistic philosophy: "... Ich will mich auch auf die Philosophie werfen." (GW VI, 2353) It is between these two poles, the real and the ideal, that Fritz and Pätus waver in all that they say and do.

From the little that he says in Scene 6, Fritz reveals himself as an inconsistent thinker and a person who is easily swayed by others. At first, he speaks against Pätus's interest in Kant, yet soon after, he declares somewhat unexpectedly — as noted above — that he would like to "fling himself" into philosophy. Bollwerk has urged the stubborn Pätus to reject Kant's teachings: "Repetiers: der Herr Kant ist ein Schwachkopf" and Fritz pleads pragmatically: "Kannst dus nicht sagen, daß du durchkommst?" (GW VI, 2351) Such an attitude apparently seems natural to Fritz, because there are no universally accepted values which would encourage him to stand firm. Lenz's Fritz, it should be noted, could neither counsel such dissimulation nor advocate expediency in place of principle. In the adaptation, it is perhaps the stalwart idealism of Pätus and his vigorous defense of Kant which change Fritz's mind and arouse in him a desire to learn more about philosophy.

The young von Berg is not yet so interested in the abstract that he turns his back completely on sex. Brecht notes Fritz's apparent inconsistency and remarks: "Fritz entscheidet sich für die Philosophie, geht aber doch mit Bollwerk, Mädchen zu sehen." (GW XVII, 1227) What now are harmless, contradictory intentions within Fritz develop later into a serious but short-lived conflict of interest in Scene 9.

Throughout the adaptation, Fritz is conceived of as an ineffectual young man. Brecht strengthens such a view of the young aristocrat by deleting a significant remark made by Frau Blitzer in Lenz's drama: "Ich weiß, daß Sie [Herr von Berg] viel Gewalt über ihn [Pätus] haben." (D I, 62) In the adaptation, however, Fritz has no influence at all over Pätus, nor does he actively seek to change Pätus's ways. The young von Berg neither advances personal ideals, nor posits a social ethic according to which he would have Pätus and others live. — Only Kant's Ethics and Frau Blitzer's stormy reproaches seriously determine Pätus's behavior. — And, as indicated in Brecht's totally new Scene 9, Fritz seems inexorably drawn to Pätus by these same ethics.

But is Fritz really attracted by his friend's espousal of (what Brecht ironically portrays as) Kant's view of duty? At first, Fritz seems so won over by the ostensibly noble and responsible attitude of Pätus toward the pregnant Jungfer Rehhaar that, in the spirit of friendship, he offers him his travel money[16] to pay for her abortion. Later, however, despite his professed desire to learn more about Kant's ideas, it is clear that Fritz really fears he would exchange his present freedom for domesticity, if he visited Gustchen during the holidays as promised. Fritz's claim that he is objective and rational about his reason for visiting her is hollow:

> ... so laß es denn keine Wallung des Gemüts sein! Das Denken entscheide! Mein Mädchen erwartet mich in den Ferien, sie gesteht es mir in diesem Briefe. *Liest:* "In den Osterferien wirst du eine kühnere Julie wiederfinden!" Empfange mein Geständnis, mein Pätus: der Passus hat mich geängstiget. Nein, glaub mir, 's ist eben besser, ich fahr nicht nach Insterburg dieses Jahr. Ich möcht der alte keusche Joseph nicht mehr sein. Hab ich mich doch auch entwickelt in eurem Halle! (GW VI, 2360)

He could not be more subjective about his decision.

Fritz is correct to suspect that Gustchen's challenge: "In den Osterferien wirst du eine kühnere Julie wiederfinden" alludes to her strong sexual desire for him. Brecht intends such an interpretation, for in an earlier version of the adaptation, BBA 541 of level B, the remark was spoken by Gustchen when, already seduced and in bed with Läuffer, she imagined a letter she would send to her absent Fritz: "Du hast mich vergessen, ich aber gedenke deiner. In den Osterferien wirst du eine kühnere Julie wiederfinden...." (BBA 541/38)

Fritz's decision appears noble and unselfish to Pätus, who sees it as a pure manifestation of Kant's Categorical Imperative: "Handle nur nach derjenigen Maxime, durch die du zugleich wollen kannst, daß sie ein allgemeines Gesetz werde." (GW VI, 2361) But the general law which Fritz posits is not that of unselfish, altruistic action independent of all inclination; Fritz's law would seem to be: Abuse your freedom of action in the name of reason.

In choosing not to visit Gustchen, Fritz fulfills the wish expressed by his father[17] in Scene 2 of the adaptation: "Daß du ... die wahre Freiheit kapierst! Als welche die Menschen von den Tieren unterscheidet. Die Hengste und Stuten müssens, aber die Menschen sind frei, es nicht zu tun ... die Vernunft ist eine gestrenge Herrin." (GW VI, 2338—39) Brecht interprets Fritz's gesture of free will — the fact that he does not wish to sleep with Gustchen — as symbolic of his self-emasculation: "Es ist der Moment seiner Selbstentmannung, und sie hat denselben heroischen Akzent, den die des

---

[16] It is hard to imagine a more grotesque distortion of Kant's idea of duty or more corrosive anti-romanticism than this episode concerning the abortion. See note 29, this chapter.

[17] In a series of notes to the *Hofmeister* adaptation, one of the junior co-directors, Alexander Koval, supports my interpretation: "Fritz findet an einem konkreten Fall die Erziehungsprinzipien seines Vaters, damit seine eigenen Anschauungen, damit seine Freundeswahl, damit seine Wendung zur Philosophie bestätigt .." (BBA 1567/78)

armen Läuffers haben wird." (GW XVII, 1231) Just as Läuffer believes he is sure to profit from his desperate act, so Fritz, too, believes he has more to gain from renouncing Gustchen: "... ich werde den besseren Teil unseres Handels gewinnen." (GW VI, 2360)

In the passage in Scene 9 of the adaptation where Fritz tells Pätus of his decision not to visit Gustchen, Brecht employs an expression suggestive of penitence in the confessional: "Empfange mein Geständnis, mein Pätus [Pater!]!" After such a suggestive opening statement, it is natural to expect that one will hear an admission of sins, a desire to avoid temptation, and a solemn resolution to atone for having sinned. Fritz's sins, if he has any, are only in the mind; for it is only in the imagination — *im Geiste,* an epithet Brecht uses repeatedly in the adaptation and his notes to it — that he has consummated his love with his sweetheart. To picture Fritz in the role of penitent and Pätus as father confessor is to render the two figures comic, if not ludicrous.

Brecht sustains this comic effect by allusion to a Biblical figure. Fritz refers to himself: "Ich möcht der alte keusche Joseph nicht mehr sein" but he does not envisage sleeping with Gustchen as an immoral, wicked act. The Biblical figure of Joseph (Genesis 39:7—20) rejects the invitations of Potiphar's wife to lie with her, saying: "... how then can I do this great wickedness, and sin against God?" (King James, Gen. 39:9) The comparison of Fritz to the Biblical Joseph has limited validity; all that the two men have in common is that each resists temptation. Their reasons for doing so are quite different. Whereas Joseph resists Potiphar's wife on strong moral and religious grounds — he would abuse Potiphar's trust, and, even worse, sin against God who constantly protects and favors him in his exile — Fritz resists Gustchen in order to preserve *his* virginity and his freeedom. But ironically, as Brecht shows, the result is something else altogether: A veritable although symbolic self-emasculation due to the tyranny of reason!

Whereas Lenz's Fritz matures into a sober and very rational, moral young man during his absence from Gustchen, Brecht's figure fails to develop similarly; he remains as emotional and subjective as ever. The adaptor is particularly careful to stress the immaturity and emotionalism of Fritz in Scenes 15 and 16. The former scene is almost all Brecht's invention except for the episode of Seiffenblase's letter to Fritz. The adaptor mocks the classic trip of education — the journey to Italy — by indicating that Fritz goes there for the wrong reasons. The Geheimrat sent his son to Italy not because he wished to familiarize him with Classical Antiquity but because he wished to prevent him from hearing of Gustchen's scandal: "Meinen Sohn schick ich nach Italien, er darfs gar nicht erfahren." (GW VI, 2373) His excitement in travelling to Rome is matched only by his feverish alarm in returning to Insterburg. After six months abroad without news of Gustchen, Fritz becomes so anxious about her welfare that he literally flees Italy.

Brecht's choice of words in this scene reveals that the emotional rather than the rational predominates in Fritz. The young aristocrat describes his feelings in such terms as "Ekstase des Reisefiebers;" "aufsteigende Besorgnis;" he explains exaggeratedly: "Eine plötzliche Unruhe in Pompeji treibt mich mit Macht zurück. Eine nicht geringere Bewegung des Gemüts läßt mich die überstürzte Heimreise — mit jagender Kutsche oft zu achtzig Meilen pro Tag — hier in Halle abbrechen...." (GW VI, 2385) The language suggests strongly that the important thing for Fritz is not what reality is like, but what he feels it is like, i.e., not what he experiences, but what he imagines.

Why is Fritz in Brecht's Scene 16 a ridiculous figure, a much less responsible individual than his counterpart in the corresponding scenes (V, 11 and 12) of Lenz's *Hofmeister?* The reasons become clear when we examine Gustchen's behavior before and after her seduction, Fritz's degree of maturity, and the didactic purpose of each author.

In Lenz's drama, Gustchen is apparently sincere in her relationship with Läuffer; he seems to be in love with her and she yields to him not without some show of affection because she is able to pretend that he is Fritz. Unlike Gustchen in Lenz's drama, Brecht's figure is not the pining, love-sick girl for long; she regains her former good health once Läuffer arrives. She flirts with him, egging him on until finally they yield to each other. There is no love between the two; each merely uses the other to satisfy physical lust.

Whereas Lenz's Gustchen experiences moral and religious guilt and tries in delirium to take her own life as atonement for what she considers her immoral behavior and betrayal of her father's love, Gustchen in the adaptation feels neither guilt nor remorse, and artfully tricks her father into rescuing her from a cleverly simulated suicide attempt.

Toward the end of Lenz's drama, Gustchen is described as a truly repentant sinner. The dramatist consciously tries to make her appear worthy of Fritz's forgiveness. In contrast, as becomes evident in Scene 16 of Brecht's adaptation, her affair with Läuffer and her motherhood have incurred neither Christian nor moral stigma. Nor is there any indication that Brecht's Gustchen feels shame or guilt for having betrayed her oath of loyalty to Fritz. She cannot, therefore, convince us that she is worthy of the young man's forgiveness. She is the artful, brazen hypocrite when she agrees with Fritz's explanation of why she was unfaithful: "O mein Fritz, so war es, nie anders!" (GW VI, 2389)

In both Lenz's drama and the adaptation, Fritz blames himself for Gustchen's seduction. There is, however, a difference, both in the characters and in their reasons for laying the blame on themselves. In the Storm and Stress play, Fritz is portrayed as the sober, mature, penitent lover. He believes that Gustchen committed suicide because Läuffer had seduced her. He blames himself for her death, admitting that he had broken his oath of loyalty and neglected her: "Schuldig war ich; einzig und allein schuldig. Gustchen, seliger Geist, verzeihe mir!" (D I, 117) Contrite and ashamed, he reproaches himself: "Ich habe geschworen, falsch geschworen...." (D I, 117) To be sure, Lenz offers a portrait of an emotional Fritz here, but it is, after all, a mature and serious person in the grip of the most powerful emotions. And if Fritz did contemplate briefly a romantic suicide ("Gustchen! Wär es erlaubt, Dir nachzuspringen! *Steht hastig auf.* Wo ist der Teich? [D I, 117]) before his unexpected reunion with a very much alive Gustchen, his wish to die in her arms is a joyous release from intense grief, self-condemnation, and the burden of sin he had assumed ("Himmel! Himmel welche Freude! — Laß mich sterben! laß mich an Deinem Halse sterben" [D I, 118]). Behind the apparent exaggerations of his rather emotional statements here, Fritz is still really the strong, resolute man with firm principles and a stout social conscience.

In the corresponding scene in the *Hofmeister* adaptation, however, Fritz cuts no such figure. Here in Scene 16, Brecht portrays the emotional, inward individual, the romantic idealist. In Lenz's drama, Fritz invokes Gustchen's departed spirit and pleads with her to forgive his severe religious and moral guilt. In the adaptation, Fritz is confronted with a flesh-and-blood Gustchen. As we shall see, his plea for forgiveness must be interpreted really only as a wish to be excused from having physically neglected her! How to react to her infidelity is his only problem, for Brecht has omitted all reference to the moral issue of Fritz's broken oath and his religious guilt.

Brecht's Fritz is even more unlike Lenz's figure because he is made to seem emasculated, in fact, he behaves more like a woman than a man. Conventional male opinion would probably claim that in Brecht's play Fritz is really the injured party in his relationship with Gustchen and that she should beg his forgiveness. Fritz gives the impression of being spineless because Brecht offers the reverse of what one conventionally expects. Hence Fritz pleads for Gustchen's forgiveness. The young von Berg's statement: "Ich weiß alles..." (GW VI, 2389) fosters in us the strong impression that he would prefer not to know what really occurred between Gustchen and Läuffer; his remark is blurted out loudly, "...daß mans hören konnte bis in die Küche" (GW VI, 2389), as though to silence Gustchen. On the spur of the moment, this may seem to him the easiest way out of a delicate situation. Uncertain of his next move, he stutters impotently, as though stalling while groping for a solution: "...und alles, was ich tue, ist — ich bitte dich um Verzeihung." (GW VI, 2389) To be sure, on the surface his words may be interpreted as a sign of his great tenderness and his magnanimous spirit — but only by such sentimental people as the maid who reports these offstage remarks. In the eyes of his cynical relatives, however, he appears somewhat the fool, the "sucker,"[18] confident that he has struck a fine bargain, yet unaware that he is the victim of his own trusting, considerate nature.

Once onstage in Scene 16, Fritz behaves much like the immature romantic hero that he was in Scene 2 of the adaptation. There, he had boasted to Gustchen: "Verlange mein Leben, meinen letzten Tropfen Bluts." (GW VI, 2338) (This exclamation is taken verbatim from the corresponding episode

---

[18] See Brecht's definition of a "sucker," GW XVII, 1206.

in Lenz's Act I, Scene 5.) Echoing this statement, he pleads in Scene 16 of the adaptation: "Mein Vater! Meine zweiten Eltern! Lasset mich kämpfen mit meinem letzten Blutstropfen um mein Gustchen." (GW VI, 2389)[19] (The fact that Fritz still uses the same clichés as he did three years earlier [in Scene 2] reveals that he has changed little; what could be important experiences in reality are for him more satisfying as the vicarious thrills of a romantic imagination.) Such exaggerated and desperate heroics are as out of place at this point in the action as they are unexpected. Like Shakespeare's Romeo, Fritz behaves as though Gustchen (Juliet) were about to be married to another man on the spot.

It is necessary to ask why Fritz must declaim so desperately in Brecht's adaptation, particularly since the corresponding scene in Lenz's drama offers no precedent. Because there are no other suitors for Gustchen's hand, because neither Fritz's father nor the Major, nor Gustchen herself, are disputing his right to marry her, Fritz's grand manner appears unwarranted. It is also incongruous, for he speaks as though Gustchen were a valuable prize rather than "damaged merchandise."

There are two dramaturgical reasons for Fritz's behavior, one of which we have already touched upon briefly above. Firstly, Brecht conceived of Fritz's emotionalism (and that of the maid) in Scene 16 as a poetic quality, as a pleasantly humorous counter-comment to the previous episode of the scene in which the aristocrats vent their scorn on the emasculated Läuffer and his petition: "Die Erzählung der Magd und die Rede Fritz von Bergs sind als Bravourstücke zu bringen: beide Personen geben sich begeistert der wohlgelittenen Innigkeit hin." (GW XVII, 1248) Given the comic "happy end," some melodrama is appropriate.

Fritz's insistence on marrying Gustchen, although comic, is also fraught with the tragic — and this reveals the shortcomings in his character. His impassioned defense of Gustchen and his idealistic explanation of her behavior "... ihrem wahren Geliebten gab sie sich wirklich hin, im Geiste, lieber Vater" (GW VI, 2389) show not only how grossly Fritz misjudges reality, but also how little importance real events have for him personally.

He is taken in completely by the "cooked-up" story which Bollwerk and Rehhaar told to Pätus; he believes that it offers a valid parallel to the Gustchen-Läuffer relationship and has no interest in learning what really went on between the two. Fritz's blindness to real problems has broad

---

[19] Contrast Fritz's heroic statement here with Ziffel's dry remark in *Flüchtlingsgespräche* (GW XIV, 1386—87): "Auch der letzte Blutstropfen ist wichtig." Here, the expression, no longer a meaningless cliché, is used in a conversation about social and military situations in which its literal, concrete meaning contrasts starkly with the shallow, romantic effervescence associated with the epithet as Fritz uses it. Although Fritz's use of the expression is superficial, it indicates that he possesses that uncritical spirit which Brecht condemned earlier in Pätus's harangue about Germans: " ... Untertänigkeit, in dem sie [the Germans] doch nur selig sind, wenn sie Knechte sein können, am liebsten Kriegsknechte, als welche sie sich für irgendein Oberhaupt aufopfern!" (GW VI, 2351)

social implications. As Elisabeth Hauptmann indicated,[20] Brecht felt that Fritz and his kind — potentially capable of initiating needed social reform — had failed German society. Now wittingly, now unwittingly, they accepted without protest infringements on their own rights and on the rights of others. Their ideal of how life should be clouded their vision of how life actually was.

A characteristic example of Fritz's self-deception occurs in Scene 16 of the adaptation when the young von Berg speaks joyfully of Gustchen as being alive: "Und sie [sic] Wirklichkeit," whereupon the Geheimrat replies significantly: "An die treulich dich zu halten ich dir lehrte — falls sie nicht dem innern Bild widerspräche." (GW VI, 2389) The idea or ideal should consistently remain the more important of the two, as far as the Privy Councillor is concerned.

That he must accept Gustchen's child by Läuffer comes as a momentary shock to Fritz. To be sure, it is, as the Privy Councillor says, the logical next step after he has already pardoned her fall: "Mein Sohn. Er hat die Ursach sanktionieret, nun fahr Er gefälligst nicht zurück vor der Folge... Wozu hat Er seine Logik studieret?" (GW VI, 2390) Although he may triumph abstractly by arguing that Gustchen is not to blame, Fritz ends as the loser in reality. Brecht's rhetorical question is implied: "How can positive steps toward social change be expected from such an individual and his class, if their idealism leads them to approve tacitly of obvious injustice?"

Because the privileges of his class and his inherited wealth spare him from having to commit himself to definite principles and an active role in society, Brecht's Fritz can remain the dreamer. He may have been disillusioned (in Scene 15) in his once high expectations of Pätus's championing Kant's ethics and pacifism but he has no ideals of his own, no mission to which to dedicate himself.

At one point early in the genesis of the adaptation, Brecht thought of making Fritz a representative of the intellectuals and teachers of the play:

GEHEIMRAT: Und was, darf ich fragen, willst du [Fritz] werden, mein Ritter von der Runden Tafel?
FRITZ: Schullehrer.
GEHEIMRAT: Aber an der Staatsschule, hoff' ich. (BBA 541/105)

But such a plan and this portion of the dialogue were dropped in subsequent levels of the adaptation. Brecht's emphasis on the aristocracy as a class which ignored social problems and scorned the middle class precludes Fritz from undertaking such a bourgeois occupation as teacher. Brecht's aristocrats are, by definition, interested only in preserving the status quo. In Lenz's drama, however, Fritz von Berg is, as we have seen, an exemplary figure and a link between the classes because the author conceives of him as a man with a mission.

---

[20] In my interviews with her on February 4 and 6, 1970.

Pätus in Lenz's "Hofmeister": A Means to a Moral End

In Lenz's drama, Pätus occupies a secondary role in the subplot and is less a character in his own right than a means to the author's didactic ends. The dramaturgical function of Pätus is to act as a foil for Fritz; i.e., it is necessary for him to err as he does, so that Fritz's development as a highly moral and rational individual may be motivated. Sociologically, Pätus is a target for Lenz's criticism of a certain type of student — the impulsive, irresponsible but colorful *Kerl*. Lenz wishes to establish high standards of ethical behavior toward women and to show how adherence to such standards benefits the individual and society.

The course of the friendship between Pätus and Fritz illustrates this goal: Pätus is forgiven by his father, receives his fortune, and can restore Jungfer Rehaar's honor by marrying her. Lenz's Pätus, like Fritz, undergoes a development toward the positive. Each becomes an exemplary figure by achieving moral self-perfection. As Lenz shows, the attainment of this improbable goal is possible only when reason and *humanitas* prevail over self-interest, and free will over external necessity.

Lenz's Pätus exhibits a rather weak character. Rowdy, and selfish in his relationship with Frau Blitzer, he is foolish and unable to govern his finances as well as his emotions. His creditors and the young women about town take him for all he is worth. Fritz comments:

> Er hat nie gewußt mit Geld umzugehen und gab jedem was er verlangte. Hätt' ihm ein Bettler das letzte Hemd vom Leibe gezogen und dabei gesagt: mit Ihrer Erlaubnis, lieber Herr Pätus, er hätt's ihm gelassen. Seine Kreditores giengen mit ihm um wie Stras[s]enräuber. . . . (D I, 71—72)

The young von Berg reminds Pätus: "Die Hamstern war eine Kokette, die aus Dir machte, was sie wollte." (D I, 92) She can manipulate him because he lacks sophistication and firm principles, definite goals and self-knowledge. But apparently he is audacious and forward with the innocent Jungfer Rehaar. Again Fritz analyzes him: "Ich kenne Dich, ich weiß, so dreust Du scheinst, bist Du doch blöde gegen's Frauenzimmer. . . ." (D I, 93) (As is discussed later, Brecht's Pätus exhibits these same traits that Fritz notes.)

Although he is loyal to Fritz and respects him, Pätus — in Lenz's drama — cowardly takes advantage of Old Rehaar's timidity, insulting and striking him. He also threatens physical violence when criticizing other people (Hanke the tailor) and actually becomes violent when Bollwerk or Blitzer criticize him. His personality is altogether unstable; his behavior fluctuates from one extreme to another. Strong when confronted with the weak, Pätus is, in turn, weak when he has to deal with the strong. Although he can verbally browbeat Frau Blitzer in Act II, Scene 3: ". . . aber potz, wenn ich auch einmal ernsthaft werde, kusch ist sie wie die Wand" (D I, 62), his show of bravado is really compensatory behavior for an acutely felt sense of inferiority and inadequacy. In part, his aggressiveness is due to his financial and social embarrassment. He has wasted his money in extravagant living and has pawned his last frock coat. As a result, he depends wholly on Frau Blitzer's extending him credit and remains virtually a prisoner in his own room.

His need to build himself up as capable and fearless, and to be accepted by Fritz borders on the compulsive. No sooner has Frau Blitzer threatened him: "Nichts als Schaden und Unglück kann Er machen. Ich will Dich verklagen; ich will Dich in Karcer werfen lassen" (D I, 63), then he reacts — once she has left the room — with threats of aggression and tells Fritz: "... wenn mirs der Mann gesagt hätte, das wär was anders, dem schlüg' ich das Leder voll — Siehst Du wohl!" (D I, 63) Indeed, Pätus tries hard to appear privately what he cannot be in public, namely, confident, successful, and respected.

The impetuous, good-natured boisterousness of Lenz's own student days is reflected in Pätus and his somewhat more belligerent friend, Bollwerk.[21] In a humorous fashion, the latter teases Pätus about Hanke who has refused to make a coat for him on credit: "Der verfluchte Hanke! Wollen wir gehn und ihm die Haut vollschlagen? ... Wollen ihm die Fenster einschlagen...." (D I, 64) Later, in II, 7, Bollwerk's pugnaciousness becomes further apparent when he tries to pick a fight with von Seiffenblase.

Given Pätus's frustrations and show of aggressive behavior, it is interesting to note that Lenz stopped short of developing the figure along two separate, i.e., schizophrenic lines but simply considered the young man's difficulties as temporary and part of the trial and error process of maturation and self-recognition. It is possible to infer from Pätus's bickerings with Frau Blitzer and his boasts to Fritz that his character could have been further developed along diverging lines. He might then have appeared as an inward-looking person who regarded his mental image of himself as the fearless, undaunted champion more real than his actual fearful and ineffectual self. To be sure, there is no such split in the Pätus of Lenz's drama but it would seem that Brecht perceived the potential dualism in Lenz's Pätus. In the adapted figure, a marked division is exhibited between his behavior as a coward dealing with or, rather, bungling real issues and as an idealist postulating ethical absolutes.

---

[21] Cf. A. Schöne, *Säkularisation als sprachbildende Kraft*, p. 90: "Die Studentenszenen, die um ihn [Pätus] und Fritz spielen, sind Nachfahren jener Studentenkomödie des 16. und 17. Jahrhunderts, die ihre Helden in den lasterhaften Vergnügungen des Universitätslebens zeigt, sie in diesem Sumpfe untergehen läßt oder aber gebessert aus ihm hervorzieht." Schöne appends a note to this statement: "Vgl. etwa Christoph. Stymmelius, Martin Hayneccius, Albert Wichgrev, Georg Mauricius, Joh. Georg Schoch."

Most of what happens to Pätus in Brecht's play is entirely the invention of the adaptor. His very different didactic goals — which will be discussed at the end of this chapter — necessitate a complete revision of the action as well as the economic conditions affecting Pätus. Actually, Brecht's Pätus is a much more interesting and significant figure than his counterpart in Lenz's drama. The adapted protagonist does, however, still possess some of the important character traits of Lenz's figure. He can cope neither with his financial affairs nor with personalities stronger than his own; and he is even more imbecilic in his behavior toward Jungfer Rehhaar than the original Pätus. Whereas Lenz portrays the basic contradiction in Pätus's behavior as a vacillation between acts of bravado and cowardice, Brecht resolves this ambivalence in the adapted figure by splitting him bodily, as it were, into his two contradictory halves and then creating two new characters: One who is essentially a coward in interpersonal relations (Pätus), and the other a loud-mouthed bully (Bollwerk). The adapted Bollwerk is no longer the unimportant tangential character of Lenz's drama but now assumes the blustery role the original Pätus played in opposition to the tempestuous Frau Blitzer. Brecht then renders the simplified Pätus more complex by adding a complication of his own: Pätus remains a physical coward but becomes a heroic figure on an intellectual level, at least for a short time.

In Brecht's adaptation, the new Pätus is depicted at first as a starry-eyed, impractical, ridiculous figure. He fails to notice that Bollwerk — now his roommate — does not contribute his share to the expenses for room and board:

PÄTUS: Wir zahlen — was zahlen wir, Bollwerk?
BOLLWERK: Nichts.
. . .
FRITZ: Helft Ihr einander aus? Ihr seid brave Burschen.
PÄTUS: Halb und halb. Ich könnt mirs allein nicht leisten. (GW VI, 2348—49)

The irony of the situation is that Pätus believes that Bollwerk does help him out. Actually, Pätus must pay the lodging for both and has no money left for personal expenses. "Bruder Bollwerk" (GW VI, 2348) was hardly brotherly in disregarding the fact that Pätus had to pawn his frock coat half a year earlier to pay Frau Blitzer the rent; nor does he now offer to help Pätus redeem the coat. Pätus, who tries to be agreeable to everybody, is blind to his exploitation by Bollwerk. The important question is: Does he voluntarily overlook the abuse he receives — in order to retain Bollwerk's friendship — or is he really so preoccupied with other things that he fails to notice how he is treated? At this point, the latter seems to be true. The idea of true friendship so possesses him that he fails to see how he is taken advantage of when he responds generously to demands made on this friendship. Later, in Scene 9, he unquestioningly pays the (borrowed) sum his roommate requests for Jungfer Rehhaar's abortion.

Brecht endows Bollwerk with the strong and domineering qualities of Lenz's Pätus; as a result the adapted Pätus from the start gives the impression that he has lost his manhood. In contrast, Brecht's Bollwerk is demonstratively oversexed. He also has the first words in the scene, words spoken formerly by Pätus in Lenz's drama. His conversation is a constant source of sexual puns. Whenever Lenz's Pätus refers to girls, now, either the adapted Pätus makes no mention of them or else Bollwerk develops the topic. The original Pätus remarks to Fritz, for example: "...ein Jahr in Halle und noch mit keinem Mädchen gesprochen..." (D I, 60), whereas in the adaptation, Bollwerk greets the young aristocrat with "Drei Monate in Halle und noch mit keinem Mädchen gesprochen!" (GW VI, 2348) In BBA 544/29, Bollwerk's remark ended with the verb "gelegen" but this was subsequently struck and Lenz's "gesprochen" restored.

If Bollwerk is shamelessly direct: "Man will nicht schlafen, weil man liebt; man liebt, weil man schlafen will" (GW VI, 2348), Pätus is foolishly defeatist and, one suspects, cerebral in his relations with women. He finds it a convenient excuse that his lack of a coat prevents him from visiting and wooing Jungfer Rehhaar. Apparently, he sublimates his sensual yearnings, a fact which Bollwerk vulgarizes: "Er träumt von ihr. Das Leintuch muß es büßen. Ich lehr Ihm [Fritz]: Sag mir von welcher du träumst, und ich sag dir, mit welcher du nicht geschlafen hast." (GW VI, 2349) Brecht's view of love and physical attraction is pragmatic. To experience life is, for him, to admit only the significance of the physical while dismissing the imaginative and spiritual as illusory.

Brecht's coarseness may amuse but — because it treats a topic normally taboo in polite conversation — it also functions as a powerful alienating effect which jars the spectator and causes him to ask how Bollwerk can be oblivious to the far-reaching social and political issues which Pätus raises. For Bollwerk, sexual satisfaction is the only goal worth striving for. By his own admission, he states that, unlike Pätus, he is unaffected by the "...Streit der Geister...." (GW VI, 2351) As he puts it: "Nein, ich werd Hofmeister, da geht's in die Klausur in einem abgelegenen Nest, ich muß mich bevor weidlich ausleben." (GW VI, 2352)

Brecht's J'accuse is partially masked here, for the conversation between the three students abruptly turns to other things. But the spectre of the Mitläufer, the traitor by default of protest, is raised, and at a very early point in the drama, too. Just as in the dramas of the mature Lessing, so also in those of the later Brecht, there is never a superfluous word; every statement is purposeful, concise, and hard-hitting. Hence, Bollwerk's rejoinder to Fritz must be examined more closely! Imposing, forceful, but apolitical, Bollwerk seems headed for a career which may parallel that of Läuffer. Probably, he will suffer like temptations, frustrations, and abuse; he may forced by economic misery to seek an accommodation with his employers, the nobility, and — like Läuffer and Galilei — expressly agree, or even volunteer, to teach their version of the truth in return for (half-hearted) assurances of the most meagre material security.

What eventually happens to Bollwerk will be less tragic for him than for his future pupils and mankind. What Brecht says of Läuffer in the epilogue also applies to Bollwerk: "Gebrochen ist sein Rückgrat. Seine Pflicht / Ist, daß er nun das seiner Schüler bricht." (GW VI, 2394) He will always find some minor, fleeting satisfaction for himself because he is an opportunist through and through. He already has no qualms about abusing Pätus. It is tragic for society that, a eunuch intellectually, this virile braggart[22] lacks any real concern for education and any desire to improve his profession; it is tragic that he accepts the status quo without the slightest protest; it is tragic that his acquiescence will prolong the devitalizing conditions to which he yields.

It is surprising that Pätus, the pure-minded idealist who — as we shall see later — courageously sets himself up as a pillar of strength in opposition to "der ganzen teutschen Untertänigkeit" (GW VI, 2351) should fail to realize that he harbors in Bollwerk the very kind of person whose servant mentality he inveighs against in the name of idealism, progress, and political liberty. It is the constant failing of Pätus that his idealism obscures his judgment of things as they are. He is the worst judge of character, and guilty of the shamefully optimistic belief that Bollwerk means well despite his actions to the contrary. In this regard, the apolitical Pätus is a symbolic figure, like Herr Biedermann in the play *Biedermann und die Brandstifter* by Max Frisch.

Pätus and his Defense of Kant:
Perpetual War or Perpetual Peace?

In the initial exposition in Scene 6, Brecht's various additions to Frau Blitzer's part in the dialogue make it explicitly clear that Pätus so loses himself in intellectual matters that he neglects equally important real situations in everyday life. What in Lenz's drama is the landlady's good-natured scolding becomes undisguised contempt:

---

[22] In the section of his notes to the *Hofmeister*, entitled "Über das Poetische und Artistische," Brecht's remarks tend to "whitewash" the biting criticism which — it would seem to me — was to be regarded seriously in the play itself: "Die Darstellung des freiheitlichen Zugs, herrschend in den Universitätsstädten der Zeit, darf nicht darunter leiden, daß die Freiheit als eine recht begrenzte gezeigt wird. Selbst die Zotenreißerei Bollwerks hat eher den Charakter des "Sich-grenzenlos-Erdreustens." (GW XVII, 1243) It is possible that Brecht did not consciously see Bollwerk as I have interpreted him. But as I have shown, Bollwerk is very much the *collaborateur*, even if only potentially at this point in his development.

Zu Pätus: Räum Er die Bücher vom Tisch, sie sind so für nichts und wieder nichts. All die schönen teuren Bücher, und Er weiß immer noch nicht, wo der Hase läuft!

. . .

Das vierte Jahr ist er im Examen Philosophikus durchgerasselt. Warum? Er begreifts nicht! (GW VI, 2350)

Frau Blitzer may be too "limited" to realize the ideological reasons for the repeated failures of Pätus, but she is right to dismiss his academic efforts as irrelevant to tangible goals. (Her adjective "teuren" is indicative of her essentially materialistic outlook.) For Pätus, the only important thing is to insist on the validity of what he believes in; thus, he bravely opposes his professor's rejection of Kantian Ethics and Pacifism.

What are the ideas which Brecht claims are so unpopular with the "establishment"? Bollwerk reads a passage from Kant's *Zum ewigen Frieden* (1795) to illustrate the radical thinking of his friend:

Nach einem beendigten Kriege, beim Friedensschlusse, möchte es wohl für ein Volk nicht unschicklich sein, daß nach dem Dankfeste ein Bußtag ausgeschrieben würde, den Himmel im Namen des Staats um Gnade für die große Versündigung anzurufen, die das menschliche Geschlecht sich noch immer zu Schulden kommen läßt — das barbarische Mittel des Krieges zu gebrauchen. (GW VI, 2351[23])

It is amusing that Bollwerk should "accidentally" select this passage, for it is contained in an obscure footnote in the treatise! It is a significant selection because it reveals how progressive and idealistic Pätus really is in contrast to the popular, simplistic, and pragmatic Wolff who taught, for example, that times of evil were a result of vice and times of good a result of virtue.

It was by a process of trial and error during rehearsals of the adaptation that Brecht and his co-directors eventually succeeded in finding just the right passage in Kant to show that Pätus was right to insist on that philosopher's idealism. Egon Monk discusses this problem in his notes about the Berliner Ensemble rehearsals of the *Hofmeister* in 1950:

Die Figur des Pätus stimmte nicht, solange nicht glaubwürdig gezeigt wurde, daß Pätus mit echter Größe *den Unterwühlungsversuchen Wolffens* stand — und das Panier Kants hochhält. In diesem Punkt muß Pätus eine echte fortschrittliche Haltung zeigen. Das hier verwendete Kantzitat wurde erst in den letzten drei Probenwochen gefunden. Zuvor hatte man an einen Abschnitt über das Ding an sich gedacht. Das Ding an sich machte jedoch dem Zuhörer einen so kon-

---

[23] Brecht's long dash in the excerpt indicates that long clauses have been omitted. The reason for the omissions is, given the length of Kant's periods, simply to improve the intelligibility of the passage when read aloud. In the omitted portions, Kant deplores both the lack of respect that belligerent nations selfishly display for the concept of non-aggression treaties, as well as the fact that war fails to assure the rights of each and every state. Cf. Immanuel Kant, *Werke* (Leipzig: Insel, 1922) Moralische Schriften, vol. 5, pp. 675–676.

fusen Eindruck, daß Pätus letztlich doch als bloßer Wirrkopf dagestanden hätte. Auch hierin hätte man es dann eher mit dem Realisten Bollwerk gehalten. In der jetzigen Fassung hat Bollwerk eindeutig Unrecht, wenn er über Kant herzieht. Auch wenn Pätus mit Kant aufwieglerisch nur im Geiste ist. (BBA 2062/11; italics mine)

Actually, Monk is thinking here of a passage used on an earlier level of the adaptation: "Über den apodiktischen und assertorischen Satz" (BBA 1561/45 and BBA 2062/86) which, in the opinion of the people present at rehearsals, made Pätus seem like a fuzzy-headed clown.[24] The short section of dialogue about the "Ding an sich" was written by Brecht himself and inserted into the *Regiebuch* (BBA 539/45). It was spoken by Bollwerk and made Pätus look silly and otherworldly rather than confused. It caused Bollwerk to appear more a teller of dirty jokes than the antagonist of progressive ideas:

> Wie kann einer schreiben, daß man ein Ding nicht erkennen kann, wo doch jeder Studiosus aus der Praxis weiß, daß er die Dinger ganz vortrefflich erkennen kann, indem man nur das Wort Erkennen richtig auslegt wie der Doktor Martin Luther in der Bibel: "Und Jakob erkannte Lea" als was bedeutet, daß er mit ihr geschlafen hat. (BBA 539/45)

The important point in Brecht's search for a telling passage was that it had to give an example of the noble, humanitarian ideals which the age failed to appreciate other than as abstractions. Neither the selection about the "apodiktischen Satz" nor the ironic interpolation about the "Ding an sich" achieved this aim. Not only does the quotation finally taken from *Zum ewigen Frieden* raise Pätus to the loftiest point in his moral idealism, it also defines more precisely Brecht's anti-war position throughout the drama. It is important to describe the progress toward the solution of this problem in detail because it illustrates how easily Brecht could have failed to develop a powerful polemic thrust and how much a part of the creative process the rehearsals of the adaptation actually were.

The eventual inclusion of this passage from *Zum ewigen Frieden* confirms how right Ruth Berlau was in her criticism early in the process of adaptation. One of her handwritten notes to Brecht reads: "Auch beim Studenten muß es mehr rauskommen wie kastriert die Professoren geworden sind durch Lehren." (BBA 543/69) The fact that Pätus is penalized by his professor for upholding the treatise on eternal peace is supposed to indicate that Wolff fails to see the significance of Kant's ideals for the improvement of social and political conditions. Wolff's opposition to Kant is a sign of his intellectual self-emasculation which — thanks to Berlau — Brecht tries to illustrate in the amusing simile of Pätus: "Wer ist Wolffen! Die Kreatur haßt die Kantschen Freiheitsschriften wie der Kapaun das Hahnenkrähn!" (GW VI, 2351) It was also on the occasion of this addition to the dialogue

---

[24] Cf. I. Kant, *Kritik der reinen Vernunft* (Leipzig: Bibliographisches Institut, 1899) p. 106, lines 17—26.

that Bollwerk's ironic epithets in praise of Pätus were inserted into the text: "[Ich nenns] Seelenstärke. Mich schaudert. Pätus, der Aufrechte! Pätus, der Furchtlose!" (GW VI, 2351)

Bollwerk calls Kant's pacifism nonsense for two reasons: Wolff has brainwashed him, and it is a new, even revolutionary idea for him. — Of course, dramaturgically, Bollwerk has to disagree because he functions as antagonist to Pätus, the protagonist. — Bollwerk reflects the (supposedly) popular belief that wars are a necessary, sure means to attain one's ends. As proof that Pätus is wrong he advances the argument: "Wenn wir beide hier einen Tag aufhörten mit der Blitzer Krieg zu führen, bestünde Ihr Kaffee nur noch aus Gerste." (GW VI, 2351) He suggests further that it is un-German, and hence unpatriotic and wrong, to believe that one can rely on other means than war to gain one's ends. His whole argument becomes invalid when Fritz remarks quietly: "Der Kaffee schmeckt nach Gerste." (GW VI, 2352) Likely, Bollwerk throws[25] the entire coffee service out of the window, not because he is angry at being wrong about war — he fails to see the irony of Fritz's remark — but because he resents being the dupe of Frau Blitzer.

Bollwerk is primarily an opportunist. Although he believes in war, he does not stop to consider the misfortune which Pätus suffers as a result of the recent Seven Years' War. Frau Blitzer informs the spectator quite pointedly: "Seine [Pätus'] Mutter kann einem leid tun, und eine Witwe dazu. Und die Witwen- und Waisenpensionen gekürzt wegen dem [sic] siegreichen Krieg." (GW VI, 2350)[26] As in *Mutter Courage und ihre Kinder,* so here too, Brecht makes abundantly clear that the little man profits nothing from war. As a result of his steadfast opposition to Professor Wolff,[27] Pätus acquires, in the eyes of Fritz, the stature of a moral hero. His resolute loyalty to an ideal is symbolized by the carving of the word "Nein" into his landlady's table. Pätus explains the full significance of his stand:

---

[25] Brecht could sometimes show his abhorrence for Imperial Germany and the Kaiser's militaristic slogans in a humorous "slap-stick" manner. The stage version of the *Hofmeister*-adaptation substituted for Bollwerk's: ""Nun, so hol dich" (GW VI, 2352) — spoken as he throws the coffee out of the window — "Mit Gott für König u. Vaterland." (BBA 2087/43 and in *BEA Eingestrichenes Exemplar*)

[26] In BBA 542/47 Brecht indicates that Pätus's father has fallen in the war and that the lad's mother is hard put to finance his unsuccessful studies for yet another year: "Sie eröffnet mir, daß sie die Pension auf Monate verpfändet. Kärglich wie die eines gefallenen Hauptmanns ist." Such textual emendations indicate how anxious Brecht was to describe intolerable conditions of economic misery that would arouse in the spectator the call for radical change.

[27] Brecht is guilty of distorting historical fact in stating that an actual controversy existed between Wolff and Kant. Freiherr Christian von Wolff (1679–1754) lectured in Halle (where the action of the Pätus subplot occurs) and was already long since dead when Kant (1724–1804) counted Lenz as one of his pupils at Königsberg in 1769–70. Kant's "Freiheitsschriften" (GW VI, 2351), which Pätus claims Wolff hated, were published between 1781 and 1793, and *Zum ewigen Frieden* as late as 1795.

Das ist meine Antwort im fünften Jahr, wenns sein muß. Und dies Nein gilt gleichermaßen der ganzen teutschen Untertänigkeit, indem sie [die Teutschen] doch nur selig sind, wenn sie Knechte sein können, am liebsten Kriegsknechte, als welche sie sich für irgendein Oberhaupt aufopfern! (GW VI, 2351)

Of course, this idealistic and determined pose contrasts starkly with his cringing submissiveness to Frau Blitzer. When she complains that the coffee service has been thrown out of the window and threatens Pätus with jail, as she does in Lenz's drama, Pätus crawls with the obsequiousness of a whipped servant: "Still Mutter, ich zahls... Lassen Sies noch einmal gut sein, Frau Blitzer, es kömmt nicht mehr vor, bitte, Frau Blitzer." (GW VI, 2352) It is already obvious that Pätus is an utter failure in his personal relations. He may not be afraid of his professor, but he cowers before his landlady: "Ich fürcht nichts als die Blitzer, sie hat keinen Verstand." (GW VI, 2353)

Scene 9 of the adaptation is a hilarious, entirely new creation of Brecht. Here the adaptor makes a fool of the idealist Pätus, who is so enamored of abstract truth that he is unable, or more accurately, *unwilling* to recognize truth in reality, i.e., that Jungfer Rehhaar cannot honestly maintain that she loves him despite having just slept with Bollwerk. Pätus is making the mistake of trying to bolster his idealism by nurturing it in a vacuum, protected from the corrective influence of reality: "Ist dann in der Beurteilung Körper oder Geist, was zählt? Es ist eine Frage in re philosophia."[28] (GW VI, 2359) The effort that it takes to believe in the greater truth of the spiritual is almost too much now for Pätus: "Berg, ich bins manchmal fast müd, Philosophie zu betreiben! *Bricht in Tränen aus.*" (GW VI, 2359)

Kant's ideals of duty, moral freedom, and good will are led *ad absurdum* when Pätus insists that he himself must pay for Jungfer Rehhaar's abortion.[29] His insistence is a sign of his moral freedom to do his "duty" and help her, despite his frustration that it was Bollwerk who slept with her. He is so sublime in expressing his good will that he is ridiculous: "Aber für mich geschah es, für wen sonst? Mich liebt sie!" (GW VI, 2359) Pätus seems to believe that Jungfer Rehhaar made love with Bollwerk in the spirit of Kant's Categorical Imperative. Preposterously, he thinks that she did so for him, Pätus, seeing him as a representative of mankind and the beneficiary of her selfless act of love, consummated disinterestedly with Bollwerk!

---

[28] As noted by a recent critic, Brecht intentionally endows Pätus with a faulty command of Latin. Cf. Rainer Pohl, *Strukturelemente und Entwicklung von Pathosformen in der Dramensprache Bertold* [sic] *Brechts* in *Bonner Arbeiten zu deutscher Literatur* (Bonn: Bouvier, 1969), vol. 20, p. 158.

[29] It is grimly ironic that the idea of abortion is not repugnant to either disciple of such a humanist as Kant! Because Pätus and Fritz are so concerned with living up to an abstraction, the ideal of duty to others, they overlook what they are advocating. Neither the moral and societal problems of abortion nor the unfortunate Jungfer Rehhaar herself concern the two students.

In BBA 1561, the earliest level of the adaptation, Brecht had not yet developed such an ironic view of Pätus; there, the hapless lover remarked: "Zu denken, daß sie im Geiste mein ist, mein, mein! Daß im Geiste ich es war, von dem sie...." (BBA 1561/55) Brecht changed this version for several reasons. Least important were dramaturgical considerations, which required that complications in the originally suggested action be omitted. Of greater importance was that the remark as it stood sought only to ridicule Pätus as someone who was completely satisfied with the vicarious experience of sexual love. Also, Pätus seemed to be thinking only selfishly of himself, for the exclamation did not contain the suggestion of the Categorical Imperative. The version which Brecht finally decided on illustrates his intention to show how misleading such idealism is. The danger in valuing the intellectual, vicarious experience more highly than the physical experience is that it obviates the necessity of having to act. The idealist is constrained intellectually to rise above social injustice and withhold protest.

Pätus comes full circle in his relationship to Kant by abjuring his philosophy in order to obtain a degree. In good conscience, Pätus reverses his former anti-militaristic stand, maintaining that he is not betraying his ideal because Kant himself is "... aufwieglerisch doch nur in der Idee" (GW VI, 2360), as he explained already in Scene 9.[30] Paradoxically, he believes here in Scene 15 that he is being true to Kant by abandoning him: "Wie hätte ich ansonsten eine Lehrerstelle gekriegt? Und ohne Lehrerstelle, wie hätt ich meine Karoline ... ehelichen können? Und es steht hier, daß ichs muß." (GW VI, 2384) Pätus is referring to Kant's *Eherecht*, from which he quotes the definition of marriage in order to explain why his action was justified.[31]

In telling Fritz about the subject of his examination, Pätus admits:

---

[30] During rehearsals of the *Hofmeister* it was discussed that Pätus should really appear only an armchair revolutionary, despite his initially vigorous enthusiasm for the humanitarian idealism of Kant. One in a series of notes in BBA 2062, " 'Hofmeister' — Textänderungen während der Proben," attests to this critical attitude: "Wir zeigten aber nicht nur die Qualität der nun von Pätus eingenommenen [moralheroischen] Haltung, sondern übten durch den kleinen Zusatz 'in der Idee' zugleich auch Kritik an ihrer Unzulänglichkeit." (BBA 2062/87)

[31] Compare the passage as it occurs in Kant, *Werke — Moralische Schriften* (Leipzig: Insel, 1922), vol. 5, p. 391 with Brecht's rendering in GW VI, 2384. The wording of the selection taken from Kant's *Eherecht* cited in Scene 15 of the adaptation has been slightly amended. Generally, whenever Brecht incorporates excerpts from well-known works into his plays, he condenses or so edits the passage that now the original message, now the style is distorted or vulgarized. In the excerpt referred to here, Brecht employs vulgarization for comic effect. Whereas Kant was inoffensive and abstract, the adaptor is intentionally provocative and concrete in defining conjugal rights. Characteristic of this distortion is the instance of "Besitz ihrer Geschlechtseigenschaften" in Kant being altered to read "Gebrauch ihrer Geschlechtsorgane" in the adaptation. Even here it would seem that the Marxist is concerned with productive use rather than mere possession! In this respect the Marxist's concern with materialism reveals itself in the addition made to this passage on page 85 of copy 2 of the "Eingestrichenes

Ich ließ die Philosophie draußen. 'Der Krieg, der Vater aller Dinge' — aber ich ließ es witzig durchblicken, in einem geeigneten dunklen Satze, daß die Vaterschaft jeweils nicht beweisbar ... (GW VI, 2384—85)

The man who once condemned war as barbarism now justifies its necessity as a first cause. He claims hypocritically that the reasons which lead to war are not identifiable. His statement is an ironic echo of Article 340 of the *Code Napoléon:* "La recherche de la paternité est interdite." Pätus implies thereby that to identify the causes for war would be counter to the interests of those who wish to profit from it. In accepting social injustice he as much as reveals his complicity.

The moral hero exchanges the heady sublimity of humanitarian idealism for the torpid materialism of middle-class mediocrity. In so doing, Pätus, like the cowardly Läuffer and Wenzeslaus, has performed the delicate operation of intellectual self-emasculation; each plucks out the eye which offends him. Ideals and moral attitudes are as easily compartmentalized and shut away or discarded as mere things which have lost their usefulness. In fact, Galy Gay in *Mann ist Mann* describes his capitulation in this manner, employing gesture and physical terms to render the abstract process concrete: "Und lege ab, was unbeliebt an mir, und bin / Da angenehm." (GW I, 361)

Pätus: A Vehicle for Brecht's Criticism of German Classical Humanism

Some of the scholars who write about Brecht's adaptation of the *Hofmeister* consider the figure of Pätus among the most interesting in the drama because he is the target for the adaptor's criticism of German Idealism.[32] Pätus has given up his rebellion against the powers that encourage German "Untertänigkeit" (GW VI, 2351) and has joined them instead. Now that he has a niche within society he tolerates the evils which he once so resolutely denounced, much the same as did Goethe and Schiller, once they saw where their futures lay:

The fact remains that the German classics, Goethe in particular, not only found generous patrons at court, but were profoundly affected in their outlook on life by the court atmosphere. They found something so valuable in the essence of aristocracy based on inherited privilege, however many defects the existing

---

Exemplar" stored in the Berliner Ensemble Archiv: The three words (which I quote from GW VI) read here „Gebrauch ihrer Vermögen und ihrer Geschlechtsorgane."

[32] Ilja Fradkin, "Die 'Bearbeitungen' von Bertolt Brecht" in *Kunst und Literatur Sowjetwissenschaft* XVI (1968), 168—169; Göran Löfdahl, "Tradition, dialektik, moral — Kring Pätus-figuren in 'Der Hofmeister'" in *Ord och Bild*, Brechtnummer (1964), LXXIII: 61—64; Hans Mayer, *Bertolt Brecht und die Tradition* (Pfullingen: Neske, 1961), p. 59.

aristocracy might have, that in spite of radical beginnings they desired no imitation in Germany of the French Revolution, and showed themselves in their mature outlook decidedly conservative.[33]

Brecht further regards Pätus's behavior symbolic of the historical failure of the German middle class to imitate their American and French counterparts of the late eighteenth century. Pätus's capitulation is supposed to teach that ethics of good will — hoping to change the world merely by wanting what is right for mankind — are socially ineffectual, even immoral in times of adverse economic and political conditions.[34]

It is important to note that, in Lenz's drama, economic necessity does not determine Pätus's character or his actions, with the exception of his flight from his creditors. Lenz allows him complete freedom of will. Brecht, on the other hand, alters the situations which affect Pätus, creates conditions of economic misery, and still asks that Pätus pratice free will! As Löfdahl puts it:

De yttre förhållandena, ekonomisk misär — ingen examen, inget arbete — tvingar så småningon Pätus att sluta en 'förnuftig' kompromiss med samhället.... Brecht nöjer sig emellertid inte med att kritiskt bedöma Pätus' handlingssätt, han — och därmed åskådaren — fördömer det. Grundtendensen i Tolvskillings operan (först käket, sedan moralen) är visserligen fortfarande sann, men enbart denna sanning räcker inte till.[35]

The propagators and popularizers of inwardness and idealism, Goethe, Kant, Klopstock, and Schiller are held responsible for creating an abstract, intellectual world which sees no need for social engagement in the real world. Ilja Fradkin, a Soviet critic, writes acidly that these authors were all involved:

... an der Propagierung ideeller Kompensationen für durchaus materielle, soziale Entbehrungen und Verluste, an der philosophischen Idealisierung des Sklavenzustandes, letzten Endes an der ethischen Lehre, die die Revolution, d.h. reale Aktionen mit dem Ziel einer gerechten Veränderung der Welt, durch geistige Illusionen und spekulative Fiktionen ersetzt.[36]

Brecht seeks to blame the apolitical schoolmaster and intellectual to a certain extent for Germany's failure to become a nation, as Klaus-Detlef

----

[33] Walter Horace Bruford, *Germany in the Eighteenth Century: The Social Background of the Literary Revival* (Cambridge, Engl.: Univ. Press, 1935), p. 71.

[34] Cf. Löfdahl, op. cit., pp. 61—62.

[35] Löfdahl, op. cit., p. 61. English translation courtesy of Juta Kovamees Kitching: "The external conditions, economic misery — no exam, no work — force Pätus by and by to make a 'rational' compromise with society .. However, Brecht is not satisfied with judging Pätus's actions critically, he — and thus the spectator, too — condemn them. The basic theme of the *Dreigroschenoper* ("Erst kommt das Fressen, dann kommt die Moral") is still true, to be sure, but this truth does not suffice by itself."

[36] Fradkin, op. cit., p. 168.

Müller explains: "Die Kontinuität zwischen feudal-absolutistischer und bürgerlicher Ordnung wird hier durch die Schulmeister vermittelt, wobei die Vermittlung auf einer Überbewertung des Geistigen beruht."[37] In Brecht's view, Pätus and Läuffer are typical of the educators of German history, as well as of the Nazi and post war periods, as is emphasized in the closing lines of the epilogue of the *Hofmeister:* "Schüler und Lehrer einer neuen Zeit / Betrachtet seine Knechtseligkeit / Damit ihr euch davon befreit!" (GW VI, 2394)[38] The German school teachers and university professors who swore an oath of loyalty to Hitler in the Third Reich were, in the adaptor's opinion, collaborators, and the heirs and descendants of Pätus. In his notes to the adaptation, Brecht writes that Pätus's development stands for ". . . die eigentliche Form der Selbstentmannung der deutschen Intellektuellen bürgerlicher Kreise, welche . . . die Revolution anderer Völker . . . nur 'im Geiste' erleben." (GW XVII, 1230—31)

Pätus is the focus for criticism of Schiller's development from his youthful political engagement and revolutionary élan to philosophical idealism and ideas about the sublimity of moral freedom. Löfdahl links the capitulation of Pätus and the general lack of resistance of the German intelligentsia against Nazism to Schiller:

> . . men dramat vill också visa, att denna kompromissvilja endast är en logisk fortsättning av en tradition, endast en följd av samma företeelse, som kom Pätus att ge upp all opposition och anpassa sig. Denna tradition skulle kanske med Brechts sätt att se kunna symboliseras av Schillers utvecklingslinje.[39]

A similar opinion is expressed by the anonymous author of the notes " 'Hofmeister' Textänderungen während der Proben:"

> Während Läuffer sich leiblich kastriert, was natürlich auch eine geistige Kastration bedeutet, nämlich den Verzicht auf die Rebellion, so ist die Kastration, die Pätus an sich vollzieht, nur geistig zu verstehen. Pätus geht im 'Hofmeister' den umgekehrten Weg Schillers. Er unternimmt im Verlaufe des Stückes den Abstieg von der überschwenglichen in die platte Misere. (BBA 2062/86)

----

[37] Müller, op. cit., p. 90.

[38] Hans Kaufmann denies that Brecht levels any criticism at the educators of the DDR: "Die Darstellung des Hofmeister-Schicksals dient also dazu, die Gegenwart von der Vergangenheit abzugrenzen. Nicht einen Vorläufer positiver Bestrebungen von heute, sondern einen charakteristischen Fall geschichtlichen und menschlichen Versagens sollen wir nach Brechts Interpretation darin erblicken." Kaufmann conveniently glosses over the uncomfortable warning earlier in the epilogue: "Und vielerorts ists auch heut noch wahr." See *Bertolt Brecht — Geschichtsdrama und Parabelstück* (Berlin: Rütten und Loening, 1962), p. 206.

[39] Löfdahl, op. cit., p. 61. Translation courtesy of Juta Kovamees Kitching: ". . . but the drama also wishes to show that this willingness to compromise is only a logical continuation of a tradition, only a result of the same phenomenon which caused Pätus to give up all opposition and conform. This tradition could perhaps, according to Brecht's way of looking at things, be symbolized by Schiller's line of development."

Schiller's dominant interest in the idea of moral freedom,[40] rather than in the reality of political freedom itself was for Brecht a prime example of the German intellectual's separation of the ideal and the real. Like Hans Mayer,[41] Klaus-Detlef Müller notes that Brecht's criticism of Kant is equally a criticism of Schiller:

> Sie [Brechts Schiller-Kritik] ist besonders deutlich in der Umfunktionierung der Schillerschen 'Jungfrau von Orleans' zur 'Heiligen Johanna der Schlachthöfe'. Die parodistischen Passagen des Schlußaktes, die außer auf Schiller auch auf Goethe und Hölderlin zielen, erläutern die Funktion einer Ethik des guten Willens und eines Kultes der Innerlichkeit in einem System der Ausbeutung: sie dienen der Aufrechterhaltung der Stabilität.[42]

To be sure, the works of Goethe and Schiller encourage moral self-perfection of the individual and as pure an aestheticism as possible. This one-sidedness, Brecht objects, stressed non-involvement in the pressing social and political questions of the age. Ronald Duncan Miller notes that real issues were irrelevant for the aesthetics of Schiller:

> In his dramatic theory Schiller repeatedly stresses the fact that the sufferings of the protagonist, the tragic conflict in which he is involved, has no other purpose than to stimulate his sense of moral freedom and to inspire the audience by his example.[43]

Man triumphs over adversity, Schiller teaches, by rising above it spiritually. In a short essay, "Ist das epische Theater etwa eine 'moralische Anstalt'?," Brecht ironically discusses how Schiller's drama, in contrast to epic theater, was preoccupied with esoteric moral attitudes rather than with moral outrage at intolerable social conditions. Nietzsche's rejection of Schiller, which is equally Brecht's, is of interest here:

> Nach Friedrich Schiller soll das Theater eine moralische Anstalt sein. . . . Zu seiner Zeit hatte das Publikum nichts gegen das Moralisieren einzuwenden. Erst später beschimpfte ihn Friedrich Nietzsche als den Moraltrompeter von Säckingen. Nietzsche schien die Beschäftigung mit Moral eine trübselige Angelegenheit, Schil-

---

[40] In his book, *The Drama of Schiller* (Harrogate: Duchy Press, 1963), p. 2, Ronald Duncan Miller summarizes the importance of Kant in Schiller's drama: "The ideal of moral freedom, fundamental in Kant, is scarcely less important in his disciple Schiller, and the group of associated ideas which cluster around this main idea — freedom of will, the power of reason to liberate man from his own sensuous nature, man as an end in himself, the principle of autonomy and the supreme importance of the human personality — all of these Kantian ideas are whole-heartedly accepted by Schiller and become, so to speak, part of his flesh and blood. It is in his drama that Schiller creates a world in which these ideas acquire living reality."

[41] Cf. Mayer, *Bertolt Brecht und die Tradition* (Pfullingen: Neske, 1961), p. 59, p. 61.

[42] Müller, op. cit., pp. 92—93.

[43] Miller, op. cit., p. 3.

ler erblickte darin eine durchaus vergnügliche. Er kannte nichts, was amüsanter und befriedigender sein konnte, als Ideale zu propagieren. Das Bürgertum ging daran, die Ideen der Nation zu konstituieren. Sein Haus einrichten, seinen eigenen Hut loben, seine Rechnungen präsentieren ist etwas sehr Vergnügliches. Dagegen ist vom Verfall seines Hauses reden, seinen alten Hut verkaufen müssen, seine Rechnungen bezahlen wirklich eine trübselige Angelegenheit, und so sah Friedrich Nietzsche ein Jahrhundert später die Sache. Er war schlecht zu sprechen auf Moral und also auch auf den ersten Friedrich. (GW XV, 270—271)

As Brecht notes as early as 1920 in the *Augsburger Theaterkritiken*, he can no longer take Don Carlos' servitude seriously after reading Upton Sinclair's novel *The Jungle:* "Auch ist die Freiheit beim Schiller immer nur gefordert, in anerkannt schönen Arien, zugegeben, aber sie könnte vielleicht auch dasein, in irgendeinem Menschen, aber Posa und Carlos und Philipp: Opernsänger, gratis für Beifall." (GW XV, 10—11)

Brecht makes of Lenz's *Hofmeister* an anti-idealistic, anti-humanistic drama. In defense of German Classicism, however, it is perhaps appropriate to acknowledge Goethe's sympathy, for example, with the poor. Walter Horace Bruford discusses the financial situation of Karl August's dukedom in the 1780's when Goethe saw, as provisional President of the Treasury, how difficult it was to make financial ends meet:

It is about this time (20 June 1784) that he [Goethe] writes in a letter that it is the poor who must always 'carry the sack, and it makes no difference whether it is too heavy for a man on his right shoulder or on his left'. A series of remarks in his letters between 1782 and 1784 show how well he understands the socially unjust world in which he lives, though he can think of no fundamental remedies, and fears disorder more than injustice. 'The class we call the lower', he says, is 'in God's eyes the higher.' 'One is ashamed at being favoured above so many thousands. We are always hearing how poor a province is, and how it is getting poorer; sometimes we tell ourselves that it isn't true, at others we put it out of our minds. But what when we see things for ourselves with open eyes, and see how incurable it all is, and how many botched efforts are made!'[44]

In this regard, Hans Mayer discusses the conflict which Goethe experienced when trying to encapsule and isolate his idealism from the economic misery surrounding him during work on *Iphigenie auf Tauris:*

. . . ein Werk, von dem Goethe, sich selbst gleichsam davon distanzierend, etwas spöttisch sagte, es sei 'verteufelt human'. Womit er das Irreale, gerade eben noch Mögliche, der geistigen Position andeuten möchte. Wir kennen gleichzeitig den erschütternden Ausbruch eines Briefes, als Goethe in Apolda sitzt und an der

———————

[44] Bruford, *Culture and Society in Classical Weimar* (Cambridge, Engl.: Univ. Press, 1962), pp. 113—114. The call for revolution is well illustrated by a remark of Friedrich Engels about Goethe: "Auch Goethe war nicht imstande, die deutsche Misere zu besiegen; im Gegenteil: sie besiegte ihn; dieser Sieg der Misere über den größten Deutschen ist der beste Beweis dafür, daß sie von innen heraus nicht zu besiegen war." Quoted in Hermann Pongs, *Das kleine Lexikon der Weltliteratur* (Stuttgart: Union Verlag, 1967), 6. Aufl., columns 1241—2.

Iphigenie [sic] arbeitet, die in der Prosaform nicht gelingt und erst unter den Eindrücken der italienischen Reise zustande kommt. Da heißt es am 6. März 1779: 'Hier will das Drama gar nicht fort, es ist verflucht, der König von Tauris soll reden, als wenn kein Strumpfwirker in Apolda hungerte.'

Damit ist die Diskrepanz angedeutet zwischen der Realität um ihn, und der exorbitanten Anforderung an sittliche Verantwortung, die in der *Iphigenie* gestellt wird: 'Wahrheit sei zwischen uns.'[45]

Goethe was painfully aware, continues Mayer, that he has Iphigenie assume an extreme position with her absolute trust in moral decisions. Her position is that of Kant's Categorical Imperative. Mayer regards the spread of Kantian Idealism as a second wave of Humanism in Germany:

Der neue große Aufschwung vollzieht sich von der Lessing-Zeit bis zu jenem entscheidenden geschichtlichen und geistigen Wendepunkt, der durch die mißglückte bürgerlich-demokratische Revolution von 1848/49 bestimmt wird. In dieser Zeit stehen guter Wille, sittliche Verantwortung des Einzelnen, sittliche Wahrheit des Einzelnen, Gutseinwollen, interesseloses Wohlgefallen am Schönen, im Mittelpunkt aller philosophischen Maximen.[46]

And Bruford, presenting the views of several German historians who write about the spirit of this age, pinpoints the very failures of German intellectuals which Brecht castigates in the *Hofmeister* adaptation:

... poetry and philosophy from Lessing to Hegel ... represent a single sustained effort of the German mind to make sense of its own peculiar world. Unlike their fellow-countrymen earlier in the eighteenth century and in the nineteenth, and unlike their French contemporaries, they were little concerned with improving the material conditions of life. Their ideal, as Troeltsch puts it, was rather 'a full and free development of the mind and heart for its own sake', and many members of the intellectual elite began to see in the realisation and propagation of this ideal the specific mission of the Germans. Culture [... personal as opposed to national ...] had become a supreme good, an ideal to live for.[47]

The weakness of Pätus and his kind, claims Brecht, consists of their unwillingness to translate their humanitarian ideals into social and political reality. How an individual is to bring about such change Brecht does not say in his dramas about anti-heroes.[48] Indeed, he was still seeking the an-

---

[45] Mayer, *Anmerkungen zu Brecht* (Frankfurt: Suhrkamp, 1967), 2nd. edn., p. 88.

[46] Ibid., p. 89.

[47] Bruford, op. cit., pp. 2—3.

[48] In contrast, Brecht's lyrics often contain, in programmatic, even doctrinaire form, the unsatisfying (Marxist) answers to problems raised but unsolved in the plays. Typical of the Marxist verse of the *Svendborger Gedichte* is the first stanza of "Keiner oder alle:"

> Sklave, wer wird dich befreien?
> Die in tiefster Tiefe stehen
> Werden, Kamerad, dich sehen
> Und sie werden hör'n dein Schreien:
> Sklaven werden dich befreien.

swer in his third version of *Leben des Galilei* in the last years of his life. Galilei's condemnation of Mucius in this drama is a moral luxury as long as he himself is not in the position of having to decide where his allegiance lies: "Wer die Wahrheit nicht weiß, der ist bloß ein Dummkopf. Aber wer sie weiß und sie eine Lüge nennt, der ist ein Verbrecher!" (GW III, 1300) Ultimately, Galilei is put into this position and must hear himself condemned with his own words. Pätus, like Galilei, also denies the truth in order to live. And just as Galilei continues to do research because it is an incorrigible vice of his, so Pätus, too, continues to believe in Kant. Neither Galilei's research nor Pätus's idealism is productive of social change.

Keiner oder alle. Alles oder nichts.
Einer kann sich da nicht retten.
Gewehre oder Ketten.
Keiner oder alle. Alles oder nichts.

GW IX, 649

CONCLUDING STATEMENT

As the discussion has shown, the BBA and BEA materials are of special value to the literary historian as well as the practicing student of the theater. They show how Brecht gradually developed, in 1950, an altogether new and entertaining comedy out of Lenz's then neglected closet drama. Since that time — and largely thanks to Brecht — Lenz has become the subject of renewed scholarly and editorial interest. In contrast, if the Berliner Ensemble and other theaters in the DDR today take little interest in Brecht's *Hofmeister* — the BE has never revived the play — the same is not true in Western theaters, as is obvious from the abundant performances reviewed in newspaper articles listed in Appendix D.

As the adaptation progressed from level A through E during rehearsals, Brecht was able to formulate more precisely his polemic thrusts against class society, war, and the apolitical intellectual, of the past and the present. Whereas Lenz shows that times are changing as well as changeable, Brecht does not, even though later he insists in his 1955 letter to the participants of the 5. *Darmstädter Gespräch* that the modern world may be presented on the stage only if it is shown to be a changeable world.[1] But his adaptation depicts a historical situation with figurative reference to the present. Brecht builds on and exaggerates Lenz's realistic beginnings, and shows that conditions are so intolerable that they must be changed. However, the adaptor indicates nowhere in his play that conditions *are* changeable, not to speak of how a different society can be brought about.

The problems of the teacher and apolitical intellectual with their lack of overt resistance to repressive authorities are among the pivotal concerns of Brecht. The adaptor is as preoccupied by the question of social responsibility as Lenz is — as Albrecht Schöne has shown[2] — with the biblical theme of the prodigal son. Both writers return again and again to their respective topics in the search for a solution to the problem. But more often than not, Brecht postulates a personal, individual solution while implying that a collective stand, revolution, is the only desirable answer. Likely, this was one reason for the cry of *Formalismus!* which greeted the BE production of the play in 1950 and which Brecht responded to with the brief essay: "Ist 'Der Hofmeister' ein 'negatives Stück'?" (GW XVII, 1250—1251) Nevertheless, Brecht advocates social reform in his adaptation. This places the work in a consistent line of development from his *Lehrstücke* onward.

---

[1] Brecht was unable to attend the Darmstadt conference; he sent a message entitled: "Kann die heutige Welt durch Theater wiedergegeben werden?" Cf. GW XVI, 929—931 and the appropriate note there on p. 14*.

[2] *Säkularisation*, Palaestra, vol. 226, pp. 76—115.

If Lenz's great tragic theme is: "Der dem Trieb und Verhängnis versklavte Mensch...,"[3] Brecht makes this equally clear but in a primarily comic manner, particularly in the case of Läuffer, and, to a lesser extent, Bollwerk. Brecht heightens the tragedy of Läuffer while also intensifying the ludicrous aspects of the tutor and his situation. On the one hand, Brecht shows in scene after scene how the young man is powerless to resist brutal exploitation and humiliation by his aristocratic employers, as well as by Wenzeslaus, ostensibly in the name of morality and duty. On the other hand, the adaptor so exaggerates Lenz's already caricatured portrayal of Läuffer and his tormentors, including Gustchen and the Geheimrat, that the tragic and the comic become subtly fused. As the adaptor indicates in "Stückwahl" (GW XVII, 1221), he lays great importance on the alternation and ambivalence of comic and tragic moments in the play.

In Läuffer's decision to castrate himself for the sake of his profession, Brecht satirizes the Germans' traditional respect for the concept of duty. As Brecht shows, only the have-nots, Wenzeslaus, Läuffer, and Pätus, deny themselves a private life and let themselves be totally governed by their ideal of *Pflicht:*

> Pflicht! Du erhabener großer Name, der du nichts Beliebtes, was Einschmeichelung bei sich führt, in dir fassest, sondern Unterwerfung verlangst, doch auch nichts drohest, was natürliche Abneigung im Gemüt erregte und schreckte, um den Willen zu bewegen, sondern bloß ein Gesetz aufstellst, welches von selbst im Gemüte Eingang findet und doch sich selbst wider Willen Verehrung (wenngleich nicht immer Befolgung) erwirbt, vor dem alle Neigungen verstummen, wenn sie gleich insgeheim ihm entgegenwirken: welches ist der deiner würdige Ursprung, und wo findet man die Wurzel deiner edlen Abkunft, welche alle Verwandtschaft mit Neigungen stolz ausschlägt und von welcher Wurzel abzustammen die unnachläßliche Bedingung desjenigen Wertes ist, den sich Menschen allein selbst geben können?[4]

The adaptation documents Brecht's desire to portray the dangers inherent in the wholehearted devotion to such an ideal of duty as conceived of by Kant. This dangerous idealism is also exorcised in the "frame" to the adaptation, the prologue and epilogue, in which Brecht alleges that the German educator has believed in such values to his own and society's detriment: "Gebrochen ist sein Rückgrat. Seine Pflicht / Ist, daß er nun das seiner Schüler bricht." (GW VI, 2394) An earlier, less ironic and hard-hitting version of the epilogue pokes fun at the educator's inwardness: "die Köpfe in die Wolken gesteckt / die Füsse aber dafür bedreckt." (BBA 543/30)

---

[3] Fritz Martini, *Deutsche Literaturgeschichte* (Stuttgart: Kröner, 1960), 10. Auflage, p. 208.

[4] From Kant, *Kritik der praktischen Vernunft*, p. 105 as quoted in H. A. Korff, *Geist der Goethezeit* (Leipzig: Koehler und Amelang, 1966), vol. 2, 8. unveränderte Auflage, p. 201.

In contrast to Lenz, Brecht shows how irresponsible such ideals of an individual's moral and ethical integrity are in a society which is desperate for social change. The pragmatist Brecht does not believe in the perfectibility of man through the exercise of reason and *humanitas*. He believes, in theory at least, in the perfectibility of society: "'Alles kann besser werden,' sagte Herr Keuner, 'außer dem Menschen'." (GW XII, 403)

Levels	A	B	C		D							E		
BBA File №.	1561	541	542	540	1900	545	544	539	1562	2087	1563	546	1167	495
GW VI Scene №.														
Prologue	+	+	+	+	+	+	+	+	+	+	+	+	+	+
1	1	1	1	1	1	1	1	1	1	1	1	1	1	1
2	4	3(4)	2(3)	2(3)	2	2	2	2	2	2	2	2	2	2
3	2	2	3 2	3(2)	3	3	3	3	3	3	3	3	3	3
4	—	5(6)	5	5	5	5	4(5)	4(5)	4(5)	4(5)	4(5)	4	4	4
5	3	4	4	4	4	4	5(4)	5(⁰/₂)	5(4)	5(4)	5(4)	5	5	5
6	8	7	7 8	7	7	7	6(7)	6(7)	6(7)	6(7)	6(7)	6⁷	7	7
7	6	6	6	6	6	6	7(6)	7(6)	7(6)	7(6)	7(6)	7	7	7
8	5	8(7)	8(⁷/₇)	8(7)	8	8	8	8	8	8	8	9	8	8
9	11	10(⁹/₁₁)	10*	10	10	10	9(10)	9(10)	9	9(10)	9(10)	8	9	9
10	10	9	9	9	9	9	10(9)	10(9)	10	10(9)	10(9)	10	10	10
11	7 & 12	11(¹³/₇)	12	11(12)	11	11	11	11	11	11	11	11	11	11
12	13	12(¹²/₈)	13	12(13)	12	12	12	12	12	12	12	12	12	12
13	14	13	14	13(14)	13	13	13	13	13	13	13	13	13	13
Entr'acte	—	+	+	+	+	+	+	+	+	+	+	+	+	+
14a	16	14(1)	15	14 15	14	14	14a	14a	14a	14	14a	14	14a	14a
b	17	14(2)	15(¹²/₃)	15b(¹⁰/₁₉)	15	15	14b(15)	14b(15)	14b(15)	14b(15)	14b(15)	15	15b	b(15)
c	18	14(3)	15(¹³/₃)	16c(¹²/₁₈)	16	16	14c(16)	14c(16)	14c(16)	14c(16)	14c(16)	16	c(16)	c(16)
15	15	15(17)	16	17	17	17	15(17)	15(17)	15(17)	15(17)	15(17)	17	15(17)	15(17)
16	20	17(¹⁹/₂₀)	18	19	19	—	17(19)	17(19)	17(19)	16(19)	17(18)	19	16(19)	16(19)
17	19	16(¹⁵/₁₉)	17	18	18	—	16(18)	16(18)	16(18)	17(18)	16(19)	18	17(18)	17(18)
Epilogue	—	—	—	—	—	—	—	+	+	+	+	—	+	+

SCENE SEQUENCE TABLE — NOTES

1. The level and the file number of each script are indicated in the first two horizontal title lines of the table.
2. The vertical title column to the left of the table indicates the scene numbers of the most recent published text of the adaptation in GW VI.
3. In the columns under the BBA file numbers, the position of the scene number (large figures) in each script is given opposite its equivalent scene position and scene number in the GW VI text. This comparative arrangement shows at a glance how the scene sequence was revised and how it gradually evolved toward the one used in the GW VI text.
4. A plus sign (+) indicates that the prologue, entr'acte, or epilogue were present in the respective BBA or BEA script. A minus sign (−) indicates the absence of a scene or of the entr'acte or epilogue in the particular BBA script.
5. The numbering of BBA 541 Scenes 9 and 10 is confused in the script, where both scenes are called number nine. Our table shows the correct order in terms of the text in GW VI; the second ninth scene of BBA 541 is renumbered as Scene 10.
6. Small numbers contained in parentheses indicate from the bottom figure to the top figure the number(s) progressively assigned to each scene as the adaptation proceeded.
7. The larger figures not in parentheses indicate the final scene number in the early versions; in the early versions, these were often written by hand.
8. BBA 1561 has an eleventh scene called "Halle im Gefängnis;" some of its context is like that of Scene 9 in the GW VI text. BBA 1561 has a ninth scene not shown in our table. See Chapter I, note 61. BBA 542 also has an eleventh scene called "Halle im Gefängnis;" the position of this scene in BBA 542 is indicated in the table by an asterisk.
9. The scene juxtaposition in BBA 546 is noteworthy. Scene 8 preceded Scene 10 in the script. This sequence is particularly effective theatrically; however, Act II would then have had only two scenes, whereas Act III would have had six.
10. The first scene 7 in the columns for BBA 1167 and BBA 495 is really the sixth scene, but was not renumbered as such in the two scripts.
11. The four BEA copies of level E have the same scene order as noted in the column for BBA 1167.

Brecht's   Condensation of   Lenz's   Drama

L e n z ' s   **Hofmeister**   Brecht's   Adaptation

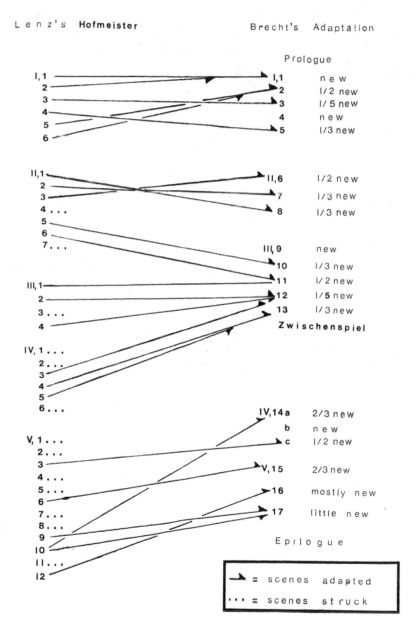

Prologue

I, 1 ——————————————————————→ I, 1   n e w
2 ————————————————————→ 2   I / 2 new
3 ————————————————→ 3   I / 5 new
4   4   n e w
5   5   I/3 new
6

II, 1 ————————————————————→ II, 6   I / 2 new
2   7   I/3 new
3   8   I/3 new
4 . . .
5
6
7 . . .   III, 9   new
10   I/3 new
11   I/2 new
III, 1 ——————————————————→ 12   I/5 new
2 ————————————————→ 13   I/3 new
3 . . .   **Z w i s c h e n s p i e l**
4

IV, 1 . . .
2 . . .
3
4
5
6 . . .   IV, 14 a   2/3 new
b   n e w
c   I/2 new
V, 1 . . .
2 . . .
3 ———————————————————→ V, 15   2/3 new
4 . . .
5 . . .   →16   mostly new
6
7 . . .   →17   little new
8 . . .
9   E p i l o g u e
10
11 . . .
12

↗	= scenes adapted
•••	= scenes struck

APPENDIX C

LENZ'S TEXT IN THE ADAPTATION

To what extent is Brecht's *Hofmeister* a literal copy of the Lenz original? By the time the level E text of the adaptation was produced, 72⁰/o of the original Lenz text had been struck out; this left only 28⁰/o of his play to be printed verbatim in the *Hofmeister* text in GW VI. This amount is equivalent to 44⁰/o of the body of the adaptation, thus the new materials make up more than half of Brecht's drama. Such facts alone indicate that the *Hofmeister* of 1950 is really another Brecht play.

The calculations in the table below are based on the number of complete and partial lines (including act and scene numbers, scene titles, and stage directions) of Lenz's text taken over bodily into the *Hofmeister* as printed in GW VI. The edition of Lenz's *Hofmeister* used in my comparison was that of Heinz Kindermann in *Deutsche Literatur in Entwicklungsreihen* (Leipzig: Reclam, 1939), Reihe 15, VIII, 134–207.

BRECHT'S INDEBTEDNESS TO LENZ

Hofmeister text as in **GW VI**	Total Number of Lines in the Adaptation	Number of Lines Occupied by Lenz's Text in the Adaptation	Percentage of Adaptation from Lenz
Prologue	22	—	—
Act I	388	180	46
Act II	319	155	50
Act III	593	299	50.4
Entr'acte	8	—	—
Act IV	285	94	33
Act V	313	128	40.8
Epilogue	27	—	—
FINAL TOTALS IN PERCENT	56⁰/o is new	44⁰/o from Lenz	44⁰/o from Lenz

APPENDIX D

THE BBA COLLECTION
OF NEWSPAPER ARTICLES AND REVIEWS
CONCERNING *DER HOFMEISTER*

The BBA does not possess a list of its collection of newspaper articles and reviews about the *Hofmeister*. To date (October 1973), no extensive bibliographical record of the reception of the stage version of Brecht's *Hofmeister* in newspapers has been published. Klaus-Dietrich Petersen's *Bertolt Brecht — Leben und Werk — Ein Bücherverzeichnis* (Dortmund: Stadtbücherei, 1966) lists only five articles on the *Hofmeister* in journals and has no newspaper entries. Walter Nubel's "Bertolt Brecht Bibliographie," published in *Sinn und Form* (Rütten & Loening: Berlin, 1957) Zweites Sonderheft Bertolt Brecht, pp. 598–599, contains entries for nine newspaper reviews and one journal article about the *Hofmeister*. In the following list, an asterisk preceding the name of the newspaper indicates that Nubel's bibliography also contains this entry; in all, only five of the ten articles Nubel records are contained in the BBA collection. Elisabeth Genton's *J.M.R. Lenz et la scène allemande,* (Paris: Didier, 1966), pp. 281—282 and pp. 285—287, cites thirty-one newspaper reviews about performances of Brecht's adaptation. Only nine of these reviews are contained in the BBA collection and are marked here by a double asterisk.

This list does not aim at completeness. It records only the major items of interest in the BBA collection, which, itself is incomplete. Short notices announcing the performance of the *Hofmeister* by the Berliner Ensemble and other theater companies are not included below. Entries are given in chronological order for articles appearing in Danish, English, French, and German language newspapers. Articles published on the same day in various newspapers are listed in alphabetical order according to the name of the newspaper. The date and place of publication, as well as the title of the article and the author's name are given to the extent that this information was available in the BBA files. Although many of the Danish articles had titles and were signed, lack of time in the BBA prevented me from copying this information. (The BBA files did not indicate volume and page numbers of the newspapers in which the articles were published.) Dates are written in the order of day, month, year. The abbreviations "s," "m," and "l" in parentheses indicate whether the article is short, moderately long, or long.

Danish Language

16.	6. 64	*Skanderborg Amts Avis Bladet* (m)
28.	7. 64	*Aarhus Stiftstidende* (m)
15.	8. 64	*Jyllands-Posten* (m)
27.	8. 64	*Holstebre Dagblad* (l)
1.	11. 64	*Aarhus Stiftstidende* (l)
		Demokraten (m)
3.	11. 64	*Politiken* (m)
4.	11. 64	*Aarhus Stiftstidende* (m)
		Odder Dagblad (m)
		Ringkøbing Amtstidende (m)
5.	11. 64	*Aarhus Stiftstidende* (m)
		Berlingske Aftenavis (s)
6.	11. 64	*Aalborg Stiftstidende* (m)
		Aarhus Amtstidende (m)
		Aarhus Stiftstidende (l)
		Aktuelt (m)
		Berlingske Tidende (m)
		Demokraten (l)
		Ekstrabladet (m)
		Folkebladet for Randers (m)
		Horsens Folkeblad (m)
		Information (m)
		Jyllands-Posten (m)
		Land og Folk (m)
		Politiken (m)
9.	11. 64	*Dannevirke* (m)
4.	12. 64	*Aarhus Stiftstidende* (s)
2.	4. 65	*Berlingske Tidende* (m)
12.	4. 66	*Demokraten* (m)
16.	1. 67	*Berlingske Tidende* (s)
		Jyllands-Posten (m)

English Language

12. 6. 57   The Times, London (m)
2. 8. 63   *The Times,* London, "A Brechtian Adaptation" (s)
8. 8. 63   *The Listener,* London, Drama Section: "The Tutor," P. N. Furbank's review of a BBC (Aug. 1, 1963) Third Programme Broadcast of Brecht's adaptation in English translation. (s)
9. 8. 63   *Palo Alto (Calif.) Times,* "Brecht Work Strong Satire," Dorothy Nichols (s)
10. 8. 63   *New York Times Western Edition,* Article about Stanford University Theater Workshop's production of Brecht's *Hofmeister* (s)
                 San Francisco Examiner, "Exciting Brecht Première by Stanford's Workshop," Stanley Eichelbaum (s)
12. 8. 63   *San Francisco Chronicle,* "A Brecht Triumph at Stanford," in section of Drama Review, Betty Janss (s)
7. 2. 66   *The Times,* London (m)

French Language

29. 6. 57   *Le Monde,* Paris (m)
7. 8. 57   *Carrefour,* Paris (l)
13. 7. 61   *Courrier de l'ouest,* Angers (l)
14. 7. 61   *Courrier de l'ouest,* Angers (l)
15. 1. 65   *Le Méridional,* Marseille (m)
11. 6. 65   *Le Dauphine* [sic] *Libéré,* Grenoble (m)
4. 12. 71   *L'Aurore,* Paris, "Le Précepteur" de Lenz. Adaptation de Brecht," André Ransan (s)
                 France Soir, Paris, " 'Le précepteur' — Une cruelle leçon," Pierre Marcabru (s)
                 Le Monde, Paris, ' "Le Précepteur' adapté de R. Lenz par B. Brecht," by B. P.-D. (s)
6. 12. 71   *Le Figaro,* Paris, " 'Le Précepteur' de Reinhold Lenz," Pierre Mazars (s)
                 Le Quotidien du Médecin, Paris, "Le 'précepteur' — une salade russe" (s)
— 12. 71   *Paris Tel,* " 'Le Précepteur' de R. Lenz, adapté par Bertolt Brecht" (s)
20. 12. 71   *La Croix,* Paris, " 'Le Précepteur' de Reinhold Lenz," by H. R. (s)
                 L'Humanité, Paris, "L'éducation soumise ('Le Précepteur'), de B. Brecht à la Gaîté-Montparnasse," France Vernon (s)
20. 12. 71   *Pariser Kurier,* " 'Der Hofmeister' von Lenz in Brechts Bearbeitung — Ein Stück mit Antihelden" (s)
27. 12. 71   *Valeurs Actuelles,* Paris, " 'Le Précepteur' pièce de Reinhold Lenz adapté par Brecht," by C.-H. L. (s)

German Language

9. 4. 50   **Der Sonntag,* Berlin, "Zwischen Shakespeare und Büchner," (Zur Lenz-Aufführung des Berliner Ensembles), Max Schroeder (m)
— 4. 50   *Freie Presse,* Berlin, "Wir sahen..." (s)
— 4. 50   *Berliner Zeitung,* "Der 'Lenz' ist auferstanden" (s)
12. 4. 50   *Täglicher Rundschau,* Berlin, "Reinhold Lenz' Geburtsstunde" (s)
13. 4. 50   ***Neues Deutschland,* Berlin, "Das ABC der deutschen Misere," Hans Mayer (l)

15. 4. 50 *Berliner Zeitung am Abend*, "Enthüllung der deutschen Misere," Walter Thomas (m)
Der Abend, Berlin, "Neuer Frühling für Lenz," Manfred Barthel (s)
Der Kurier, "Das ungesunde Klima," Edwin Montigo .(m)
Nacht-Express, Berlin, "*Der Hofmeister* im Deutschen Theater," by R. W. N. (m)
Vorwärts, "*Der Hofmeister*, Deutsches Theater," (s)

16. 4. 50 *Berliner Anzeiger*, "Lenz erlebt einen neuen Frühling," Herbert Hans Grassman (s)
Der Morgen, Berlin, "Komödie der Urnatur," Erich Krafft (m)
Neue Zeit, Berlin, "Aufgefrischter Sturm und Drang," by I. E. (s)
**Neue Zeitung*, "Ein ABC der deutschen Misere," Friedrich Luft (m)
* & ** *Neues Deutschland*, "Beispielgebendes Theater, Bertolt Brechts Neubelebung des *Hofmeisters* von Reinhold Lenz im Deutschen Theater," Fritz Erpenbeck (m)
RIAS 11:50 a.m. to 12:05 p.m., Radio Talk on the Program "Die Stimme der Kritik," Friedrich Luft, carbon copy of typescript (l)
Telegraf, Berlin, "Die deutsche Misere, *Der Hofmeister* im Deutschen Theater," Heinz Ritter (m)

17. 4. 50 *Berliner Montag*, "ABC der deutschen Misere" (s)
Der Abend, Berlin, "*Der Hofmeister*," Konrad Haemmerling (s)
Neue Zeitung am Montag, "Brecht gab ein neues Beispiel" (m)
Vorwärts, "*Der Hofmeister*" (s)

18. 4. 50 * & ***Berliner Zeitung*, "Brecht und Lenz, Zur dritten Prèmiere des Berliner Ensembles: *Der Hofmeister*," Paul Rilla (l)
**Der Tagesspiegel*, Berlin, "Reinhold Lenz: *Der Hofmeister*," Herbert Pfeiffer (m)
Die Tagespost, Potsdam, "Das ABC der deutschen Misere," Paula Steiner (m)
Die Welt, "Bert Brecht inszeniert J. M. R. Lenz," Walter Busse (m)
**Tägliche Rundschau*, Berlin, "Des deutschen Schulmeisters Ahnherr," Wolfgang Harich (m)

19. 4. 50 *National-Zeitung*, Berlin, "Musterbeispiel liberalistischer Kritik," Franz Fühmann (m)
Schleswig-Holsteinische Volkszeitung, "Berliner Theaterbrief" (s)

20. 4. 50 *Tribüne*, "Die deutsche Misere" (s)

21. 4. 50 *Bauern-Echo*, Berlin, "*Der Hofmeister*" (s)
Berlin, Berlin, "*Der Hofmeister*" (s)
Deutschlandstimme, Berlin (s)
Westdeutsche Zeitung, Düsseldorf, "Die Ballade von der deutschen Misere" (s)

22. 4. 50 *Theaterdienst*, "*Der Hofmeister*" (l)
Weser-Kurier, Bremen (s)

23. 4. 50 *Roland von Berlin*, Berlin, "Lenz: brechtisch-prächtig!" Walter Kaul (m)
Sie, Berlin (s)
Sonntag, Berlin, "Schöpferisches Theater," Max Schroeder (m)

24. 4. 50 *Frankfurter Allgemeine Zeitung*, "Am Beispiel eines Hofmeisters," Sabina Lickmann (m)
Montag, Berlin, "Berlins jüngstes Bühnenpaar" (m)

25. 4. 50 *Deutsche Tagespost*, Augsburg, "Lenz' *Hofmeister*" (s)
Deutsche Woche, Berlin (s)
Hamburger Echo, "*Der Hofmeister*" (s)

26.	4.	50	*Die Weltbühne, Berlin, "Die Tragikomödie des deutschen Schulmeisters," Leo Menter (l)
			Nacht-Express, Berlin, "Neue Kulturaufgaben Berlins" (s)
27.	4.	50	Hannoversche Allgemeine, "Erregendes Berliner Theater," Christa Ratzold (m)
			National-Zeitung, Berlin, "Sturm gegen die deutsche Misere" (m)
28.	4.	50	Berliner Palette, Berlin (m)
1.	5.	50	**Illustrierte Rundschau, Berlin, "Der Hofmeister," Magritz (m)
4.	5.	50	Stuttgarter Nachrichten (m)
17.	5.	50	Rhein-Neckar-Zeitung, Heidelberg, "Berliner Brief" (m)
5.	7.	50	Die Union, Dresden, "Musik und Theater in Berlin" (m)
7.	8.	50	Stuttgarter Zeitung, "Von Brecht bis Kafka" (s)
18.	8.	50	Rhein-Neckar-Zeitung, Heidelberg (m)
7.	9.	50	Deutsche Tagespost, Augsburg, "West-östliche Spielzeit in Berlin" (m)
13.	10.	50	Neue Zeit, Berlin, "Serienerfolge im Deutschen Theater" (m)
9.	2.	56	Hamburger Echo, "Übung über Brecht" (m)
4.	7.	57	Die andere Zeitung, Hamburg, "Neuentdeckter Sturm und Drang" (m)
17.	7.	57	Carrefour, Frankfurt (m)
26.	8.	57	Hannoverische Allgemeine, "Der Hofmeister und die junge Elektra" (m)
24.	3.	58	Gießener Anzeiger, "Willst du dich nach Sodom umsehen?" (l)
			Gießener Freie Presse, "Der Hofmeister" (l)
27.	3.	58	Mitteldeutsche Neueste Nachrichten, Halle (m)
29.	3.	58	Leipziger Volkszeitung, "Von Sinn und Wirkung eines Gastspiels" (m)
9.	4.	58	**Die Union, Leipzig, "Das ABC der deutschen Misere" (m)
11.	4.	58	Abendpost, Frankfurt, "Brecht und die Vokabeln der Satire" (m)
			Kieler Nachrichten (m)
15.	6.	59	Frankfurter Allgemeine Zeitung (m)
27.	8.	59	Wiesbadener Tageblatt, "Was bringt das Schauspiel?" (m)
4.	3.	60	Sächsisches Tageblatt, "Das ABC der deutschen Misere" (m)
22.	8.	60	Kieler Nachrichten, "Deutsche Premieren zum Saisonstart" (m)
14.	9.	60	**Hamburger Echo, "Brecht und die deutsche Misere" (m)
15.	9.	60	**Die Welt, Essen, "Mensch und Rolle wurden eins" (s)
17.	9.	60	Düsseldorfer Nachrichten, "Gründgens-Theater-ferngelenkt" (m)
20.	9.	60	Allgemeine Zeitung, Mainz, "Gründgens-Theater-ferngelenkt" (m)
			Der Mittag, Düsseldorf, "Der Hofmeister" (s)
25.	9.	60	Lübecker Nachrichten, "Noch einmal Thema: Brecht" (s)
27.	9.	60	Kölner Stadt-Anzeiger, "ABC der deutschen Misere" (s)
12.	10.	60	Abendpost, Frankfurt (m)
			Deutsche Woche, München, "Hofmeister"
4.	11.	60	Hakidmah, Tel-Aviv, "Theater in drei Ländern" (m)
18.	12.	60	Sonntag, Berlin, "Bühne hinterm neuen Glanz" (l)
5.	11.	61	Nationalzeitung, Basel (m)
13.	9.	62	Sächsische Neueste Nachrichten, Dresden (m)
13.	10.	63	Lübecker Nachrichten, "Das ABC der deutschen Misere" (m)
14.	10.	63	Lübecker Morgen (m)
17.	10.	63	Schleswiger Nachrichten, "Lübecker Kulturbrief" (s)
12.	8.	64	Tages-Anzeiger, Zürich (s)
—	10.	64	Vaterland, Luzern, by I. F. H. (s)
4.	10.	64	Radiozeitung, Schweiz-Zofingen, "Der Hofmeister" (l)
22.	10.	64	Tages-Anzeiger, Zürich, "Vielfältiger Spielplan in Zürich" (m)
19.	2.	65	Neue Züricher Zeitung, "Theater in Luzern" (l)
24.	5.	65	Tages-Anzeiger, Zürich (m)
3.	6.	65	Offenburger Tageblatt (m)
23.	10.	65	Frankfurter Rundschau (m)

28. 10. 65	*Frankfurter Allgemeine* (m)

28. 10. 65   *Frankfurter Allgemeine* (m)
          Frankfurter Neue Presse, "Brechts Satire auf dem deutschen Idealismus" (m)
          Frankfurter Rundschau, "Untertan ohne Harm," Erich Lissner (m)
          Höchster Kreisblatt (m)

2. 11. 65   *Die Welt,* Ausgabe B, "Revolte gegen sich selbst," Rudolf Krämer-Badonie (m)

3. 11. 65   *Westfälische Rundschau,* "Brechts *Hofmeister* in Frankfurt," Gunter Schäble (m)

4. 11. 65   *Badische Volkszeitung,* Karlsruhe, "Weder Lenz noch Brecht" (s)

5. 11. 65   *Stuttgarter Zeitung,* "Umsonst," Gunter Schäble (m)

11. 11. 65   *Bad Sachsaer Nachrichten,* "Von Brecht geknetet" (m)

28. 12. 65   *Aachener Nachrichten,* "Was die Obrigkeit aufträgt" (s)

16. 2. 66   *Westdeutsche Rundschau,* Wuppertal (m)
          Westdeutsche Rundschau, Wuppertal (l)

25. 3. 66   *Lippische Landes-Zeitung,* "Junge Generation anders als ihre Großväter" (m)

— 4. 66   *Die Welt,* Hamburg, "Von US bis Ghelderode" (s)

16. 4. 66   *Allgemeine Zeitung,* Karlsruhe (m)
          Badische Zeitung, Freiburg, "Das ABC der deutschen Misere" (s)

21. 4. 66   *Stuttgarter Nachrichten,* "Lenz von Brecht" (s)

11. 5. 66   *Badische Neueste Nachrichten,* Karlsruhe, "Engagiertes Theater" (m)

8. 6. 66   *Göttinger Tageblatt,* "Spiel der deutschen Misere" (s)

23. 6. 66   *Mindener Tageblatt,* "Bielefelds neuer Spielplan liegt fest" (s)

8. 10. 66   *Gevelsberger Zeitung* (m)

27. 7. 67   *Schleswig-Holsteinige Landeszeitung,* Rendsburg, "Neue Theaterpolitik in Schweden" (m)

21. 10. 67   *Berner Tageblatt,* "Theaterherbst in Schweden" (m)

13. 4. 68   *Thüringer Neueste Nachrichten,* Erfurt, "Schweden ehrte Bertolt Brecht" (m)

10. 5. 68   *Wochenpost,* Berlin, "DDR in Stockholm" (m)

30. 5. 68   *Die Glocke,* Oelde, "Theater aus komödiantischer Lust," Dr. Guckow (m)

20. 2. 69   *Westfälischer Zeitung,* Bielefeld, "Diskussion um den *Hofmeister,*" short articles continued in the issues of 7. 3. 69, 8. 3. 69, and 15. 3. 69.

14. 3. 69   *Westfälische Zeitung,* Bielefeld, "Spottgesang auf den Untertanengeist," part of series above (m)

5. 11. 71   *Oberhessische Presse,* Marburg, "Praeceptor Germaniae," Wolfgang Grunewald (m)

25. 11. 71   *Fuldaer Volkszeitung,* " 'Der Hofmeister' — Symbol der deutschen Misere," Hans von Specht (m)

11. 2. 72   *Husumer Nachrichten* & *Schleswiger Nachrichten,* "Das Abc der Teutschen Misere — 'Der Hofmeister' von Lenz/Brecht im Stadttheater Flensburg," Wilhelm Hambach (m)
          Norddeutsche Rundschau, Itzehoe, "Brecht Première in Flensburg," Paul Paulsen (s)

20. 1. 72   *Fuldaer Zeitung,* "Komödie 'Der Hofmeister' im Kurtheater" (s)
          Bergsträßer Anzeigeblatt, Bensheim, "Teutonische Charakterfehler — Brechts Komödie 'D. H.' am 27. Januar im Parktheater" (s)

27. 1. 72   *Lauterbacher Anzeiger,* "War dies nicht erschröcklich?" Werner Stephan (m)

SOURCES CONSULTED

Unpublished Documents in Bertolt Brecht's Posthumous Papers

It would be repetitious to list here the file numbers and titles of the folders examined in the Bertolt Brecht-Archiv and the Berliner Ensemble Archiv. A detailed classification of these documents for reference purposes has been given in Chapter I, pp. 2ff., and in the footnotes pertinent to these pages.
For the index to the dramaturgical materials in the BBA consult:„

Bertolt Brecht-Archiv Bestandsverzeichnis des literarischen Nachlasses, Band I, Stücke, herausgegeben von der deutschen Akademie der Künste zu Berlin, bearbeitet von Herta Ramthun. Berlin: Aufbau, 1969.

Bunge, Hans J. "Über das Bertolt Brecht-Archiv." *Sinn und Form,* XI (1959), 140–145.

Editions of Brecht's Works

Brecht, Bertolt. *Bertolt Brecht Arbeitsjournal,* ed. Werner Hecht. 2 vols. with a vol. *Anmerkungen* by the editor. Frankfurt: Suhrkamp, 1973.
—. *Gesammelte Werke.* 20 vols. Frankfurt: Suhrkamp, 1967.
—. *Stücke,* 12. vols. Frankfurt: Suhrkamp, 1959.
—. *Versuche,* Heft 11. Berlin: Suhrkamp, 1951.
—. *Versuche,* Heft 11. Berlin: Aufbau, 1952.

Bibliographies of Works about Bertolt Brecht

Nubel, Walter. "Bertolt-Brecht-Bibliographie." *Sinn und Form,* Zweites Sonderheft Bertolt Brecht, 1957.
Petersen, Klaus-Dietrich. *Bertolt Brecht — Leben und Werk — Ein Bücherverzeichnis.* Dortmund: Stadtbücherei, 1966.

Suvin, Darko, M. Spalter & R. Schotter. "A Selected Brecht Bibliography." *The Drama Review,* XII (1967), 156—169. (Lists English language items only.)

Editions of Works by Jakob Michael Reinhold Lenz in Chronological Order of Publication

Gesammelte Schriften von J. M. R. Lenz, ed. Ludwig Tieck. 3 vols. Berlin: Reimer, 1828.
Stürmer und Dränger. Zweiter Teil. Lenz und Wagner, ed. A. Sauer. Deutsche National-Litteratur, Vol. 80, ed. J. Kürschner. Berlin: Spemann, [1880].
Weinhold, Karl. *Dramatischer Nachlass von J. M. R. Lenz.* Frankfurt: Rütten & Loening, 1884.
Jakob Michael Reinhold Lenz, Gesammelte Schriften, ed. Franz Blei. 5 vols. München: Müller, 1909.

Gesammelte Schriften von Jacob Michael Reinhold Lenz, ed. Ernst Lewy. 4 vols. Berlin: Cassirer, 1909.
Briefe, von und an J. M. R. Lenz, eds. Karl Freye und Wolfgang Stammler. 2 vols. Leipzig: Wolff, 1918.
Der Hofmeister. Kampf um das soziale Ordnungsgefüge, ed. Heinz Kindermann. Deutsche Literatur ... in Entwicklungsreihen, Reihe 15, vol. 8. Leipzig: Reclam, 1939.
Lenz, Jakob M. R. *Der Hofmeister — Komödie — Anmerkungen übers Thea-*

ter. Mit einem Nachwort von Klaus Hammer. Leipzig: Reclam UB 1375/76, [1962].

Lenz, Jacob M. R. *Der Hofmeister.* Mit einem Nachwort von Karl S. Guthke. Stuttgart: Reclam UB 1376, 1963.

Lenz, Jacob Michael Reinhold. *Der Neue Menoza oder Geschichte des cumbanischen Prinzen Tandi — Eine Komödie,* in *Komedia,* ed. Walter Hinck. Berlin: Walter de Gruyter, 1965, with valuable section "Material zum Verständnis des Textes," pp. 73—95.

Lenz, Jacob M. R. *Gesammelte Werke in vier Bänden,* mit Anmerkungen, hrsg. von Richard Daunicht. München: Fink, 1967, Dramen I.

Lenz, Jacob M. R. *Werke und Schriften,* eds. Britta Titel und Hellmut Haug. Stuttgart: Goverts, 1967, vol. 2.

Works about Brecht and Lenz

Brock-Sulzer, Elisabeth. "Lenz/Brecht 'Der Hofmeister,'" *Theater Heute,* V (1964), Heft 12, p. 42.

Busse, Christa. "Brecht Bibliografie — Nicht veröffentlichte wissenschaftliche Arbeiten über Bertolt Brecht, die an Universitäten und Hochschulen der DDR geschrieben wurden," *Theater der Zeit,* XXIII (1968), 1—5. (Thirteen "Arbeiten" about Brecht's *Hofmeister* are listed on p. 5. All are unavailable outside the DDR and were not consulted for this study. The bibliography is noted here only for the sake of completeness.)

Erpenbeck, Fritz. "Beispielgebendes Theater." *Neues Deutschland,* Berlin, April 16, 1950, p. 3.

Fradkin, Ilja. "Die 'Bearbeitungen' von Bertolt Brecht." *Kunst und Literatur — Sowjetwissenschaft,* XVI (1968), 159—170.

Genton, Elisabeth. *Jacob Michael Reinhold Lenz et la scène allemande.* Paris: Didier, 1966, pp. 199—217.

Gyssling, Walter. "Basel: Lenz/Brecht 'Der Hofmeister.'" *Theater Heute,* II (1961), Heft 10, p. 34.

Kaufmann, Hans. *Bertolt Brecht — Geschichtsdrama und Parabel-Stück.* Berlin: Rütten & Loening, 1962, pp. 195—215.

Löfdahl, Göran, "Tradition, dialektik, moral — Kring Pätus-figuren i *Der Hofmeister.*" *Ord och Bild,* Brechtnummer, LXXIII (1964), no. 1, 61—64.

Lutz, Regine, "Wie die Darstellerin des Gustchens die 7. Szene, Katechismusstunde, auffaßt," *Theaterarbeit,* ed. Ruth Berlau et al., Berlin: Suhrkamp, 1961, 2nd rev. & enlarged edition, pp. 96—99.

Mayer, Hans. *Bertolt Brecht und die Tradition.* Pfullingen: Neske, 1961, pp. 52—61.

—. "Das ABC der deutschen Misere." *Neues Deutschland,* Berlin, April 13, 1950, p. 3.

—. "Lenz oder die Alternative." Afterword in *J. M. R. Lenz — Werke und Schriften,* eds. B. Titel & H. Haug. Stuttgart: Goverts, 1967, vol. II, pp. 795—827.

Menter, Leo. "Die Tragikomödie des deutschen Schulmeisters." *Die Weltbühne,* Berlin, V, 17, April 26, 1950.

Müller, André. "Den Reaktionären zum Trotz — Drei Brecht-Inszenierungen in Westdeutschland." *Theater der Zeit,* XV (1960), Heft 11, p. 66—70.

Petr, Pavel. "Člaňek — K Brechtovu Zpracovani Lenzovy Hry O Hofmistrovi." (German summary has title "Lenz' Drama *Der Hofmeister* in der Bearbeitung Bertolt Brechts.") *Časopis pro Moderni Filologii,* XXXIX (1957), 221—226.

Rilla, Paul. "Analyse der Bearbeitung." *Theaterarbeit,* ed. Ruth Berlau et al. Dresden: VVV Dresdner Verlag, [1952], pp. 80—82.

Spalter, Max. *brecht's tradition.* Baltimore: Johns Hopkins Press, 1967, pp. 3—203.

Works about Brecht

Beckley, Richard. "Adaptation as a Feature of Brecht's Dramatic Technique." *German Life & Letters,* XV (1961—1962), 275—284.

Brecht Dialog 1968 — Politik auf dem Theater, ed. W. Hecht. Berlin: Henschelverlag, 1968.

Eisler, Hanns. "Zwei Briefe an Bertolt Brecht." *Sinn und Form,* Sonderheft Hanns Eisler. 1964, pp. 14—16.

Ekmann, Bjorn. *Gesellschaft und Gewissen — Die sozialen und moralischen Anschauungen Bertolt Brechts und ihre Bedeutung für seine Dichtung.* Kopenhagen: Munksgaard, 1969.

Esslin, Martin. *Bertolt Brecht,* Columbia Essays on Modern Writers, vol. 42. New York: Columbia Univ. P., 1969.

—. *Brecht — The Man and his Work.* New York: Doubleday Anchor, 1961.

Fradkin, Ilja. "Brecht, die Bibel, die Aufklärung und Shakespeare." *Kunst und Literatur — Sowjetwissenschaft,* XIII (1965), 156—175.

Fuegi, John B. "The Artful Artificer, Bertolt Brecht: A Study of Six Bearbeitungen." Dissertation, Univ. of So. Calif., 1967.

—. *The Essential Brecht.* Los Angeles: Hennessy & Ingalls, 1972.

Grimm, Reinhold. *Bertolt Brecht.* Stuttgart: Metzler, 1971, 3rd. rev. edn.

Henneberg, Fritz. *Dessau-Brecht-Musikalische Arbeiten.* Berlin: Henschelverlag, 1963.

Hinck, Walter. *Die Dramaturgie des späten Brecht.* Palaestra, vol. 229. Göttingen: Vandenhoeck & Ruprecht, 1959.

Hoffmann, Charles W. "Brecht's Humor: Laughter while the Shark Bites." *Germanic Review,* XXXVIII (1963), 157—166.

Klotz, Volker. *Bertolt Brecht — Versuch über das Werk.* Bad Homburg v.d.H.: Gehlen, 1967, 3rd rev. edn.

Kohlhase, Norbert. *Dichtung und politische Moral — Eine Gegenüberstellung von Brecht und Camus.* München: Nymphenburger, 1965.

Mayer, Hans. *Anmerkungen zu Brecht.* Frankfurt: Suhrkamp, 1967, 2nd edn.

Melngailis, Valda D. "*Leben Eduards des Zweiten von England* — Bertolt Brecht's Adaptation of Marlowe's *Edward II.*" Dissertation, Harvard, 1966.

Mueller, Carl R. "Brecht and the Marxist Nature of Man." *Medieval Epic to the 'Epic Theater' of Brecht.* Univ. of So. Calif. Studies in Comparative Literature, vol. 1, eds. Rosario P. Armato & John M. Spalek. Los Angeles: Univ. of So. Calif. P., 1968, pp. 203—217.

Müller, Klaus-Detlef. *Die Funktion der Geschichte im Werk Bertolt Brechts — Studien zum Verhältnis von Marxismus und Ästhetik.* Tübingen: Niemeyer, 1967, pp. 89—95.

Münsterer, Hans O. *Bert Brecht — Erinnerungen aus den Jahren 1917—1922.* Zürich: Arche, 1963.

Pohl, Rainer, *Strukturelemente und Entwicklung von Pathosformen in der Dramensprache Bertold* [sic] *Brechts.* Bonn: Bouvier, 1969.

Rülicke-Weiler, Käthe. "Bemerkungen Brechts zur Kunst — Notate 1951—1955." *Weimarer Beiträge,* Brecht Sonderheft, 1968, pp. 5—11.

Schrimpf, Hans J. *Lessing und Brecht — Von der Aufklärung auf dem Theater.* Opuscula, vol. 19. Pfullingen: Neske, 1965.

Schumann, Klaus. "Themen und Formenwandel in der späten Lyrik Brechts." *Weimarer Beiträge,* Brecht Sonderheft, 1968, pp. 39—60.

Schwabe, Willi. "Beschreibung der Figur des Grafen Wermuth durch den Darsteller." *Theaterarbeit,* ed. Ruth Berlau et al. Berlin: Suhrkamp, 1961, 2nd rev. & enlarged edn., p. 100.

Sinor, Irene M. "The Adaptor Adapted Shakespeare's *Coriolanus* in two Adaptations attributed to Bertolt Brecht." M. A. Thesis, Indiana Univ., 1967.

Sokel, Walter H. "Brecht's Split Characters and his Sense of the Tragic." *Brecht — A Collection of Critical Essays,* ed. Peter Demetz. Englewood Cliffs: Prentice Hall, 1962, pp. 127—137.

Stern, Guy. "Brechts *Trommeln in der Nacht* als literarische Satire." *Monatshefte,* LXI (1969), 241—259.

Theaterarbeit — 6 Aufführungen des Berliner Ensembles, ed. Ruth Berlau et al. Dresden: VVV Dresdner Verlag, 1952, and Berlin: Suhrkamp, 1961, 2nd rev. and enlarged edn., pp. 68—119.

Tracy, Gordon L. "Das 'Gestische' and the Poetry of Brecht." *Essays on German Literature in Honour of G. Joyce Hallamore.* Toronto: U. of Toronto P., 1968, pp. 218—235.

Weisstein, Ulrich. "From the Dramatic Novel to the Epic Theater — A Study of the Contemporary Background of Brecht's Theory and Practice." *Germanic Review,* XXXVIII (1963), pp 257—271.

—. "The First Version of Brecht/Feuchtwanger's *Leben Eduards des Zweiten von England* and Its Relation to the Standard Text." JEPG LXXIX (1970), 193—210.

—. "Two Measures for One, Brecht's *Die Rundköpfe und die Spitzköpfe* and its Shakespearean Model." *Germanic Review,* LIII (1968), pp. 24—39.

Williams, Raymond. *Modern Tragedy.* Stanford: Stanford Univ. Press, 1966, Part II, Chap. 7, "A Rejection of Tragedy: Brecht," pp. 190—204.

Woods, Barbara A. "A Man of Two Minds." *German Quarterly,* LXII (1969), pp. 44—51.

—. "The Function of Proverbs in Brecht." *Monatshefte,* LXI (1969), pp. 49—57.

Works about Lenz

Burger, Heinz O. "J. M. R. Lenz: *Der Hofmeister.*" *Das deutsche Lustspiel I,* ed. H. Steffen. Göttingen: Vandenhoeck & Ruprecht, 1968.

Friedrich, Theodor. *Die "Anmerkungen übers Theater" des Dichters Jakob Michael Reinhold Lenz* (Nebst einem Anhang: Neudruck der "Anmerkungen übers Theater" in verschiedenen Typen zur Veranschaulichung ihrer Entstehung). Leipzig: R. Voigtländers Verlag, 1908.

Genton, Elisabeth. *Jacob Michael Reinhold Lenz et la scène allemande.*" Paris: Didier, 1966.

Girard, René. *Lenz 1751—1792 — Genèse d'une Dramaturgie du Tragi-comique.* Paris: Librairie C. Klincksieck, 1968.

Guthke, Karl S. *Geschichte und Poetik der deutschen Tragi-Komödie.* Göttingen: Vandenhoeck & Ruprecht, 1961.

—. "Lenzens *Hofmeister* und *Soldaten.* Ein neuer Formtypus in der Geschichte des deutschen Dramas." *Wirkendes Wort,* IX (1959), pp. 274—286.

Harris, Edward P. "Structural Unity in J. M. R. Lenz's *Der Hofmeister:* A Revaluation." *Seminar,* VIII (1972), pp. 77—87.

Hausdorff, G. *Die Einheitlichkeit des dramatischen Problems bei Lenz.* Dissertation, Würzburg, 1913.

Heinrichsdorff, Paul. *J. M. R. Lenzens religiöse Haltung.* Germanische Studien, Heft 117. Berlin: Ebering, 1932.

Kossmann, Alfred. "Reinhold Lenz." *Tirade,* VIII (1964), pp. 682—694.

Markwardt, Bruno. *Geschichte der deutschen Poetik, Band II, Aufklärung, Rokoko, Sturm und Drang.* Grundriß der germanischen Philologie, ed. Hermann Paul. Berlin: de Gruyter, 1956, pp. 404—418; pp. 470—471; pp. 630—633.

Meyer, Willy. *Lenz's 'Hofmeister' — Ein Kapitel aus der Entwicklungsgeschichte der deutschen Literatur.* Dissertation, Erlangen, 1933.

Rosanow, M. W. *J. M. R. Lenz, der Dichter der Sturm- und Drangperiode, sein Leben und seine Werke.* (Leipzig: Verlagsbuchhandlung Schulze & Co., 1909).

Rudolf, Ottomar. *Jacob Michael Reinhold Lenz — Moralist und Aufklärer.* Bad Homburg v.d.H.: Gehlen, 1970.

Schmidt, Erich. *Lenz und Klinger — Zwei Dichter der Geniezeit.* Berlin: Weidmannsche Buchhandlung, 1878.

Schöne, Albrecht. "Wiederholung der exemplarischen Begebenheit — Jakob Michael Reinhold Lenz," in *Säkularisation als sprachbildende Kraft — Studien zur Dichtung deutscher Pfar-*

rersöhne, pp. 76—115. Palaestra, vol. 226. Göttingen: Vandenhoeck & Ruprecht, 1958.

Stammler, Wolfgang, *'Der Hofmeister' von Jakob M. R. Lenz.* Dissertation, Halle, 1908.

General

Benz, Richard, *Die Zeit der deutschen Klassik — Kultur des achtzehnten Jahrhunderts 1750—1800.* Stuttgart: Reclam, 1953.

Bickert, Hans G. *Studien zum Problem der Exposition im Drama der tektonischen Bauform — Terminologie — Funktionen — Gestaltung.* Marburger Beiträge zur Germanistik, vol. 23. Marburg: Elwert, 1969.

Bramsted, Ernest K. *Aristocracy and the Middle-Classes in Germany — Social Types in German Literature 1830—1900.* Chicago: Univ. of Chicago P., 1966, rev. edn.

Bruford, Walter H. *Culture and Society in Classical Weimar 1775—1806.* Cambridge, Engl.: Univ. P., 1962.

—. *Germany in the Eighteenth Century: The Social Background of the Literary Revival.* Cambridge, Engl.: Univ. P., 1935.

Crumbach, Franz H. *Die Struktur des Epischen Theaters — Dramaturgie der Kontraste.* Schriftenreihe der pädagogischen Hochschule Braunschweig, Heft 8. Braunschweig: Waisenhaus, 1960.

Dosenheimer, Elise. *Das soziale Drama von Lessing bis Sternheim.* Konstanz: Südverlag, 1949.

Escarpit, Robert. " 'Creative Treason' as a Key to Literature." *Yearbook of Comparative and General Literature,* X (1961), pp. 16—21.

Freytag, Gustav. *Die Technik des Dramas.* Darmstadt: Wissenschaftliche Buchgesellschaft, 1965, unveränderter, reprographischer Nachdruck der 13. Auflage, Leipzig, 1922.

Frye, Northrop. *The Educated Imagination.* Bloomington, Ind.: Indiana Univ. P., 1964.

Garland, H. B. *Storm and Stress.* London: Harrap, 1952.

Gellert, Christian F. *Sämmtliche Schriften — Erster Theil.* Leipzig: M. G. Weidmanns Erben und Reich, und

Caspar Fritsch, 1775, neue, verb. Auflage.

Gundolf, Friedrich. *Shakespeare und der deutsche Geist.* München: Küpper, 1959, XI. Auflage.

Guthke, Karl S. *Modern Tragicomedy — An Investigation into the Nature of the Genre.* N. Y.: Random House, 1966.

Hinck, Walter. *Das deutsche Lustspiel des 17. und 18. Jahrhunderts und Die italienische Komödie.* Germanistische Abhandlungen, vol. 8. Stuttgart: Metzler, 1965.

—. "Das deutsche Lustspiel im 18. Jahrhundert," *Das deutsche Lustspiel I,* ed. H. Steffen. Göttingen: Vandenhoeck & Ruprecht, 1968.

Kant, Immanuel. *Gesammelte Schriften,* ed. by Königlich Preußische Akademie der Wissenschaften, Band VIII: Abhandlungen nach 1781. Berlin: de Gruyter, 1923.

—. *Kritik der Reinen Vernunft.* Leipzig: Bibliographisches Institut, 1899.

—. *Perpetual Peace.* intro. by Nicholas M. Butler, first English edition of 1796. New York: Columbia Univ. P., 1939.

—. *Sämtliche Werke.* Band V: Moralische Schriften. Leipzig: Insel, 1922, Großherzog Wilhelm Ernst Ausgabe.

—. *Zum ewigen Frieden — Ein Philosophischer Entwurf.* Königsberg: Fr Nicolovius, 1796, neue vermehrte Auflage.

Kayser, Wolfgang. *Das Groteske — Seine Gestaltung in Malerei und Dichtung.* Oldenburg: Stalling, 1957.

—. *Das sprachliche Kunstwerk.* Bern: Francke, 1962, 8th edn.

Kerr, Walter. *Tragedy and Comedy.* New York: Simon & Schuster, 1967.

Kistler, Mark O. *Drama of the Storm and Stress.* New York: Twayne, 1969.

Kließ, Werner. *Sturm und Drang.* Velber: Friedrich, 1966.

Klopstock, Friedrich G. *Oden.* Leipzig: Göschen, 1798, 2 vols.

Klotz, Volker. *Die geschlossene und offene Form im Drama.* Reihe Literatur als Kunst. München: Hanser, 1960.

Korff, H. A. *Geist der Goethezeit.* Leipzig: Koehler & Amelang, 1966, 8. unveränderte Auflage, vols. 1 & 2.

Mann, Thomas. *Buddenbrooks — Verfall einer Familie.* Stockholm: Fischer, 1959, Stockholmer Gesamtausgabe.

Mattenklott, Gert. *Melancholie in der Dramatik des Sturm und Drang.* Studien zur Allgemeinen und Vergleichenden Literaturwissenschaft, Band I. Stuttgart: Metzler, 1968.

Mayer, Hans. *Zur deutschen Literatur der Zeit.* Reinbeck: Rowohlt, 1967.

Meier, Werner. *Der Hofmeister in der deutschen Literatur des 18. Jahrhunderts.* Dissertation. Zürich: Gebr. Lehmann, 1934.

Mercier, Louis Sébastien. *Du Théâtre ou Nouvel Essai sur l'Art Dramatique.* Geneva: Slatkine Reprints, 1970, Réimpression de l'édition d'Amsterdam 1773.

Miller, Ronald D. *The Drama of Schiller.* Harrogate: Duchy Press, 1963.

Nist, John. "The Three Major Modes of Literary Art: Comedy, Tragedy, Pathedy." *Southern Humanities Review,* II: pp. 70—88.

Pascal, Roy. *Shakespeare in Germany 1740—1815.* Cambridge, Engl.: Univ. Press, 1937.

—. *The German Sturm und Drang.* Manchester: Univ. P., 1959.

Peacock, Ronald. "Tragedy, Comedy and Civilization." *The Poet in the Theatre.* N. Y.: Hill & Wang, 1960, pp. 151—159.

Price, Lawrence M. *English Literature in Germany.* Berkeley: U. of Calif. P., 1953.

Richter, C. G. *Der Hofmeister nach der Mode — Ein Lust-Spiel* [sic] *in drey Aufzügen.* Hamburg: [n.p.], 1763. (Xerox copy available from BM. Cf. BM Catalogue vol. 105, p. 235).

Robertson, J. G. *Schiller after a Century.* Edinburgh: Wm. Blackwood, 1905.

Rose, William. "The Psychological Approach to the Study of Literature," *German Studies presented to Leonard Ashley Willoughby.* Oxford: Blackwell, 1952.

Selver, Henrik. *Die Auffassung des Bürgers im deutschen bürgerlichen Drama des 18. Jahrhunderts.* Engelsdorf-Leipzig: Vogel, 1931.

Stallknecht, Newton P. and H. Frenz, eds. *Comparative Literature: Method and Perspective.* Carbondale: So. Ill. Univ. P., 1961.

Steiner, George. *The Death of Tragedy.* New York: Knopf, 1961.

Styan, John L. *The Dark Comedy — The Development of Modern Comic Tragedy.* Cambridge, Engl.: Univ. P., 1968, 2nd edn.

—. *The Dramatic Experience.* Cambridge, Engl.: Univ. P., 1965.

Symington, Rodney T. K. *Brecht und Shakespeare.* Studien zur Germanistik, Anglistik, Komparatistik, vol. 2 Bonn: Bouvier, 1970.

Szondi, Peter. *Theorie des modernen Dramas.* Frankfurt: Suhrkamp, 1966.

Thompson, Alan R. *The Anatomy of Drama.* Berkeley: U. of Calif. P. 1946, 2nd edn.

Wekwerth, Manfred. *Notate — Über die Arbeit des Berliner Ensembles 1956 bis 1966.* Frankfurt: Suhrkamp, 1967.

Wellek, René and Austin Warren. *Theory of Literature.* New York: Harcourt, Brace (Harvest Book), 1959, 2nd edn.

Wiese, Benno von. *Friedrich Schiller.* Stuttgart: Metzler, 1959.

Willoughby, Leonard Ashley. *The Classical Age of German Literature 1748—1805.* N. Y.: Russell & Russell, 1966, 2nd edn.

Wolffheim, Hans. *Die Entdeckung Shakespeares. Deutsche Zeugnisse des 18. Jahrhunderts.* Hamburg: Hoffmann & Campe, 1959.

INDEX OF NAMES

(References to Bertolt Brecht and J. M. R. Lenz and their works are not included here.)

TABLE OF CONTENTS

Chapter